Why do you call me 'Lord, Lord' and not do what I tell you?

(Luke 6.46)

Contents

INTRODUCTION   5

PART ONE: FAILED PROPHECIES
1. HOW JESUS REPEATEDLY GETS IT WRONG   12

PART TWO: FALSE PROMISES
2. BROKEN PROMISES, WORTHLESS GUARANTEES   32

PART THREE: IMPOSSIBLE MORALITIES
3. JESUS' TRIBAL MORALITY   49
4. ON BEING PERFECT   89
5. MORALITY AND SALVATION 113

PART FOUR: RE-BRANDING THE MESSAGE
6. BIBLE WORSHIP   121
7. THE CHRIST FANTASY   138
8. CHRISTIANS' FAVOURITE DELUSIONS   157
9. LIVING IN A WORLD OF MAKE-BELIEVE   192

PART FIVE: LOSING SIGHT OF TRUTH
10. GOD IS NOT THE DEFAULT SETTING 197
11. HOW CHRISTIANS INFLICT THEIR EXTRA-CURRICULAR BELIEFS ON US ALL (AND WHY WE SHOULDN'T LET THEM)   203

PART SIX: CONCLUSIONS
12. FACING THE TRUTH   219

GLOSSARY OF CHRISTIAN TERMS   226

Why Christians Don't Do What Jesus Tells Them To

...and what they believe instead

Neil Robinson

For
Cephas Chapelwife

INTRODUCTION

This book, which, discerning reader and searcher after truth that you are, you will want to read from cover to cover, began life as a series of email messages between two old friends. One of these friends (let's call him Simon) is a born-again Christian. The other, me, is a former believer, now an atheist. For Simon this is a problem that prompts him to send me messages from time to time that implore, beg and bully me to return to the faith, for the sake of my 'mortal and eternal state'. I respond to these messages in what I hope is a reasoned and reasonable way, explaining to Simon why I no longer believe. From his perspective, however, my responses represent nothing more than rebellion against God. I would like to reproduce here some of his messages, or at the very least his first, but he is angry with me because of my supposed rebellion and would not, I know, give his permission. So, instead, here is my first epistle to Simon to give you a flavour of our differing positions:

I don't mind you sharing your faith, though I do remember a time when I had it and you didn't. Of course that also means I know for myself what it is you're saying, even if I don't hold with it any more.

I cannot now believe in, or kowtow to, or ask forgiveness of the violent despot of the Old Testament - the same deranged personality, presumably, who makes it through to the sequel. He's clearly a very bad idea; no more than a tribal deity who reflects the harshness and brevity of life in the iron age. He doesn't exist in reality. I'm equally unconvinced by the way he's represented in the New Testament - supposedly opposed to human sacrifice but resorting to it to 'save' mankind from his own annoyance with it. I am absolutely certain there is no god like this. As I see it, I'm not rejecting a being who is out there somewhere and who will be upset with me in some way as a result. There is no such being... no personal god of the Christian/Jewish/Muslim type. I am, therefore, an atheist. And before you say that that is a faith position in itself, let me say - borrowing a phrase from American commentator, Bill Maher - that atheism is faith in precisely the same way that abstinence is a sex position.

There are, I have to say, many reasons why I can't believe in the god of the bible: for example, where you see creation screaming of his presence, it speaks just as much to me of the necessary but cruel wastefulness of natural selection, the endless struggle for survival, the need to kill or be killed and the way life evolves through sex (a subject which seems to exercise the Christian god, or at least Christians, a great deal when it comes to humans). In addition, there's the phenomenal inconsistency of believers ('by their fruits shall ye know them'), from the appalling paedophila of the Catholic church, for which, shamefully, it has tried to position itself as victim, to other Christians claiming persecution because they can't wear graven images to work (when doing so is in contravention of the second commandment which expressly forbids them). And that's not to mention the absurdities and atrocities of Islam. I cannot subscribe any more to such inconsistent 'principles' and standards.

No, this life is all there is, and once it's gone, it's gone - there is no evidence at all that we go on beyond the grave. Our 'self' is a product of the brain, and that, like the rest of our bodies, dies; the essence of who we are, our 'self', dies with it. It isn't a bad thing that we enjoy only this brief existence - it's certainly better than nothing - and knowing it's all there is can lead us to make the most of it. It's even possible to know peace that truly does pass understanding and to find real purpose too, without having to believe life is something it's not. So don't worry about my eternal salvation: quite literally there is no need, because there is no such thing to be had.

I trust you won't mind me saying all this in response to what you call 'sermonising' - it's what I believe and indeed what I know to be true. I didn't casually give up Christianity: much thought, reading and soul-searching went into it. I can, ultimately, only believe in truth, wherever that takes me. Consequently, I am not a Christian for the same reasons you are not a Muslim or a Mormon. All three, as well as other religious belief systems, are neither rational nor true.

This was a good start, but as far as this book is concerned, covers ground more than capably covered elsewhere. Richard Dawkins, for example, is unbeatable when considering the redundancy of theology in 'creation' and evolution; Sam Harris explains the impossibility of the soul or self existing separately from the brain much better than I can; Dan Barker of the *Freedom From Religion Foundation* systematically highlights the absurdities of the ancient Yahweh cult in *Godless*. In addition, there are numerous websites that explore these areas, many written by former Christians and ministers, notably *Debunking Christianity*, *Christianity Disproved* and *Infidels*. Consequently, while I will refer to these authors and websites in what follows, I won't be concentrating on the same areas. Simon, like most Christians, is unmoved and unconvinced by arguments from outside his faith as it were. For him and many other Christians, the existence of God is a given: they are not swayed by arguments against His existence and any such attempts are seen as mere rebellion against our mutual Father in Heaven, who, whether anyone else believes in him or not, remains ever-present and ever-constant.

I wanted a way to break through the rigidity of this mindset, inculcated and reinforced in Christians by innumerable years in church, listening to sermons, reading the Bible and other Christian books, and living the Christian life, whatever that may mean. My approach is not therefore about the feasibility of God's existence, unlikely as that is, nor about how the Bible as we know it came to be. Bart Ehrman is far better qualified to deal with this, in any case, demonstrating, as he does, how unreliable 'scripture' actually is. Instead, I want to approach the Bible as Simon views it, as the Word of God, and to concentrate on the promises, prophecies and moralities Christians believe this Word makes known. There seems to me, as a former believer, to be insurmountable difficulties in believing the fantastic claims and promises purportedly made by Jesus in the gospels. It also seems to me, from years of experience with Christians, that most of them don't believe a significant number of these improbable things either, whatever they may claim to the contrary. It is this lack of belief that I want to explore in this book.

It was not my aim in originally writing to Simon to de-convert him (though I would have been happy if that had happened) but I wanted him to think and reflect on his beliefs, to ask himself, 'Can I believe this? Do I believe this?', 'Do I believe it to the extent it makes a difference in my life?'. I hoped that a chink of light, of rationality, might break through as he asked himself these questions. I hoped too he would recognise the absurdity of many of the claims of Christianity and face up the fact that as an intelligent human being he can't and doesn't believe the failed prophecies, false promises and impossible moralities of the Bible. It is my contention that no Christian really believes these fanciful notions; if they did the world would be a very different place, they would be very different people. It is my hope that you too, dear reader, might, if you haven't already, respect your own intelligence by seeing through the absurdity that is Christianity.

A note about some of what follows: firstly, I will maintain the capitalisation of 'God' and 'Bible' when referring to the evangelical/fundamentalist conceptions of both terms, as believers do. However, the fact I follow their practice does not indicate either belief in or acceptance of their perspective. Secondly, I will inevitably make a number of generalisations, claiming, for example, that Christians believe this or that. No doubt there are Christians who don't believe this but do believe that, others who believe this but not that, and plenty who will be quick to point out how I am misrepresenting *their* beliefs, and that that invalidates all that I have to say. (They seem to think this criticism of their collective inability to agree on the Truth is a criticism of their opponents when it's actually a Christian own goal). Consequently, I make no apologies for saying 'Christians believe', particularly when I provide evidence of a representative group or individual doing so somewhere.

Second, I will make references to statements that Jesus makes in the gospels usually by saying 'Jesus said'. I am aware, however, that much of what he said he probably didn't, and that the concerns and interests of his followers in the period when the gospels were written, between 40 and 90 years after Jesus' death, are put into this mouth. However, most Christians who view the gospels as the Word of God, are in denial about this established fact. Consequently, I will, more frequently than not, represent Jesus' supposed utterances in the synoptic gospels (Mark, Matthew and Luke) as if he actually made them. That is, after all, what Christians believe.

Christians will also tell you that the depiction of Jesus' 'earthly ministry' in John's gospel is as faithful as the synoptic writers are in theirs. In fact, John, being the last and latest of the four gospel to be written, represents a much more developed theology than that of its synoptic brethren and conflicts in many places with them, particularly in the way that Jesus regards himself. The synoptic gospels are focused on what he says about the coming Kingdom and qualifications for being part of it; John has Jesus talk almost exclusively about himself, with the Kingdom relegated to a single mention (John 3.5). The conspicuous non-appearance of Jesus' predicted Kingdom accounts, therefore, for much of the changed perspective of the fourth gospel. Consequently, while cognitive dissonance allows Christians to believe that John and the synoptics are in harmony, they are not. There is, as a result, less reliance in what follows on John's gospel and its super-human Jesus.

Third, I will use the Anglicised Revised Standard Version of the Bible for quotations, except where indicated. I recognise that some Christian groups will only accept certain translations; some, for example, are inordinately fond of what they (mistakenly) believe is the King James authorised version of 1611, on the basis that if its language was good enough for God, it is good enough for them. However, later translations, as opposed to paraphrases, more accurately reflect the oldest manuscripts that are now available. Biblical references are included in the text itself, but I want to avoid footnotes (and those annoying little numbers that would otherwise litter the text) for other sources. Because I wouldn't want you to think I am making all of this up, these references can be found listed by page number at the back of the book.

Fourth, this is not a book about Islam. Christians are fond of rebutting criticism of their beliefs by accusing the critic of cowardice: 'he wouldn't dare say these sorts of things about Islam. It's only because we Christians are meek and accepting that authors like this think they can get away with it'. Christians are far from being meek and accepting, but what follows is not a critique of Islam because of some supposed fear of reprisals from Muslims. It is not about Islam because I was not once Muslim. Consequently, I do not know that faith as intimately as I know Christianity. It was not Islam that consumed twenty years of my adult life, it was the Christian faith. There are critical examinations of Islam available to those who think this book should be about Islam – I'd recommend Araan Sufi Ali's *Infidel* and Sam Harris's *The End of Faith* – but please don't think, if you're inclined to do so, that you have answered all of the criticisms of Christianity in this book by recourse to 'he wouldn't dare...'.

The book is divided into six parts. The first examines Jesus' prophecies, the pronouncements he makes about what lies in the future for believers, the world in general and the consequences of his radical vision. We will see here that these prophecies have systematically failed to materialise and that Christians choose to ignore the fact that Jesus consistently locates them in a time immediately following his ministry, pretending instead that they still might occur, two thousand years later. The second section looks at the promises of Jesus - what he says his followers can expect to receive, achieve or claim as their own because they believe in him. I will demonstrate how little Christians themselves believe in these promises, however much they may say they do. This leads, in part three, to a consideration of the morality of the Bible, and that of Jesus in particular, exploring how much of his moral teaching is practised by believers today. All Christian groups claim to derive their morality from the Bible, and exhort others to follow its teaching, castigating those who don't: we will conclude that there is reason to thank God that the morality of the Bible does not prevail in the twenty-first century.

Having determined the extent to which Christians subscribe to the tenets of their good book, and their good shepherd in particular, I take a look in parts four and five at some fundamental beliefs of contemporary Christianity that many assume are 'scriptural', even though they cannot be found in the Bible. Some, indeed, conflict with it and the words ascribed to Jesus. The book finally considers whether Jesus would recognise what Christians believe today as having anything to do with him, why Christians continue to believe what they do, and why their proselytising and moralising should be resisted.

PART ONE: FAILED PROPHECIES

Chapter 1
How Jesus Repeatedly Gets It Wrong

Jesus knew his world was about to end. He understood that the old order, the way everyone had lived up to that point, was shuddering to a halt. A new age was about to begin. As a result, all he had to say, every bit of teaching, every challenge to live a better life came from his utter conviction that this incredible change was imminent. God was about to establish his Kingdom on earth, reversing the social order and bringing freedom to the captive, justice to the poor and sight to the blind (Luke 4.18 & 19). Jesus felt compelled to share the good news of the coming Kingdom with all who would listen: all you had to do to be part of the new age was to be ready, to mend your ways and align yourself with God's priorities (Matthew 3.2) by feeding the hunger, clothing the poor, caring for the sick and visiting the imprisoned (Matthew 25. 35-40). When the time was right - and the tipping point would be reached once enough people had signed up - God would be sending his special envoy, 'the Son of Man', to herald the new age and God's Kingdom would appear in all its glory.

All of Jesus' message, every single bit of it, is directed to this end, addressed solely to the conditions necessary for the new age, the Kingdom, that he so evidently anticipates when he prays 'your Kingdom come, on Earth as it is in Heaven'. He urges those he encounters to change their lives, to adopt a radical lifestyle that entails giving their possessions to the poor, abandoning their families and demonstrating love for their enemies in the dying days of the old system. Only in this way will God know that they are in earnest about being part of his new world order. Jesus dedicates his life to this mission, even casting himself as God's specially chosen herald, the Son of Man. Once the right conditions are reached, he will, he tells his followers, be propelled through the heavens by God's almighty power, making a spectacular entrance at the exact point of transition from the old system to the new.

And when is all of this going to happen? Very soon. If not in the months ahead then within a few short years, certainly within the lifetime of his associates. How do we know this? We know it because the Bible preserves Jesus saying so in numerous places. Here are a few of them:

> *For the Son of Man is going to come in his Father's glory with his angels... I tell you the truth,* **some who are standing here will not taste death** *before they see the Son of Man coming in his Kingdom.* (Matthew 16:27-28)

> *For as the lightning comes from the east and flashes as far as the west, so will be the coming of the Son of Man... and then all the tribes of the earth will mourn, and they will see the Son of Man coming on the clouds of the sky with power and great glory. I tell you the truth,* **this generation will certainly not pass away until all these things have happened**. (Matthew 24:27, 30-31, 34)

> *Then they will see "the Son of Man coming in a cloud" with power and great glory. Now when these things begin to take place, stand up and raise your heads, because your redemption is drawing near. Truly I tell you,* **this generation will not pass away until all things have taken place**. *Heaven and earth will pass away, but my words will not pass away.* (Luke 21:27-28, 33-34)

[Emphases mine]

As we know from our vantage point, two thousand years later, none of this happened: God didn't initiate his Kingdom on earth, Jesus didn't fly through the air accompanied by a heavenly host and his mission didn't end in power and glory. And as for the time-scale for these events... well, that has been a problem for Jesus' followers ever since.

We can, as Bart Ehrman demonstrates, be certain that these incredible guarantees emanate from Jesus himself; the fact he hadn't returned by the time the later gospels were written, when Jesus' contemporaries were dead or dying out, was a potential source of embarrassment to second generation Christians. They could have eliminated the promised imminence of Jesus' return from their accounts. The earlier gospel authors didn't, however, because it was widely known that he had made such a promise; it would have been alarmingly conspicuous by its absence if they had removed it. We know from Paul's first and only letter to the church in Thessalonica, the earliest of the New Testament books, written in 51CE or thereabouts, that fledgling believers were aware of the promise of their Lord's return and were confident it would be soon, just as he said he would :

> *For this we declare to you by the word of the Lord, that **we who are alive**, who are left until the coming of the Lord, will by no means precede those who have died. For the Lord himself, with a cry of command, with the archangel's call and with the sound of God's trumpet, will descend from heaven, and the dead in Christ will rise first. Then **we who are alive, who are left**, will be caught up in the clouds together with them to meet the Lord in the air; and so we will be with the Lord for ever.* (1 Thessalonians 4.15-17)

Note how Paul talks about 'we' who are left, not 'those' of the very far future. He does so again a few years later when he assures the church in Corinth that Christ would soon be returning to give them new bodies:

> *Listen, I will tell you a mystery! **We will not all die**, but we will all be changed, in a moment, in the twinkling of an eye, at the last trumpet.* (1 Corinthians 15.51-52)

As more time passed, adherents of the new faith become even more convinced the end must be imminent. After all, Jesus had promised he would come back soon, and the passage of several decades could only mean he would be arriving at any moment.

While they are starting to come up with excuses for the lateness of Jesus' appearance, nonetheless the excitement felt by second-century biblical writers is palpable:

> *Children,* ***it is the last hour****! As you have heard that antichrist is coming, so now many antichrists have come. From this we know that* ***it is the last hour****.* (1 John 2:17-18)

> *The end of all things* ***is near****.* (1 Peter 4.7)

So, the one whom Christians believe to be the Son of God prophesies that he will return while his audience is still alive; his apostle, Paul, ordained by God according to Romans 1.1, declares that Jesus will be returning soon. Similarly, later writers, also inspired by God according to Christians, proclaim that Jesus' return is 'near'.

Significantly, the equally late gospel of John eliminates all mention of the second coming and the arrival of the Kingdom: its writers can get away with so significant an omission when so few first, and even second generation Christians remain alive. Nonetheless, the New Testament couldn't be clearer about when the Lord is going to return; and it is not two thousand years into the future. That is not what terms like 'this generation', 'some who are standing here', 'we who are alive' and 'the end is near', uttered two millennia ago signify. There is no escaping the fact that Jesus failed to materialise as the Son of Man, in the heavens or anywhere else, when he said he would. He has failed to do so at any time since, as he was bound to do. Given that he failed to kick-start God's Kingdom on earth when he was alive, it is hardly surprising he couldn't manage it after his death. This is not 'doubting the Word of God', as present day believers might claim. It is facing the evidence, the reality that Jesus failed to do what he said he would. This central tenet of his 'good news', therefore, is demonstrably false: he was wrong about the Kingdom and his own triumphant return through the clouds; his followers were wrong to preach that he'd be back soon; early converts were wrong to think the end was near and Christians today are wrong in thinking he's going to return at this late date. And the reason they are wrong is that, as we all really know, dead men don't return as super-heroes, except in comic books.

What do Christians do about this problem? What they don't do is look to Deuteronomy 18:20-22 where God insists that false prophets be put to death (though this might explain why the religious authorities of his day were so eager to execute Jesus):

> *Any prophet who... presumes to speak in my name a word that I have not commanded the prophet to speak - that prophet shall die.' You may say to yourself, 'How can we recognise a word that the Lord has not spoken?' If a prophet speaks in the name of the Lord but the thing does not take place or prove true, it is a word that the Lord has not spoken. The prophet has spoken it presumptuously; do not be frightened by it.*

Instead, most Christians deny there is a problem; it is, they say, only the misinterpreting of scripture that leads to such erroneous conclusions. No *literal* reading is allowed here, oh no: when Jesus said he would be back within the lifetime of his disciples, that is not what he meant and his words are not to be understood literally. 'This generation', Christians explain, doesn't mean the generation of people Jesus was addressing. It means, rather, the generation living at the end of time, whenever that is, when certain conditions, like the gospel being preached 'throughout the world' (Matthew 24.14), have been met. Christians believe those conditions still haven't quite been met - but as ever Jesus' return is only a matter of time!

David Wenham suggests that the Bible verses that emphasise 'the unknownness of the time of the Lord's coming return (derive) from the church as it was faced with the embarrassment of Jesus' mistaken predictions of a near end', though is confident that such sayings and parables appeared very early in church tradition. It is true that a certain 'unknownness' about the timing of Jesus return creeps into some New Testament passages that deal with it – no doubt because of growing embarrassment - but even when Jesus is made to profess ignorance about precisely when he'll be back (as he does in Matthew 24.36), he is still talking in terms of events and conditions of the first century - specifically the destruction of Jerusalem in 70CE by the Romans - and he still includes the prediction that they will take place within 'this generation', referring to the one 'destined' to live through the traumas of the Roman assault; almost all of Matthew 24 is given over to this scenario. Other New Testament contributors, like the writer of 1 John, express the conviction, under the supposed inspiration of the Holy Spirit, that *his* generation is living in the very end times predicted by their Lord.

It takes some very convoluted exegesis to interpret away Jesus' failed prophecy about his second coming; but as we might expect, modern Christians are up to the job. Tom Wright, until recently the UK's Bishop of Durham, thinks we can get round the problem of Jesus' Son of Man prophecies by arguing that they don't refer to the 'second coming', when Jesus will inaugurate the Kingdom, but to his Ascension at the end of his thirty-three years on earth. To do this, Wright has to maintain that the word 'coming' in sayings like 'you will see the Son of Man coming in glory' really mean 'going', referring to Jesus' return to his Father: 'the coming', he says, 'is an upward not a downward movement'. In this way, the pronouncements cease to be failed prophecies of Jesus' imminent return as inaugurator of God's Kingdom, and instead fulfilled prophecies of his Ascension. Related in Mark 16.19 and Acts 1.9-11, the Ascension is indeed realised while all of the disciples, with the exception of Judas, are still alive. The author of Acts tells us: 'as the disciples were watching, Jesus was lifted up, and a cloud took him out of their sight. While he was going and they were gazing up towards heaven, suddenly two men in white robes stood by them'.

The problem for Tom Wright and this particular interpretation, however, is that 'coming' does not mean 'going'. It means the opposite. The only way the very clear use of 'coming' in the Son of Man prophecies would make any directional sense would be if Mark and Luke were giving us the perspective of Jesus' Ascension as it might be viewed by a resident of heaven looking down.

Evidently they are not doing this when the perspective in both accounts is that of the earthbound disciples who stand *'looking up towards heaven'* as Jesus ascends (Acts 1.9). In any case, Jesus' Ascension is remarkably low key; angel voices and heavenly trumpets are conspicuously absent. Even if Jesus was foretelling his Ascension in the Son of Man prophecies, he would be somewhat wide of the mark with regard to the bells and whistles he says will accompany it. Moreover, no New Testament writer interprets the prophecies in the way Wright proposes; Acts 1.11, for example, makes clear within a single verse that the Ascension and second coming are two separate and distinct events, the white-robed men telling the disciples, 'this Jesus, who has been taken up from you into heaven, will **come** in the same way as you saw him **go** into heaven'.

The prophecies Jesus makes of his return, then, are predictions not of departure, but of arrival. This is the way the New Testament authors understood them and it is how the Bible represents them. That Jesus and his early followers believed his return would occur within their lifetimes is a significant difficulty which most Christians prefer to ignore, or, if they're Tom Wright, attempt to get round by altering the meaning of words. So much for literal interpretation!

The Reverend exercises more verbal sleight-of-hand when he considers the nature of the Ascension itself. He proposes that Jesus did not 'ascend' to heaven in any way that we understand the term, in spite of Acts' insistence that Jesus 'was lifted up' and the disciples 'were gazing up towards heaven' as he completed his trajectory (Acts 1.9-10). However, Wright is of the view that the language of upwardness used of heaven and Jesus' return to it, is entirely metaphorical: metaphorical, that is, for 'sideways'. Apparently, at his Ascension, Jesus moved bodily into a parallel dimension, which Wright informs us, is where God's domain actually is. 'Heaven' exists 'tangentially' to the earth; that is, alongside it but invisible to it, while being everywhere at once (which, according to Wright, is how Jesus also pulls off the trick of being omnipresent). On the last day, however, 'heaven' will appear, as will Jesus once again, in the same dimension as the earth.

Heaven will then envelop the earth, along with all of the rest of creation, and regenerate everything in this earthly plane.

It's a nice idea, all this phasing in and out, but in the end, 'ascend' simply will not comply with the attempt to make it move sideways, even when compelled by a Bishop of the Church of England. Significantly, Wright himself can't even sustain it, informing us that God's heavenly city will come *down* to the earth, though no doubt he means this metaphorically. Jesus' Ascension is, as the word used of it tells us, upward. For those living in the first century, including Jesus and the New Testament authors, heaven was above the earth and synonymous with the sky; a canopy, pin-pricked with stars, where God made his home, and from where Jesus is made to say he 'came down' (John 6.38). In order to return to heaven, he must, of necessity, ascend skyward. In the end, Wright's idea about Jesus' shifting planes from the earth to a parallel, heavenly dimension that will one day phase over into this plane is completely alien to the Bible. It is more at home in *Star Trek* than Scripture.

Tom Wright also has to downplay the fact recorded in the Bible - which I feel sure he must have read - that Christians in the first century were already becoming concerned about Jesus' failure to return. If the Reverend is right, and they weren't much bothered about Jesus' non-appearance, then it is difficult to understand why Paul feels the need to reassure them that everything is going to plan, and that the Lord's return is going to happen soon. He devotes an entire letter, again that to the church in Thessalonica, addressing just such concerns. In what is Paul's earliest surviving letter, he is already having to tell a fledgling Christian community that those who have died while waiting for the Jesus' return will nonetheless experience resurrection. His words in 1 Thessalonians 4.15-17, quoted at the start of this section, read very much like a response to questions raised by a worried church. Almost a hundred years later, the author of 2 Peter is still addressing the issue, which is still a matter of concern among the faithful, as well it might be:

> *...in the last days scoffers will come, scoffing and*

> *indulging their own lusts and saying, 'Where is the promise of his coming? For ever since our ancestors died, all things continue as they were from the beginning of creation!' ...But do not ignore this one fact, beloved, that with the Lord one day is like a thousand years, and a thousand years are like one day. The Lord is not slow about his promise, as some think of slowness, but is patient with you not wanting any to perish, but all to come to repentance.* (2 Peter 3.3, 8-9)

What this demonstrates is that the Christian practice of compelling words to mean something other than what they do mean is not new. One day is not 'like a thousand years'; or at least if it is, Jesus seemed unaware of it while on earth. These verses are not spiritual insight into what the Lord 'really' meant, but rather a complete re-casting of his prophesy to return soon. The community to which the letter of 2 Peter was addressed was justified in feeling let down. The 'scoffers', history has shown, had a very good point.

What these second-century attempts at encouragement and Paul's earlier reassurances make clear is that the prophesies of Jesus' imminent return in glory were a significant problem for the early church. They remain so; Jesus gave no indication that his return would be thousands of years in his future. Quite the contrary. Consequently, some today take a different tack from Wright in trying to manoeuvre around the problem, by attempting to demonstrate that the term 'this generation' in the prophecies, refers not to the one Jesus was addressing, but to that which followed the restoration of a Jewish state. They work out this equally unlikely and non-literal interpretation of events from Jesus' parable of the fig tree in Matthew 24. Having apparently predicted the terrible events that will precede his second coming, Jesus says:

> *From the fig tree learn its lesson: as soon as its branch becomes tender and puts forth its leaves, you know that summer is near. So also, when you see all these things, you know that he is near, at the very gates. Truly I tell you, this generation will not pass away until all these things have taken place. Heaven and earth will pass*

> *away, but my words will not pass away. (*Matthew 24:32-35)

Ignoring the fact that the events he is made to predict relate to the destruction of Jerusalem by the Romans in 70CE, modern believers maintain he is instead talking about the future restoration of the Jewish nation. Here is an 'explanation' of the idea as it appears on *RaptureAlert.com*:

> *As Jesus reveals (in the parable), Israel will be given a final chance to exhibit faith in Him in the last days, just prior to His Glorious Appearing. To do so, Israel must first become a nation once again, a miraculous feat which took place in May 1948. The re-establishment of Israel as a nation is the foremost sign to our generation that Christ's return is imminent. And that's why the fig tree is the key to understanding which generation will witness the Second Coming of Jesus Christ. Through the nation of Israel, God has given the world a sign that is impossible to ignore. Nevertheless, most of the world has chosen to ignore it.*

… and not without good reason. Jesus is purportedly delivering his prophesy, known as the Olivet discourse, sometime early in the fourth decade. Israel, while chafing under Roman rule, existed as a nation; it would not make any sense to his disciples for him to be talking about a restoration of Israel. Of course Matthew's gospel was written after the destruction of Jerusalem – in all probability all of the gospels were – between 80 and 85CE. That is why the account of the destruction, described in Matthew 24.15-31 is accurate and detailed and it's also why, as a believer in Jesus-as-Messiah, Matthew claims Jesus' return is bound to follow hot on the heels of such a catastrophe: '*immediately* after the suffering of those days', he says, 'the Son of Man will appear (Matthew 24.29-30). However, this is not enough for today's believers, still frustrated by Jesus' non-return. His words need to be reinterpreted – they cannot accept that Jesus, the gospel writers and other New Testament contributors were simply wrong - and applied to an event almost two thousand years later. It remains the case that it is now over sixty years since the Jewish nation was restored, which, at the very least, is *two* generations ago, and he still hasn't appeared.

Let us though, for the sake of argument, accept for a moment that this is the scenario to which Jesus refers. The generation to whom Israel was restored in 1948, was already adult. While children undoubtedly followed their parents into the new nation, it was their parents' generation, that which had suffered so much under the Nazis, for whom the restoration was made. Assuming an average age on the low side for this generation of, say, 25 then the individuals who comprise it are now, if they are still alive, approaching 90. In his apocalyptic best seller *The Late, Great Planet Earth*, Hal Lindsey, writing in the 1970s, confidently predicted that the second coming would take place in 1988, the fortieth anniversary of the restoration and the end, technically, of the restored generation. But Jesus didn't make it in 1988 and he is now cutting it very fine indeed if he plans to return while 'this generation', and not just a few long-lived individuals, is still alive. Those who promote this version of the second coming must do so then with some sense of urgency. But a sense of urgency does not make an improbable event more probable.

Other groups of believers, like the *Renew America* organisation, read different portents of Jesus' return:

> *While trying to make sense of our world's current political and social disarray, many are led to believe that something extraordinary is about to happen. We could use some good news for a change. The Second Coming of our Saviour is imminent. The signs are all around us. America's life, liberty, and the pursuit of happiness are quickly eroding. It makes people tremble in righteous indignation.*

These creative interpretations of Jesus' announcements hinge on the perceived (but non-existent) imprecision of the phrase 'this generation'. But the term appears elsewhere in the gospels in contexts where it is transparently clear that he is referring to those around him – his own generation. Not even Christians argue to the contrary when in Mark 8.12, for example, he refuses to give a 'sign' to the sceptics of 'this generation', or in Luke 11.30 where he offers the story of Jonah as a sign to those around him (again referring to 'this generation') or in Luke 17.25 when he predicts the generation of which he is part will reject him. What too of those verses where he doesn't refer to 'this generation' but indicates the shortage of time in other ways? Clearly anachronistic, with details invented at a time when Christians were beginning to experience persecution, Matthew 10 sees Jesus sending out the twelve disciples to proclaim the Kingdom (verse 5) and telling them that the Son of Man will have appeared before they've been able to visit all the towns of Israel (verse 23). Lo and behold, by the start of chapter 12, they're back from their mission, the Son of Man hasn't materialised and both Jesus and the gospel writer have forgotten all about his earlier prediction. These indisputable references in the New Testament to Jesus' imminent return *are* disputed by Christians unable to face the (gospel) truth: that Jesus and his early followers were spectacularly wrong about the end of the age, the Second Coming and the inauguration of God's Kingdom on Earth. Like Jesus himself, later Christians have persisted in seeing his return as imminent, injecting misplaced excitement into the innumerable failed predictions of the last two thousand years. As writer Ken Daniels, an ex-evangelical minister, says:

> *It is ironic that some who most ardently defend the authority of scripture and object to loose interpretations that justify homosexuality, for example, tend to reverse course when presented with passages that clearly teach the return of Jesus in the first century. If it is a matter of defending the moral high ground against sexual impurity, the Bible must be taken at face value, but if it comes to defending the authority of the Bible itself, reinterpreting what it appears to say is not only permissible but mandatory and laudable.*

Those who fail to see this think that, like Jesus before them, they can initiate the Kingdom of Heaven on earth right now. As the founder of *Christian Voice,* Stephen Green, puts it: 'We believe the Holy Bible to be the inspired, infallible, written Word of God to whose precepts, given for the good of nations and individuals, all man's laws must submit' and 'Jesus urges us to be dangerous, to take a risk, to challenge the ruling clique. He invites us to join Him as He establishes His Kingdom, to play the man and stand up for Him'. This bullying rhetoric is a made-in-the-UK version of a Christian movement known as Dominionism, the more extreme form of which is, predictably, prevalent in America, where it is known as Reconstructionism.

Dominionists and Reconstructionists believe that the Church 'should cause the whole earth to come under the Lordship (dominion) of Jesus Christ, that the laws of the State, of human governments, should eventually conform to the Law of God as an expression of that dominion'. The Kingdom thus established, Jesus will return to rule over an earth already purified and sanctified for him. This is actually the same mistake Jesus himself made: believing that a tipping point can be reached when humanity will be sufficiently holy for God to intervene and for Christ to return to rule the earth as its king.

While the Jesus of the gospels was, perhaps, modest enough to limit himself to the restoration of Jewish society, Reconstructionists believe they can convert the entire earth, so that all governments and all people willingly subject themselves to God's commandments. Where Reconstructionists can't convert governments, they will replace them. Where they can't convert individuals, they will execute them. There will be no place in the Kingdom for adulterers, homosexuals, abortionists, women who have had an abortion, rebellious children, liars and blasphemers, all of whom will be subject to the death penalty. Stoning is the favoured method of prominent Reconstructionist Gary North, on the basis that if it was good enough for ancient tribesmen, it is good enough for those living in the twenty-first century. Jesus suggests in Matthew 11.12 that the coming of the Kingdom will be associated with force and violence: Reconstructionists want to make sure it is. The entire Dominionist movement, from Gary 'stones are cheap and plentiful' North to the whingeing *Christian*

Voice, arrogantly presume that they will be able to do what Jesus couldn't, and usher in God's Kingdom on earth themselves.

In the end though, however much Christians re-interpret, spiritualise and twist the words of verses that prophesy the second coming, there is no escaping the fact that Jesus - God himself according to most Christians - was entirely mistaken about his imminent return. And if he could be wrong about this, what else was this God-man wrong about?

Nothing less than his claim that he would rise from the dead after three days; again assuming the mantle of the Son of Man, an Old Testament figure anticipated to appear at the end of the age (Daniel 7.13-14), Jesus makes this prophecy about himself:

> *the Son of Man will be handed over to the chief priests and the scribes, and they will condemn him to death; then they will hand him over to the Gentiles; they will mock him, and spit upon him, and flog him, and kill him; and after three days he will rise again.* (Mark 10.33-34)

On the surface of things, this seems pretty accurate for a prediction of events made some time before they actually happen (they wouldn't be a prediction otherwise). Except, of course, this prophecy, like others of Jesus', was written forty years or more after the event. Even then, Mark or whoever wrote the earliest gospel, can't get it right. It was a constant source of irritation to me as a Christian that fellow-believers, both ancient and modern, would proclaim that Jesus spent three days in the tomb before his miraculous resurrection. He did not: from the time he dies - 9am on Friday according to Mark (15.25) and his fellow synoptics - to his reappearance very early on the Sunday morning (16.2), the time Jesus spent playing dead is less than 48 hours; not three days, not even two.

What is the cause of this failed prophecy? For some reason, Mark assumes that 'on the third day', when he believed Jesus to have arisen, means the same as 'after three days', the words he has Jesus prophesy. The third day after the crucifixion would indeed be the

Sunday, but it wouldn't be, and isn't, three full days after it, as Mark's Jesus seems to think. The problem is not Mark's alone, however. Matthew's Jesus is even more emphatic that he will be buried for the three complete days:

> *For just as Jonah was for three days and three nights in the belly of the sea monster, so for three days and three nights the Son of Man will be in the heart of the earth.* (Matthew 12.40)

Thanks to Jesus' insistence in the earlier gospels that he would spend three days in the tomb, the belief that he must have done so, contrary to the 'evidence' in those same accounts that it was less than two, appears to have become securely established by the time of the fourth gospel. Its writers, however, find their own unique way round the problem. Their thinking seems to have been along the lines that 'if Jesus said he was going to be buried for three days and three nights, then he must have been. He's the Son of God so wouldn't get a thing like this wrong. Therefore, if, as we know, he rose on the Sunday, then he cannot have been crucified on the Friday. He must therefore, have died on the Thursday'. And so the writers of John's gospel shift the crucifixion back a day, to the afternoon of Thursday (19.14). It's an ingenious solution. Thursday to Sunday – near enough three whole days. There's even some neat symbolism as a bonus: the earlier execution equates with the slaughter of the sacrificial lambs on the Thursday, ready for Friday's Passover. Problem more than solved!

Except it creates a whole raft of new ones, not least the glaring inconsistency between the synoptic gospels' accounts of the crucifixion on Passover Friday and John's gospel's portrayal of it on the preceding day. Significantly, no-one in the history of Christendom has ever been persuaded by John's Thursday crucifixion, otherwise we'd remember it on Good Thursday instead of Good Friday, with an extra day off work.

Does any of this matter? Probably not, but it does demonstrate that:
- if Jesus' words in the synoptic gospels are to be interpreted literally, then either he can't count or he badly misjudges

the timing of his resurrection. If scheduled for three days after the crucifixion it should have occurred on the Monday;

- the resurrection didn't happen at all – we'll see what probably did later - and more than forty years later, Mark and Matthew trip themselves up desperately trying not only to convince others that it did, but that Jesus knew it would;

- the gospel writers are prepared to rearrange already highly improbable events to make equally unlikely prophecies appear true;

- because the Bible cannot get its own faked, after-the-supposed-event prophecies right it can't possibly be trusted about other claims it makes.

The problem of dodgy prophecy doesn't just arise in the words Jesus is made to utter, however. Christians believe that the Bible is full of prophecy and that most of it is fulfilled in Jesus himself. Jewish sacred scripture - the Old Testament - only made it into the Christian Bible because of its supposed predictions of the coming of the Messiah, which of course Christians maintain is Jesus. Even then it was altered so that its supposed prophecies 'fit' the events of Jesus' life more closely. At the same time, other events were invented for the Jesus story to make it seem as if he fulfilled still other Old Testament prophecies. A closer look at a couple of these prophecies, central to what Christians believe about Jesus, reveals them to be as shaky as a house built on sand.

First of all, there's those 'Son of Man' statements themselves. Jesus, with no sense of irony, seems to assume the role as his super-hero alter-ego; the Superman to his Clark Kent, the Ziggy Stardust to his David Bowie. When you think about it, and generally Christians don't, this is a peculiar title for him to have awarded himself or to have bestowed post-deification. The only person ever to be born, supposedly, without a human father chooses a title that highlights nothing less than his human origins; a son of 'man' is, by definition, the antithesis of a son of god. Even more bizarrely, the gospel writers always have Jesus refer to his imagined, alternate identity in the third person: in Matthew 26.64, for example, he tells the high priest that 'from now on, you will see the Son of Man seated at the right hand of Power and coming on the clouds of heaven'. Overlooking the fact that this is another of Jesus' failed predictions about what he wanted to happen when God rebooted the entire system, is it not more than a little delusional to cast oneself in a more expansive role, and then to refer to that role as if it were a real identity? Is it not bordering on the schizophrenic, even, to see oneself as two entities, one of which is so much more powerful and exciting than one's ordinary mortal self?

Despite Jesus referring to himself as the Son of Man a total of forty-three times in the gospels, Paul makes no mention of the title, nor indeed do any other New Testament authors with the exception of the fantasist behind Revelation. Paul prefers 'the Christ' as the name of his super-hero Jesus and it is easy to gloss over the fact that the two titles - 'the Son of Man' and 'the Christ' - do not mean the same thing. Furthermore, if 'the Son of Man' was central to how Jesus saw himself, why do Paul and the other New Testament writers seem to be so unaware of it? Why doesn't it transfer across to their writing, some of which is contemporaneous with the gospels and some even earlier? There are four possibilities:

1. Like Jesus' real name - Joshua Bar-Joseph - the term is very Jewish. It occurs a number of times in the Jewish scriptures (the Old Testament) though it is rarely applied to the prophesied Messiah there. In fact, it is most frequently used to distinguish mortals from the inhabitants of heaven. Paul is determined his version of the gospel will appeal to a gentile (i.e. non-Jewish) audience and so eliminates as many Jewish elements from it as he can.

2. Many early Christians either didn't know that Jesus used the Son of Man title of himself, or they didn't care. Given the growing belief in the first century of Christianity that Jesus was the Messiah or the Son of God or even, eventually, God himself, it seems improbable his early followers would disregard what Jesus was known to call himself. It is more likely they didn't know. But how could this be? Didn't they have the gospels that told them? The

answer is 'no'; many did not and what they had instead was Paul's fantasy version of what Jesus was about. Paul's message of salvation is the result of his own mystical experiences; he has little knowledge of the gospels, including what Jesus did, said (with the exception of a version of his words at the last supper) and what he called himself.

In other words, the two strands of the gospel tradition and Paul's good news developed separately and had little to do with each other. This accounts for the fact they present very different versions of Jesus. It also explains why there are two different Pauls as well, one conveyed in his letters and the other in Acts. The author of both Acts and Luke's gospel does his best to harmonise the disparate versions of Jesus – Paul's Christ and the Son of Man from the gospel tradition – but can only do so by compromising both: he all but abandons the Son of Man title in Acts, using it only once, while altering Paul and his theology so radically that the apostle of Acts bears little relation to that of the letters. No other New Testament writer, apart from the author of Revelation, seems to be even aware that Jesus called himself the Son of Man, suggesting they too developed or heard a very different interpretation of Jesus from that contained in the gospels.

3. Jesus didn't call himself the Son of Man at all and the notion that he did is a later development that evolved with the gospel tradition. It is possible that with his reputation after death growing, those who developed the oral tradition, later to become the gospels, needed something with which to mark his significance. Not yet thinking of him as the Son of God or divine in any way, those responsible for the oral tradition that later became the gospels settled on an enigmatic title from their scriptures: 'the Son of Man', served their purpose.

The difficulty with his explanation is that Jesus is made to assume the title in all four gospels; while Mark, Matthew and Luke share common source material, John reflects something of a separate tradition and is very late (possibly as late as 125CE). If 'the Son of Man' was an early attempt to suggest Jesus' importance, the John tradition would, in all likelihood, have eliminated it by this time, as it expunges other material incompatible with a semi-divine Jesus.

Nonetheless, the fact remains Jesus is only the Son of Man in the gospels and Revelation.

And finally in this chapter on dodgy prophecy and faulty predictions, what are we to make of the Bible's conflicting claims that the Messiah is to be born of David's line and also the product of that common means of delivery, a virgin birth. The writer of Acts is at pains to remind his readers that Jesus is descended directly from the Jewish King David. It is important that he is, because the Jewish scriptures clearly state that the Messiah will be a descendant of David's. Those looking for the appearance of the Messiah knew that, for the prophecies to be fulfilled, he had to be of David's line. Acts' author, whom we'll call Luke for convenience though we do not know if this was his name, is also keen to impress on his largely Roman audience that his new religion has an ancient pedigree, because, as Barrie Wilson points out in *How Jesus Became Christian*, the Romans were unimpressed by novelty, preferring their religions to have a respectable vintage. A new belief system, therefore, needed to ground itself in an old one if it was to stand any chance of survival in the wider Roman world.

Consequently, Luke reminds his readers that King David was 'a prophet, and knowing that God had sworn with an oath to him, that *of the fruit of his loins, according to the flesh*, he would raise up Christ to sit on his throne'. (Acts 2.30, KJV; my emphasis). The reference is to 2 Samuel 7:12, where Yahweh does indeed appear to tell David that he 'will raise up your offspring after you, who shall come forth from your body, and I will establish his Kingdom'. Notice again the emphasis in the original prophecy on the physical connection between David and his Kingdom-establishing descendant.

It is important to Luke to show that it is through the all-important male-line that Jesus can trace his ancestry to King David. Therefore he is at pains to stress that it is Joseph, not Mary, who is descended from David; this is how he contrives to get both of them to Bethlehem, 'royal David's city', in his nativity story: 'Joseph also went from the town of Nazareth in Galilee to Judea, to the city of David called Bethlehem, because he was descended from the house and family of David' (Luke 2.4).

The problem for Christians who want to claim, as Paul does in Romans 1.3, that Jesus is David's physical descendant and therefore the Messiah, is that Jesus was supposedly conceived and born of a virgin who was impregnated, not by David's descendant Joseph, but by the Almighty himself. But Jesus cannot be descended from David when he isn't descended from Joseph. It is only through Joseph that any descendancy from David, 'according to the flesh', is possible. Why doesn't Luke know that, according to the doctrine of the virgin conception, Jesus was not the fruit of any human male's loins? He includes the virgin conception and birth in his gospel (Luke 1.32-35), yet, in both the gospel and his fanciful account of the early church, Acts, makes much of Jesus being the Messiah because he is a physical descendant of David (see, for example, Luke 1.27, 1.32, 1.69, 2.4, 2.11, 3.31, 18.38, 20.41).

Luke wants it both ways: he wants his audience to know that Jesus is the Son of God, created by the Almighty's impregnation of Mary, *and* that through Joseph he's King David's descendant 'according to the flesh'. But he can't have it both ways: *either* Jesus is physically descended from David *or* he is a being conceived through divine rape, like other mythical god-men of the ancient world. He cannot be both - though he could, of course, be neither.

PART TWO: FALSE PROMISES

Chapter 2
Broken Promises, Worthless Guarantees

It's a very bad start. The Messiah gets it wrong about when he'll make his comeback tour, his supporters tell confused stories about his background and influences and, in truth, no-one's really sure if he's the artist formerly known as the Son of Man or not. However, many a star has risen on the strength of their material above such unpromising beginnings and certainly Jesus has enjoyed a long and illustrious career on the basis of his. But just how good is it? We need to take a closer look.

In several places in the gospels, Jesus promises that believers with only the smallest amount of faith will be able to move mountains and perform greater miracles than he himself did:

> *Truly I tell you, if you say to this mountain, "Be taken up and thrown into the sea", and if you do not doubt in your heart, but believe that what you say will come to pass, it will be done for you. So I tell you, whatever you ask for in prayer, believe that you have received it, and it will be yours. (*Mark 11:24, also Matthew 21.21-22)

> *For truly I tell you, if you have faith the size of a mustard seed, you will say to this mountain, "Move from here to there", and it will move; and nothing will be impossible for you.* (Matthew 17.21)

> *Very truly, I tell you, the one who believes in me will also do the works that I do and, in fact, will do greater works than these, because I am going to the Father. I will do whatever you ask in my name, so that the Father may be glorified in the Son. If in my name you ask me for anything, I will do it.* (John 14.12-14)

Shouldn't we, as a result, see Christians raising the dead, healing the blind, walking on water, turning water into wine, as well as being able to move physical objects by the power of faith, just as Jesus promises in these verses? Shouldn't they regularly demonstrate even greater feats, even if Jesus is cagey about what these actually might be? Of course, we don't, so perhaps it's the case that Christians lack sufficient faith; perhaps they don't really believe Jesus when he makes such outlandish promises, or, more likely - and this is the most plausible explanation - he was just plain wrong. No Christian has ever been able to move so much as a mustard seed through the power of wishful thinking, and these promises are simply fraudulent.

This gives Christians a problem: how to explain verses like these? How do Christians excuse the fact that they don't out-perform Jesus, or even come close to working miracles themselves? We're not talking here about the occasional psychosomatic healing nor the emotional frenzy that accompanies some churches' extreme worship; we're not talking about these because they are not what Jesus is talking about. Christians, when they bother to address these verses at all, do their utmost to wriggle around them using a range of spurious strategies – 'Biblical Exegesis' in Christian-speak. We'll look at each of these in turn, starting with their favourite excuse: 'Jesus is speaking metaphorically'.

As we are going to see throughout this book this hoary old chestnut is regularly used to explain away any awkward parts of the Bible. It is also rather inconsistent of Christians, hypocritical even, when at other times many of them spend their time asserting that the Bible is the 'literal' word of God. Can a text be absolutely literal and yet metaphorical at the same time? Not really: it can be literal in places and metaphorical in others, but this is not what literalists claim. Figurative readings of parts of the Bible, sometimes proposed by more liberal Christians, create other problems: how do we know when God is being literal and when he's speaking figuratively? In some verses it's clear - Jesus does not, for example, offer his disciples slices of his flesh to eat nor open a vein so they can drink his blood – but in other cases it cannot be that just because a verse is difficult or unrealistic, as these ones are, it must be figurative. To be sure, Jesus does sometimes use simile and metaphor to illustrate a point, but that doesn't mean the point itself is to be understood figuratively. 'The figurative language' as one Christian web-site puts it, 'is always intended to convey a literal truth'. Nonetheless, Christians resort to figurative interpretations when a literal one is too awkward or uncomfortable. We can see this in the desperate attempts by our old friend, the former Bishop of Durham, Tom Wright, to interpret some of Jesus' ask-and-receive pronouncements metaphorically.

Wright suggests in *Jesus and the Victory of God* that when Jesus talks about moving mountains he is actually referring to the temple in Jerusalem, prophesying the overthrow of the temple's system of worship as it existed at the time. Certainly Jesus disapproved of this system, as his symbolic 'cleansing' of the temple earlier in Matthew 21 attests, but how does Wright get from an extravagant promise about moving mountains to this? Easy: the temple, he points out, was situated on a mount, the eponymous 'temple mount', and it is to this that Jesus refers; the 'moving mountains' promise really means that the temple system ('the mountain') will be overthrown (the 'thrown into the sea' part) when the new Kingdom bursts on to the scene.

This really is ingenious, except the temple *mount* was not, and is not, a *mountain,* mounts and mountains being significantly different in scale. And, while the temple and its system were eventually destroyed by the Romans in 70CE, this was hardly the act of faith Jesus refers to. Those who accomplished it were not believers, they were pagans and could not possibly have been who Jesus had in mind when telling his followers it would be *their* faith and prayer that would lead to change. Had the Roman destruction of the temple been what Jesus had in mind, Matthew in particular would have ensured he said so clearly - he was after all composing his gospel some time after 70CE - and is more than happy elsewhere to show the fulfilment of Jesus' prophecies by writing them up after the event. Pro-Roman Luke could even have got bonus points for doing so, by showing that the Romans too were all part of God's great plan. But no, even as a prophecy 'moving mountains' is a failure and all that Wright achieves is to shift it from one category to another, from false promise to failed prophecy. In any case, the remainder of the verse, and all the others Wright doesn't take into account, are not open to the kind of torturous interpretation he prefers. When Jesus says directly and precisely, 'whatever you ask for in prayer with faith, you will receive', he means, presumably, what he says. 'Whatever' takes us beyond the realms of mounts, beyond mountains even, and means what it says - anything at all. What can be metaphorical about that? To drive the point home, the gospel writers keep repeating this same promise, often without any figurative language at all (emphases mine):

> *Again, truly I tell you, if two of you agree on earth about **anything** you ask, it will be done for you by my Father in heaven.* (Matthew 18.19)
>
> *I will do **whatever** you ask in my name, so that the Father may be glorified in the Son.* (John 14.13)
>
> *Very truly, I tell you, if you ask **anything** of the Father in my name, he will give it to you.* (John 16.23)

It becomes increasingly more difficult for Christians to manoeuvre around these verses. But, in spite of the all-encompassing nature of the promise, manoeuvre they do. God loves a trier, which leads us neatly to trying excuse number two: 'we don't ask for the right things'.

If Jesus says we can ask for 'whatever' and 'anything', how is it possible to ask for the wrong things? Assuming, however, that we can, and that God is unlikely to meet requests for lottery wins and Porsches - Jesus is, after all, opposed to riches in spite of what those who espouse the prosperity gospel might say – what are the right things to ask for? Jon J. Cardwell of *Justification by Grace* explains all:

> *We never read anywhere in Scripture, or even in any extra-biblical historical accounts that any of the Lord's*

> *disciples ever said to a mountain, "Be thou removed, and be thou cast into the sea" (Mark 11:23). When Jesus taught that we would receive whatever we desired when we prayed, He spoke of those whose sinful and desperately wicked hearts had been replaced with new hearts; He spoke of those who were once spiritually dead, now having been resurrected with a new spirit unto newness of life; He spoke of the praying soul who was now regenerated, having an entirely new disposition, with a heart that has turned to God and panting hard after Him, to love Him with all the heart, all the soul, all the mind, and all the strength. Is your desire the God who has saved you? Is it the Lord that you want?*

Really? What Jesus means by 'anything' is this woolliness? A buzz or blessing from working ourselves up into a state of adoration? Forgive me, Jon, but no, that's not what Jesus says. Elsewhere, it's true, he speaks clearly about loving God with all of one's heart, but that's the point - he says so clearly. If this is what he is saying in the many places he's made to make this promise, why obfuscate it to the extent it takes a paragraph to explain the simple directness of the three words, 'ask and receive'? Jesus' illustrations all concern physical reality – mountains, doors, bread - and, though I'm now repeating myself, absolutes like 'whatever' and 'anything'. He is not talking obliquely about modern day spritual 'blessings'.

So, this doesn't help. Perhaps an example of the right kind of asking prayer would help us here. There's the 'Lord's prayer' of course, which has a fair amount of asking in it - for the kingdom to come to earth, for daily bread, forgiveness and protection from temptation, all of which reflect physical as well as spiritual needs – but let us take a closer look at a different prayer of Jesus':

> *Father... I ask not only on behalf of these (the disciples), but also on behalf of those who will believe in me through their word, that they may all be one. As you, Father, are in me and I am in you, may they also be in us, so that the world may believe that you have sent me. The glory that you have given me I have given*

> *them, so that they may be one, as we are one, I in them and you in me, that they may become completely one, so that the world may know that you have sent me and have loved them even as you have loved me.* (John 17.20-23)

I think you'll agree that this asks for the right sort of 'anything': for believers to be one with the same unity the gospel writer imagines Jesus has with his heavenly father. And this being a prayer of Jesus' it is probably safe to assume it has enough faith behind it to ensure the unity asked for becomes a reality. It might well be the case, of course, that the writers of John's gospel, alarmed by the absence of love and unity among believers (see Galatians 2.11-14, 1 Corinthians 1.10-13, Ephesians 4.25-32) placed this prayer on Jesus' lips retrospectively, but whether his or theirs, one thing is apparent: the prayer went unanswered. The early church remained riven with dissent and in the two thousand years that followed, Christians denounced, totured and eradicated fellow Christians over doctrinal differences.

Today there are 34,000 Christian movements, denominations, churches, cults and sects, many of whom express hatred for the 'apostasy' of the others, reflecting the disunity of believers. Hardly what Jesus had in mind! So much then for asking for the right things and having mountain-moving faith to ensure they happen. If the one who promised this couldn't make it work, what hope is there for anyone else?

Another approach attempted by Christians as they try to get round the failure of this promise is to argue that God has a number of responses at his disposal when petitioned. 'God' they tell us, 'doesn't always answer prayers in the way we want him to'. He can, if we ask for he right things and he is feeling generous, say 'yes' to requests, but he can also say 'no', 'not now', or 'have this instead', offering us an alternative to what we've asked for rather like the child who receives a pair of socks for Christmas when he really wanted a bicycle. Of course, all of this contradicts what Jesus says – when he says 'ask and you shall receive' he doesn't make provision for any of the spiritual hedging that is necessary when the promise doesn't actually 'work' (which is always). Jesus is prepared to acknowledge that it may take a little time - but only a little - for God to respond to our petitions, but even the point of this teaching is that persistence pays off and God will give you what you ask for:

> *Suppose one of you has a friend, and you go to him at midnight and say to him, "Friend, lend me three loaves of bread; for a friend of mine has arrived, and I have nothing to set before him." And he answers from within, "Do not bother me; the door has already been locked, and my children are with me in bed; I cannot get up and give you anything." I tell you, even though he will not get up and give him anything because he is his friend, at least because of his persistence he will get up and give him whatever he needs.* (Luke 11.5-8)

Many Christians have no faith in this special offer of Jesus'. When they are ill, for example, they may pray and ask for healing, but not really expecting to receive it, they turn to science – the doctor and the surgeon – for more efficacious treatment. There are occasionally instances of Christians relying entirely on faith for a cure, just as Jesus – and James - suggest. Far from the promise that 'the prayer of faith will save the sick, and the Lord will raise them up' (James 5.15), results are frequently disastrous, as these recent cases illustrate:

> Rather than seeking medical help when he developed an inflammation in his urinary system, Neil Beagley's parents and members of the church they belonged to prayed for him. During the few days in which they did so, the boy 'filled up with urine, (which) eventually ruined his bladder and kidneys and resulted in heart failure'. Neil died, aged 16.

> Madeline Neumann developed a diabetic complaint. Her parents did not take her to a doctor but prayed for healing, recruiting others to join them as Madeline's

condition worsened. A month later, Madeline died. She was 11. Her parents said the reason their prayers went unanswered was because they did not have enough faith. Her mother told police there was a chance Madeline could be resurrected.

When their son's appendix burst, Zachery Swezey's parents followed the advice in James 5.14-15, anointing him with oil and praying for healing. As a result, Zachary died. He was 17.

Ava Worthington was 15 months old when she developed pneumonia. Instead of taking her to a doctor, which they didn't believe in, her parents prayed, fasted and anointed her with oil, which they did. Six days later she was dead.

As Francis Collins, the Christian *Director of the National Institutes of Health,* admits when considering prayed-for cures, 'as a physician I have not seen evidence for such medical miracles in my own experience'. After all those promises in the Bible? Who'd have thought it?

The Christian alternatives to Jesus' promised receiving are efforts to explain (away) the fact that in reality, it is much more probable that asking will not lead to receiving. There is perhaps some slim chance that what has been asked for will appear, and from time to time it will, but this will be no more than chance allows. Ask enough and the odds are that sooner or later the requested 'blessing' will turn up anyway. And how then the Christian praises the Lord! But since there is no God to respond in the first place, not even one in a night-shirt, how can this be anything other than coincidence?

Prayer doesn't work, certainly not in the way Jesus promised it would. Not even the most devout of Christians can get it to, demonstrating emphatically that, in fact, it doesn't work at all. Perhaps Jesus will do better with another of his guarantees, because he doesn't give up easily. He's got other offers to make, as well as trotting out the 'curing the sick' shtick one more time. In

Mark 16:17 he promises: 'these signs will accompany those who believe: by using my name they will cast out demons; they will speak in new tongues; they will pick up snakes in their hands, and if they drink any deadly thing, it will not hurt them; they will lay their hands on the sick, and they will recover'.

Of course we see this sort of thing all the time. When they're not swigging back bottles of sparkling cyanide, *Draino* and domestic bleach, Christians regularly show anacondas and rattle-snakes who's boss. Sure enough, it's a sign of just how great the Lord is when they suffer no ill effects from either snake venom or liquid poison - it's as if they're immune to the stuff. Taking a break from playing with snakes and drinking deadly substances – though sometimes they take the snakes along with them - Christians seek out those who are ill, lay hands on them and witness their instant recovery, just like Jesus says they will. It's not just specially gifted 'healers' who can do this, no sir, because that's not what Jesus promises! All believers can, which is why we've had no need for medicine or hospitals these last two thousand years. And as for demons, well, they don't even bother possessing anyone these days - not really worth their time, you see, with all of these miracle-working Christians about.

On the other hand, maybe Christian can do none of this stuff. When is the last time you saw them drinking poison with no ill-effect? Or handling serpents without coming to harm? There are those 'Holiness' churches in the Appalachians that do play with snakes, but members are frequently bitten and poisoned, with fatalities among their number now in the region of a hundred. Even they don't go for the drinking bleach option, though don't let that put you off asking any Christians you know to demonstrate this particular sign. There is, as we've already conceded, the occasional unattested 'healing' of psychosomatic ailments reported at evangelical rallies, where believers are hyped up to such a degree that they'd believe anything (and do) and even the odd exorcism of imagined demons, with the Catholic church employing specially trained exorcists in the present day. But the evidence - the signs – that Jesus talks about, as manifested by 'those who believe', simply doesn't exist. Apart from the easiest and most useless one of all, the babbling in 'new' and non-existent languages, believers don't and can't demonstrate these largely idiotic behaviours, and, indeed, why should they? Because Jesus says they will, that's why. If signs from snake handling and poison drinking to exorcisms and widespread healing were to be testimony to Jesus' and God's power, then lack of them can only demonstrate its absence.

We should, in fairness, note that most scholars regard these verses, and all of those following verse 8 in this final chapter of Mark, to be later additions. This should let Jesus off the hook, but since when do Christians listen to scholars? They're of the unshakeable opinion that all of the Bible is God's word, these suspect verses included. So Jesus, and his conspicuously miracle-free followers, are stuck with them - and we can chalk up another set of false promises. Better luck next time...

Jesus tells his followers in several places in the gospels that they need not worry about either their material needs or the future. He promises God will take care of both. Because his argument is less than persuasive, it is less pithy than usual. Here it is as Matthew records it:

> *Therefore I tell you, do not worry about your life, what you will eat or what you will drink, or about your body, what you will wear. Is not life more than food, and the body more than clothing? Look at the birds of the air; they neither sow nor reap nor gather into barns, and yet your heavenly Father feeds them. Are you not of more value than they? And can any of you by worrying add a single hour to your span of life? And why do you worry about clothing? Consider the lilies of the field, how they grow; they neither toil nor spin, yet I tell you, even Solomon in all his glory was not clothed like one of these. But if God so clothes the grass of the field, which is alive today and tomorrow is thrown into the oven, will he not much more clothe you – you of little faith?*

> *Therefore do not worry, saying, "What will we eat?" or "What will we drink?" or "What will we wear?" For it is the Gentiles who strive for all these things; and indeed your heavenly Father knows that you need all these things. But strive first for the Kingdom of God and his righteousness, and all these things will be given to you as well.* (Matthew 6.25-7.1)

Evidently life is more than food and clothing, but that doesn't reduce in any way the need for such necessities. Granted Jesus is here stressing the need to 'let go and let God', as they say in evangelical circles, because he is mindful of our need for food and clothing, but really this advice is worse than useless. Your worry or concern about fulfilling life's basic needs is inversely proportional to your ability to supply them for yourself; the less your needs are met, the more you will be inclined to worry about them. It is quite fatuous, therefore, to tell people not to be concerned about their physical needs if they are unable to meet them. Wasn't it Marie Antoinette's equally trite, 'Let them eat cake!' that led her to the guillotine? God, when all is said and done, is notoriously inconsistent when it comes to providing for people – just ask the impoverished and starving in the world today – as Jesus seems to recognise in his peculiar analogy with cut grass and birds of the field.

Elsewhere, in Matthew's gospel (10.29-31), Jesus promises that God cares for people more than he cares for sparrows. Given that the sparrows in his illustration are being sold as food to those who can afford nothing better, this is not saying very much. It almost looks as if Jesus is being cruelly ironic, pointing out, in effect, that as God isn't really bothered about preserving the life of a few inconsequential birds, he's not going to do much more for human beings. If only he were saying this. At least then he would be demonstrating some honesty, because no amount of chasing the Kingdom of God is going to manifest food and clothing. Jesus must know this because he acknowledges in Matthew 25 that there are people who are hungry, thirsty and without clothes. So why doesn't God provide for them? Is it because they don't strive strenuously enough for the Kingdom? In fact, the extent to which a person has their basic needs met is entirely dependent on where they are born. Western Christians today know this; they don't rely on God to provide for them while they spend their time pursuing his Kingdom. Instead they work to put food on the table and clothes on their children's backs. By the sweat of their own brows they meet their needs; God has nothing to do with it.

Once the Kingdom comes, on Earth as in Heaven, God will be looking for a particular kind of person to populate it (Jesus and his mates will *rule* it, so need to worry about how that's going to pan out). Jesus reassures his followers in Matthew 5 that, when the time comes, 'the meek will inherit the Earth', his promise (or perhaps it's another failed prophecy) being part of the so-called Sermon on the Mount. This catalogue of pronouncements, also known as the beatitudes, expresses Jesus' vision for the world once God's Kingdom comes into force: not only will the meek inherit the Earth, but those who mourn will be comforted, the poor in spirit blessed and those who thirst after righteousness fulfilled. What cold comfort for the impoverished, the meek and the grief-stricken among his immediate audience when he forgets to mention that they'll be long dead by the time the Kingdom makes its appearance, millennia into the future (he doesn't add this because he labours under the illusion that the Kingdom is just around the corner). So the meek he's talking to here can forget inheriting the Earth... as we now know, it didn't happen for them, nor for the meek in ensuing centuries.

Jesus makes related remarks elsewhere in the gospels where he promises, for example, that many who are first shall find themselves last and those currently last, first (Matthew 20.16). Again, he is looking towards the time when the Kingdom of God bursts on to the scene, and social hierarchies are over-turned, justice prevails and those at the bottom of the pile find themselves elevated to the top. Did this happen? Did the poor find themselves rich? Were the oppressed set free (Luke 4.18)? Did the working class – Jesus' disciples in particular - find themselves ruling over others, as he says they will in Matthew 19.28? Has any of this happened in the two thousand years since he said it would? Not, it has to be said, to the extent that anyone has noticed. Of course, we can spiritualise all of these pronouncements, as Christians do, glossing over the obvious fact that Jesus is talking about a revolution in his own here-and-now, and arguing instead that he is referring to rewards in the life to come: as the *Online Bible Study* declares, 'the 'First-last, Last-first' doctrine is an eternal rewards concept for believers'.

There are lots of reasons, which we will explore later in this book, why Jesus is emphatically not saying any such thing. Suffice to say at this point, if he meant to teach that 'you will get your reward after you die', then he forgets to mention it on every occasion when he talks about the last being first and the meek inheriting the Earth. That is because 'inheriting *the Earth*' is entirely the point and has nothing to do with an after-life in an entirely different place, in a heaven that Jesus has very little to say about, anywhere. No, he clearly teaches that the reversal of the way things are will happen on this Earth, and within a short time of his announcing them. Spirtualising his pronouncements can only be achieved by ignoring what he actually says.

So what are we to make of his promises that the world was about to be turned upside down, if we are not to spiritualise them or write them off, yet, as false promises and failed prophecies? It could be argued, I suppose, that what Jesus was talking about was the Christian era that he knew would follow his life's work, when believers would take charge of the world, salvation would be taken up by all and the Earth would become a Christian utopia.

Even a cursory glance at the history of the two millennia since Jesus' ministry shows that whenever Christians have inherited the Earth and taken control of it, disaster has ensued, as sure as night follows day, for almost everybody else living in it. The meek - assuming Jesus means 'Christians' when using the term - have frequently been far from gentle. Whenever they've gained the upper hand, they've shown themselves as capable of suppression and cruelty as any totalitarian regime, initiating campaigns of terror and persecution, crusades and pogroms. We can be sure that should today's meek souls get their chance, it would be no different, as Dominionist pastor Gary North makes clear:

> *The long-term goal of Christians in politics should be to gain exclusive control over the franchise. Those who refuse to submit publicly to the eternal sanctions of God by submitting to His Church's public marks of the covenant – baptism and holy communion – must be denied citizenship, just as they were in ancient Israel. The way to achieve this political goal is through successful mass evangelism followed by constitutional revision.*

If this is what the meek are capable of, then God save us from their inheriting. Thankfully, Jesus' promise in this instance, as in others, is hopelessly false; the meek did not inherit the Earth when or in the way he promised, and we can only hope that they never do.

He has more words of wisdom for the meek and others who take up their cross to follow him in Matthew 5.11-12 where he says: 'Blessed are you when people revile you and persecute you and utter all kinds of evil against you falsely on my account. Rejoice and be glad, for your reward is great in heaven, for in the same way they persecuted the prophets who were before you'.

Jesus may have thought so, but today's western Christians don't. They react aggressively to criticism, which, as the bishop of Croydon, Nick Baines, has pointed out, is a long way from true persecution; they whinge if mildly slighted and see themselves as a persecuted minority on the rare occasions they fail to get their own way. Instead of counting the blessings that Jesus tells them result from being reviled in his name, they prefer to sue. Either modern, western Christians fail spectacularly to claim this promise of their Lord and Saviour, or he showed little understanding of human psychology in the first place, when suggesting that persecution brings its own reward. It's probable, of course, that both parties are wrong and that Christians are as fallibly human as the rest of us, in spite of the supposed 'indwelling' of the Holy Spirit. This is a topic to which we will return later but it's sufficient to note at this point that Jesus and several New Testament writers have much to say about persecution. Consequently, there is much for Christians to ignore.

But whatever fate befalls them, Christians need have no worries about one particular aspect of their physiognomy. Yes, they may have limbs lopped from their bodies and they may be crucified just as he was, but – blessed assurance! - not a single hair on their heads will come to harm. Isn't that fabulous?

The context of this strange promise is a prophecy about the persecution of early Christians that began in earnest under the emperor Nero, some thirty years after Jesus' death. Jesus explains to the disciples what it will be like:

> *...they will arrest you and persecute you; they will hand you over to synagogues and prisons, and you will be brought before kings and governors because of my name. This will give you an opportunity to testify. So make up your minds not to prepare your defence in advance; for I will give you words and a wisdom that none of your opponents will be able to withstand or contradict. You will be betrayed even by parents and brothers, by relatives and friends; and they will put some of you to death. You will be hated by all because of my name. But not a hair of your head will perish. By your endurance you will gain your souls.* (Luke 21.12-19)

Either Jesus is remarkably prescient or, as with much of his prophecy, his predictions have been created retrospectively, once the events he refers to have come to pass. I'll leave it to you, reader, to decide which it is here. Regardless, Jesus, or whoever created this particular part of his script, is wrong in one crucial respect, when he tells those who will suffer needlessly in his name that not a hair on their heads will perish. Many early Christians were tortured and executed, including Jesus' own brother and leader of the church in Jerusalem, James (circa 62CE), several of the disciples and the self-appointed apostle, Paul (circa 64CE). And we can be fairly certain that whatever hair they had on their heads 'perished' when they did.

Perhaps Jesus suffered from male pattern baldness, which might explain his fixation with hair, because as well as promising that not a single hair on a persecuted believer's head would perish, he declares equally improbably in Matthew 10.30 that all the hairs on the disciples' heads are counted. God really does have too much time on his hands. Consequently and predictably, Christians, starting with Augustine in the fifth century, have tied themselves in tangled knots trying to explain Jesus' bizarre claim that not a single, numbered hair would be lost. What he means, some of them tell us, is that the *souls* of persecuted believers will be unharmed, safe in God's care, whatever they endure. But hair, it has to be said, seems a highly incongruous metaphor for the soul, and isn't one that the gospel writers or other New Testament authors use anywhere else.

So maybe, Christians argue, because hair is a part of the physical body, Jesus means it to stand for the whole body, and yes, this might be put to death, but it will live again as a resurrected super-body. God will then reinstate even the hair of those who have died for Jesus' sake. Which means there are going to be a lot of hirsute people in the Kingdom when all the hair they've ever possessed is returned, post-mortem, to their heads. This *is* what Jesus promises. Paul, though, says in 1 Corinthians 11.14 that long hair degrades a man, while Augustine argues tortuously that, come the resurrection, any excess hair will be incorporated into the body somewhere else. Perhaps, though, God doesn't intend acting as divine hair-restorer at all, but plans to keep all the hair ever lost, alive and vibrant, in a special heavenly hair-museum. Or maybe Jesus' guarantee that even the hair of persecuted Christians will be saved is, like the rest of his promises, nothing more than errant nonsense.

The idea that believers won't perish is resurrected by the writers of John's gospel in what is considered to be the most famous verse in the Bible, even though it fails to mention hair. John 3.16 says that '...God so loved the world that he gave his only Son, so that everyone who believes in him may not perish but may have eternal life'. As we've already established, Christians die like everyone else: with the exception of those of those alive today (whose day will come), all Christians who have ever lived have perished. Eventually they have ceased to have any physical existence at all, even as decomposed matter: if the word is to have any meaning at all, death and eventual obliteration constitute all the 'perishing' you could wish for.

'Ah, but', says the Christian, 'what the verse really means is that the believer doesn't remain in a perished state, because God will, on the last day, or when the soul reaches heaven, or in some other incredible scenario designed to argue away the inevitable, resurrect the Christian in a new body': as Paul puts it in 1 Corinthians 15.54, the perishable will then put on the imperishable (the perishable? Doesn't he understand that Christians are supposed to be perish-proof?).

Being given a new post-mortem body doesn't change the fact that the old one perishes, and with it, its brain; with the brain, the very essence of the individual is extinguished. Believers, contrary to the promise of John 3.16, must go through this perishing, just like the rest of us. Expecting that a belief like being 'washed in the blood of the lamb' will enable them to escape death is to trust in magical incantation. To the surprise of no-one except the born-again, it doesn't work and never has.

PART THREE: IMPOSSIBLE MORALITIES

Chapter 3
Jesus' Tribal Morality

Christians claim their morality is derived from the Bible, the supposed eternal and unchanging word of God. Some go as far as to say that it is impossible to have any morality at all *unless* following that which is 'laid down in God's word'. The *Exploring Christianity* website puts it like this:

> *The only satisfying foundation for a stable personal and social morality is found in the biblical understanding of God as just and as love. Any idea of morality that does not take this God into account is doomed to failure.*

Similarly, Ray Cotton, 'a minister to international students', claims that:

> *only the God who created us knows what is best for us and only God is capable of revealing to us the ethical standards that can ultimately bring the peace we so desperately seek.*

We might justifiably take exception to the idea that the God of the Bible is portrayed as just and loving when he spends much of his time, particularly in the Old Testament, flying into rages, ranting and smiting. We might wonder too how this sort of behaviour can possibly inspire personal and social morality. Nonetheless the idea persists, at least amongst Christians, that ethical standards are really only attainable through an 'understanding' of and allegiance to this God. In Jesus, they believe, we see God manifest himself in human form and so what Jesus says about morality must be what God himself expects from us. We might be filled with anger, jealousy and murderous thoughts, but with God's help we can overcome them. If it worked for God, who has 'issues' with this kind of behaviour all the way through the Old Testament, then it can work for us too.

This section, then, takes a close look at the moral guidance offered by Jesus and by New Testament writers. As you might guess from its title, however, we will find that this bears little resemblance to that which Christians suppose Jesus advocates. As a result, they fail to meet Jesus' moral requirements, even with the Holy Spirit's help. This might be because:

a) they don't understand or choose to ignore what Jesus says is moral behaviour;
b) they are incapable of meeting his ethical standards;
c) the Holy Spirit doesn't exist and therefore cannot help them meet his standards;
d) the morality offered by Jesus is utterly impossible in the first place;
e) all of the above.

So let's take a closer look at Jesus' morality, beginning with what he has to say about the old Jewish law. According to Jesus, this law is intended to remain in place and be binding until he returns, when the present heaven and earth will pass away:

> *Think not that I have come to abolish the law and the prophets; I have come not to abolish them but to fulfil them. For truly I say to you, till heaven and earth pass away, not an iota, not a dot, will pass from the law until all is accomplished.* (Matthew 5.17-18)

As we have seen, he is somewhat behind schedule, the earth and the heavens are still in place, and the Kingdom has not yet materialised. Consequently, Christians should still be following the law, as Jesus insisted, while they wait for him to reappear. In fact, most Christians ignore most of the supposed moral precepts advocated in the Old Testament, and, predictably, a good deal of those in the New.

The fact Jesus believed that he, as the Son of Man, would return within a short time of his delivering these words, is also why he gives people such impractical advice about life: sell all you have, give no thought for tomorrow, if anyone asks you for something, give it and more to them... and so on. These are instructions for living in a system that isn't going to be around much longer, when none of the old, some might say sensible, ways of living matter any more. Priorities are different, Jesus is saying (or is made to say) when the end is only a short time away. But then, of course, he contradicts himself, or rather the gospel writers contradict each other, because in Matthew, the most Jewish of the four gospel accounts, Jesus appears to give the opposite advice - live with even stricter adherence to the law while you wait for the end:

> *Whoever then relaxes one of the least of these commandments and teaches men to do so, shall be least in the Kingdom of heaven; but whoever does them and teaches them shall be called great in the Kingdom of heaven.* (Matthew 5.19)

This leaves modern Christians in a quandary: if they won't concede that Jesus was wrong about his imminent return - and I'm guessing they won't - then they have to accept instead that the Jewish law, from the time Jesus spoke until now, remains in force. Never mind what Paul said (though arguably he said it before these words were placed in Jesus' mouth); the law, according to the Son of God, God incarnate, stands until he returns. *Either* he thought he was coming back soon, and the law was to remain in place only a short time, *or* the law remains in place to this day. Again, you can't have both. So why, given Jesus' failure to return, don't Christians follow the Jewish law?

Because Jesus' death abolished it? Jesus is quite explicit in several places in the gospels that this is not the case. Moreover, when asked in Matthew 19:16-24 how one gains eternal life, Jesus does not say 'Repent of your sins, believe in my imminent sacrificial death and the atonement it brings, and you will have eternal life', as Paul had preached years before this gospel was written. Instead he says 'obey the commandments' and whether you want to construe this as just 'the ten commandments' or the entire law, it is inescapable that Jesus thinks eternal life is gained by adhering to the rules of Judaism.

Now isn't that strange? It could be that Jesus is trying here to keep his true nature, as an instigator of God's Kingdom, a secret, as the gospels suggest he tries to do elsewhere (for example in Mark 5.43). But this raises more questions than it answers: *why* does he keep what he sees as his true identity a secret on some occasions but not on others? And why, if that's what he's doing here, does he give an answer that conflicts so significantly with Paul's creed and the beliefs of Christians today? Who is right? Jesus, who says the way to eternal life is to obey the commandments, or Paul and other New Testament writers who claim that the only way to be saved is through Christ's redeeming blood (Romans 5.9 etc). Quite clearly Christians don't think it's Jesus or they would be 'obeying the commandments' and following the laws of Judaism as he categorically tells them they should.

Here is a small sample of what these laws, of such importance to Jesus, include:

> *Stone to death anyone who works on the Sabbath.* (Exodus 35.2 and Numbers 15.32-36)
>
> *Kill publicly children who dishonour their father or mother.* (Leviticus 20.9);
>
> *Stone to death anyone who blasphemes the name of the Lord.* (Leviticus 24.16);
>
> *Execute a married couple who have sexual intercourse during the woman's period.* (Leviticus 18.19);
>
> *Put to death those involved in adultery.* (Leviticus 20.10);
>
> *Execute any man who lies with another man, as with a woman.* (Leviticus 20.13)

> *Stone to death at her father's door any woman who is not a virgin on her wedding night.* (Deuteronomy 22.13-14 and 20-21).

> *Cut off 'without pity' a woman's hand if, during a fight, she seeks to rescue her husband by grabbing his opponent's testicles.* (Deuteronomy 25.11-12)

The modern equivalent of this kind of barbarism is the 'morality' demonstrated by the Taliban in their brutal 'laws'. The good news for the Taliban is that Jesus approves! He fully endorses the Old Testament versions, citing obedience to them as the way to gain eternal life. Their morality is so valued by Jesus that in Matthew 5.19 he is moved to say that 'whoever breaks one of the least of these commandments, and teaches others to do the same, will be called least in the Kingdom of heaven; but whoever does them and teaches them will be called great in the Kingdom of heaven'. So shouldn't Christians be basing *their* morality on the barbaric pronouncements of uneducated, savage tribesmen? They should, if they are adhering to the Bible as the inerrant word of God, with the Mosaic law still in operation (until Jesus returns, remember?).

There are those who would like to, of course, but most ignore Jesus' edict about keeping the law because they know, not from their Bibles and not from their faith or the church, but from modern, socially-determined morality, that stoning people because of their sexual conduct or because they fail to treat their parents with respect, is barbaric and positively *im*moral. They acknowledge in so doing that the Bible is, in all of these respects, as in many others, simply wrong. Quite rightly, they don't believe it - whatever they may claim to the contrary - and don't, for which we should be grateful, enact it.

They do, however, make a special case for the ruling that 'a man who lies with another man, as with a woman is an abomination and shall be put to death'. In this they are aided and abetted by Paul who, in his letter to the fledgling Christian community in Rome, demonstrates his customary restraint, when describing same sex relations as 'unnatural', degrading' and 'shameful' (Romans 1.26-27 NIV).

It has to be said that this is easy 'morality' for the majority of people. As Gilbert Parker once remarked, 'there is no virtue in not doing what we don't want to do. There's no virtue in not falling, when you're not tempted': if you're not gay what sort of trouble can you possibly have in avoiding sleeping with another man (or woman)? Rather, this is 'projectile morality', that Christians use on others, making frequently vitriolic pronouncements about their perceived morality, judging where they should not judge and criticising the mote in others' eyes while ignoring the beam that blinds their own. Most, it is true, ignore the second part of the Leviticus ruling about executing those who sleep with their own sex, though there are some extremists ('nuts', to use a technical term) who argue it should be upheld. Bradlee Dean, for example, self-appointed 'shepherd' of *You Can Run But You Cannot Hide*, a Christian rock group beloved of churches in North America, offers the following:

> *(Homosexuals) molest 117 people before they're found out. How many kids have been destroyed, how many adults have been destroyed because of crimes against nature... Muslims are calling for the executions of homosexuals in America... They themselves are upholding the laws that are even in the Bible of the Judeo-Christian God, but they seem to be more moral than even the American Christians do* [sic].

Less extreme than Dean and those like him - such as Martin Ssempa, the Ugandan church minister behind his country's anti-homosexuality laws - are those who apply, with relish, a mean-spirited, diluted form of punishment for homosexuals, seeking to denigrate them at every opportunity. These Christians claim, for example, that granting gay people the same rights as non-gay people will destroy traditional marriage and family life, though they never tell you how this might happen. Pope Benedict XVI (not his real name), for example, believes that same sex marriage is one of the 'most insidious and dangerous challenges that today confront the common good'.

The Ugandan Anti-homosexuality Bill, 2009, therefore, while asserting that homosexuality is not an innate condition, states as its object:

to establish a comprehensive consolidated legislation to protect the traditional family by prohibiting (1) any form of sexual relations between persons of the same sex; and (2) the promotion or recognition of such sexual relations in public institutions and other places through or with the support of any Government entity in Uganda or any non-governmental organization inside or outside the country.

Elsewhere, others claim that society's acceptance of gays brings down God's wrath on the world, in the form of tsunamis, terrorist attacks and volcanic eruptions, to name but a few:

European deputies propose that all states of the Council of Europe should introduce a subject on peculiarities of homosexual behaviour in the school curriculum... Is it possible that Europe further abandoning its Christian heritage does not see that the eruption of the Iceland volcano with its ash cloud that paralysed life of the "most progressive" society is a menacing sign of God? (Association of Orthodox Experts *[sic]* in Moscow)

It is difficult to know whether Christians actually think in such a primitive manner or whether they're merely out to vilify gay people in any way they can, as in the past they have vilified Jews, black people and women. Either way, it's hardly the 'love thy neighbour as yourself ' and 'do unto others' that Jesus also preached.

Let us give Christians the benefit of the doubt, however, and suppose that in Matthew 19, Jesus is referring only to the Ten Commandments, that if followed lead to eternal life. If he is, though, which ones does he mean? The set in Exodus 20 or the replacement batch in Exodus 34? The second group is the only one called 'The Ten Commandments' in the Bible itself, but they are not the ten injunctions that everyone knows by that name - that's the first lot in Exodus 20. Only three commandments are the same in both sets, though God says explicitly that the two are the same (in Exodus 34.1). Missing from the 'real' Ten Commandments of Exodus 34 are those about adultery, theft and killing, replaced with stipulations about observing the feast of weeks and boiling baby goats in their mothers' milk (you shouldn't apparently). But don't take my word for it - read the two accounts for yourself. I'll wait...

What is going on here? It's as if The Ten Commandments are not as immutable as Christians claim. Are they allowed to pick and mix between the two sets? Or should they reject one and use only the other? Obey both lots - The Seventeen Commandments? It's far from clear and yet eternal existence depends on getting it right. Is it any wonder that the Pharisees of the gospels became so tied up with what Yahweh's laws required and what they didn't - only to have Jesus lambaste them for their troubles? Maybe it would have helped if God had been a little clearer in the first place.

Be that as it may, in Mark 10.19, Jesus seems to be of the view that it's the first set of commandments that matters, not the ones actually referred to as the Ten Commandments, but the ones to do with, he says, 'stealing, lying and defrauding' (defrauding? That's not in either set!); those that are frequently written around the altar in Anglican churches in the UK, that American Republican, Roy Moore, is keen to erect in public places and Albert Mohler, President of the Southern Baptist Theological Seminary, says should be prominent in the lives of every Christian. Let's see if they are prominent in the sense that Christians consistently apply them in their lives.

Number 1. Do not have any other gods before me. (Exodus 20.3)

The first commandment concedes that Yahweh is not the only god in existence. Stretching the concept of 'existence' to its limit, this is true; there are other deities both in the Bible (Baal, for example) and in other mythologies. Christians still interpret this commandment as prohibiting worship of any of the other supernatural entities on offer - Allah, for example - but this commandment has, in modern times, a far greater sweep.

In my days as a Christian, I endured innumerable sermons telling me and my fellow believers, that we did not enjoy 'victory' in our Christian lives because we put other things before God; family, possessions, career, status... you name it, we idolised it. Switch to any Christian station on satellite TV and you'll hear the same; the website *Workers For Jesus* lists money, sex and celebrities as other, possible objects of worship. As Christian activist Ronald J. Sider notes in *The Scandal of the Evangelical Conscience,* 'most 'Christians' regularly commit treason. With their mouths they claim that Jesus is their Lord, but with their actions they demonstrate their allegiance to money, sex, and personal self-fulfilment'. If their own leaders, preachers and commentators are to be believed, Christians do worship other gods - albeit not supernatural ones - that are, at least some of the time, of greater importance to them than the God of the Bible. They wouldn't need to be admonished about it if they didn't.

In Matthew 6.24, Jesus picks up this idea and warns that one cannot serve both God and wealth. Clearly times have changed because, it turns out, you can! Here, from the Ohio Sceptics website, are recent annual incomes, not including profits from book sales, of some prominent Christian evangelists and leaders:

W. Franklin Graham III, Chief Executive Officer
$633,722
Billy Graham Evangelistic Association 1 (Charlotte, N.C.)

Paul Irwin, President
$358,654
American Bible Society 1 (New York)

Richard Stewart, Executive Vice President
$257,954
American Bible Society 1 (New York)

Billy Graham, Chairman
$204,607

Billy Graham Evangelistic Association 1 (Charlotte, N.C.)

Gordon Robertson, Chief Executive Officer
$326,820
Christian Broadcasting Network 1 (Virginia Beach)

Michael Little, Director
$321,084
Christian Broadcasting Network 1 (Virginia Beach)

Mike Novak, President
$280,607
Educational Media Foundation 1 (Rocklin, Calif.)

Jon Rivers, K-LOVE On-Air Talent
$218,836
Educational Media Foundation 1 (Rocklin, Calif.)

James Daly, President
$240,002
Focus on the Family (Colorado Springs)

Charles F. Stanley, President
$226,704
In Touch Ministries 1 (Atlanta)

Paul F. Crouch, President
$419,500
Trinity Christian Center of Santa Ana (Trinity Broadcasting Network)

Janice Crouch, Vice President
$361,000
Trinity Christian Center of Santa Ana (Trinity Broadcasting Network)

These are not modest sums of money. They buy a luxurious lifestyle of multiple properties and jet planes. The appropriately named Creflo Dollar (catchphrase, 'it's all about money'), who is not listed above, boasts of owning 'Rolls-Royces, private jets, a million-dollar Atlanta home and $2.5 million Manhattan apartment', where he is prone to beating his teenage daughter. Showman evangelist Benny Hinn, meanwhile, was reported by the Canadian Broadcasting Company's *Fifth Estate* programme in

2007 to have generated '$250 million a year in donations and sales of such items as stainless steel dog tags engraved with the Lord's Prayer and vials of "Anointing for Prosperity Oil"'. (More recently, Mr Hinn spent time at a hotel with a woman who was not his wife, but this involves a different commandment altogether).

These amounts pale into insignificance, however, beside the Vatican's 'incalculable' billions. This is a church so wealthy that even its supporters say the actual sums owned are unknown; its vast real estate, collections of art and other treasures are priceless, and so the church's true worth can never be known (and, some Catholics say, it is 'arrogant' even to ask).

These accumulations of wealth are all in the name of the man who didn't even own his own donkey. The same one who adjures would-be-followers to sell all they have and give to the poor (Matthew 19.21). Do Christians believe he meant this? How many do you know who sell all their possessions and give to the poor? There are some who do, no doubt, but the vast majority do not. They don't even have the sincerity of the young ruler in Matthew's story, who goes away saddened after Jesus tells him to sell everything, 'for he had great possessions'. He could, of course, have avoided feeling down altogether if he had done what most Christian today do, and ignored Jesus entirely. Selling all you have and giving to the poor is far too radical so, Christians will tell you, Jesus can't possibly mean it literally, or, if he does, then he is speaking only to the young ruler's situation at the time. Significantly, it is likely that, in spite of his wealth, the young man was nowhere near as rich as Christians living a comfortable western existence today.

If Jesus is speaking metaphorically here (and isn't he always when Christians don't particularly care for what he's saying?), he makes clear in numerous other places the spiritual dangers of materialism. In Luke 6.24 it's 'woe to you who are rich'; in Luke 12.15, 'be on your guard against all kinds of greed; for one's life does not consist in the abundance of possessions'; in Luke 14.33, 'none of you can become my disciple if you do not give up all your possessions'; in Mark 10.25 his most famous observation that 'it is easier for a camel to go through the eye of a needle than for a rich man to enter the Kingdom of God'. Indeed, sometimes it seems that Jesus preaches about nothing else but the dangers of wealth.

The theme is also taken up by other New Testament authors, so that the love of money is seen as the root of all evil by the writer of 1 Timothy, while Paul ranks 'the greedy' alongside 'fornicators, idolaters, adulterers, male prostitutes, sodomites, thieves... drunkards, revilers, robbers', none of whom will make it into the Kingdom of God (1 Corinthians 6.9-10). Christians are quick to condemn the other behaviours in Paul's list, but you'd be hard pushed to hear any sermons criticising greed: Christians are not about to condemn their God-given right to wealth and the unfettered worship of materialism, no matter how much their Lord and other New Testament luminaries rant about it. In Matthew 6:21, Jesus notes that 'where your treasure is, there will your heart be also' and in rejecting his radicalism, those who claim they belong to him show where their hearts' interest truly lies.

Number 2. You shall not make for yourself an idol, whether in the form of anything that is in heaven above, or that is on the earth beneath, or that is in the water under the earth (Exodus 20.5), or, if you prefer: **You shall not make cast idols.** (Exodus 34.17)

The King James' version of this commandment uses the phrase 'graven image' in Exodus 20.5 and 'molten image' in Exodus 34.17. A graven image is one that is carved or sculpted, while cast and molten indicate an object made by melting metal to fit a mould. Yahweh, being the old stuffy he is, presumably likes neither, or maybe he changes his mind between Exodus 20 and Exodus 34. Either way, one can't help but think this is a remarkably inconsequential commandment, not at all in the same league as killing and stealing. After all, no-one suffers because of carvings and ornaments, apart from one very over-sensitive god, and as a result Christians down the ages have, by and large, disregarded this second commandment.

As we have seen in discussing the first commandment, modern Christians are not, in any case, averse to idols. Do they have any truck with graven or molten images? Yes, they do. In 2009, a nurse in the UK, Shirley Chaplin was asked not to wear a silver crucifix while at work in hospital. The hospital authorities were not opposed to the crucifix as a religious symbol, but considered it a hazard when dealing with patients - easily grabbed or snagged and not what patients wanted dangling in their faces. They did suggest nurse Chaplin wear her cross inside her uniform or that she pin it to her clothing, but Mrs Chaplin found this compromise unacceptable. According to *The Sunday Times*, she 'suggested that her religious beliefs would be "violated" if she took off the necklace because she felt that she was being asked to hide her faith'. She had the support of a number of bishops who claimed that 'Christians are being persecuted in an increasingly secular society'. Mrs Chaplin was flouting the second commandment, not undergoing persecution. If silver crucifixes are not graven images made, as they are, from molten silver, then what is? But neither nurse Chaplin, nor her defenders, seemed to think this relevant enough to mention.

Mrs Chaplin took her employers to an employment tribunal over the matter and lost. Her religious beliefs, she said afterwards, had indeed been 'violated'. As *The Sunday Times* reported: 'after the judgement Mrs Chaplin said that every Christian would now be afraid to reveal their beliefs at work, adding: "This is a very bad day for Christianity".' One can only wonder how wearing a necklace 'reveals' Christians' beliefs. Isn't it their behaviour, and not their jewellery, that is supposed to do that?

Mrs Chaplin is not the only Christian to insist on wearing graven images; archbishops do themselves, as do many ordinary believers. Churches of several denominations are replete with them: statues of saints, angels, eagles, doves, crosses and Jesus himself, all made of stone, plaster and metal; images in stained glass (made from molten sand); even monuments portraying, of all things, the ten commandments. These despite the fact that in the Acts of the Apostles, which of course is New Testament and not so easy to ignore as the Old, we read: 'forasmuch then as we are the offspring of God, we ought not to think that the Godhead is like unto gold, or silver, or stone, graven by art and man's device'. (Acts 17:29, KJV).

Clearly then, the second commandment, as well as Acts' reminder of it, is of no interest to modern Christians. They prefer to gamble that their unchanging God is no longer quite so touchy about graven images.

Number 3. You shall not make wrongful use of the name of the Lord your God, for the Lord will not acquit anyone who misuses his name. (Exodus 20.7)

Or, as the King James version puts it 'do not take the Lord's name in vain', this is another commandment designed to protest Yahweh's vanity. He really is a sensitive soul if he can't bear to hear any of his creation utter the occasional 'Goddammit'. Stretching the application of the commandment several hundred years into its own future, Christians also like to claim it prohibits the use of Jesus' name and title as oaths and profanities. So exclaiming 'Jesus H. Christ!' when the computer crashes is also a no-no. Let's be honest, Christians don't have too much trouble with his directive, though like me you may have been taken aback to hear a believer let slip the occasional 'God knows' or 'God Almighty'.

The difficulty with this commandment, as with several others, is that it meant something else to the ancient Jews who originally concocted it. *The IVP Bible Background Commentary* informs us that it 'is intended to prevent the exploitation of the name of Yahweh for magical purposes or hexing', thus pointing to its redundancy except in cultures where people have faith in magic and hexes. In so doing it would suggest that Yahweh himself thought these things valid - the commandment is not about avoiding them altogether - but didn't want to endorse them with his brand name. It is truly remarkable how like an ancient tribesman's his thinking is.

Attempts have been made down the years to inject this commandment with some relevancy. *The Church of God Online Daily Bible Study* suggests that, 'ignoring the actual Word of God while claiming to be Christian is taking the Son of God's Name in vain'. This interpretation chimes with Jesus' own thinking when he makes the analogy between serving him and a marriage in which the bride takes her husband's name as her own. Should the bride do this lightly, without the intention of honouring her marriage commitments, she is literally taking her future husband's name in vain. With the third commandment interpreted in this way, it comes to mean 'don't become a follower of God unless you intend doing it seriously, otherwise you're just wasting everybody's time'. Casting himself as bridegroom, Jesus tells the parable of the wise and foolish virgins to show how some who would take his name are not fit to be his bride:

> ...*the bridegroom came, and those (virgins) who were ready went with him into the wedding banquet; and the door was shut. Later the other virgins came also, saying, "Lord, lord, open to us." But he replied, "Truly I tell you, I do not know you."* (Matthew 25.10-12)

Given that there are ten virgins at the start of the story, the suggestion is that half of those who would take Jesus' name, represented by the five foolish virgins, do so without any real intention of doing as he says. The evidence of this book demonstrates how, while many assume Christ's name, they repeatedly ignore his commands and teaching, and in so doing take his name entirely in vain.

Number 4. Remember the Sabbath day and keep it holy. For six days you shall labour and do all your work. But the seventh day is a Sabbath to the Lord your God; you shall not do any work—you, your son or your daughter, your male or female slave, your livestock, or the alien resident in your towns. (Exodus 20.8-10)

'For *six* days you shall labour'? Which Christian these days advocates working six days a week? Don't most of them, like the rest of us, take two days off and work only five? This is nothing less than a flagrant contravention of God's fourth commandment which tells them they should be labouring for a full six. Employers take note.

As if that's not bad enough, with the exception of one or two groups (the Seventh Day Adventists, for example) no Christian today honours the Sabbath referred to in the commandment. This began at sunset on Friday and ended at sunset on Saturday. Originally it marked the day of rest that the Creator God enjoyed after six days of creation, and like all Jewish days began in the evening; hence Genesis' repeated refrain about 'the evening and the morning' making a day. Christians will tell you that the day was moved in commemoration of Jesus' Sunday resurrection (as we've seen, not quite the third day after his death, but who's counting), though you will search in vain for his command to make it so, and, indeed, for any biblical injunction authorising the change. Rather, the move from Saturday to Sunday, and to morning from evening, took place under Constantine in 321CE, before his infamous, suspect conversion to Christianity. His decree announcing the change reads:

> *On the venerable day of the Sun let the magistrates and people residing in cities rest, and let all workshops be closed. In the country however persons engaged in agriculture may freely and lawfully continue their pursuits because it often happens that another day is not suitable for gain-sowing or vine planting; lest by neglecting the proper moment for such operations the bounty of heaven should be lost.*

The Church Council of Laodicea formalised Christian acceptance of Sunday as the Sabbath around 364CE, distancing Christian religious observance from Jewish tradition, which by this time had become abhorrent to the Jewish messiah's followers.

Overlooking pagan and political reasons for the Sabbath's move from Saturday to Sunday, and accepting the fact that for Christians Sunday has been the Sabbath for some sixteen hundred years now, how successful are they at 'keeping it holy'? 'Holy' means 'set apart' and it probably is the case that most Christians do set apart a couple of hours each Sunday to attend church. Surely God isn't asking for more than this? Having given their two hours, believers are surely free to shop, fix the car, do some DIY, go to the beach, have a barbecue and generally do as they wish? Alas, no, as the Bible spells out acts specifically prohibited on the Sabbath: these include no trading (Amos 8.5); no shopping (Nehemiah. 10:31); no travelling (Exodus 16:29) and no kindling of fires (Exodus 35.3), so there go the trips out, the grocery shopping and the barbecue. And in case you're tempted to do a little work around the house on the Sabbath, here's a little cautionary tale from Numbers 15:32-36:

> *When the Israelites were in the wilderness, they found a man gathering sticks on the sabbath day. Those who found him gathering sticks brought him to Moses, Aaron, and to the whole congregation. They put him in custody, because it was not clear what should be done to him. Then the Lord said to Moses, 'The man shall be put to death; all the congregation shall stone him outside the camp.' The whole congregation brought him outside the camp and stoned him to death, just as the Lord had commanded Moses.*

You work Sunday shifts in an essential service? Try telling that to the Lord. You'll find it's no excuse at all. And if that seems severe, it's because the two parts of the fourth commandment are related – keeping the day 'holy' means both avoiding work and dedicating the entire day to God instead: that is the meaning of its phrase 'a Sabbath to the Lord your God'. Quite how you accomplish this apart from punctuating an otherwise indolent day with a visit to church (which probably involves travelling) is a mystery to me, but shouldn't be to Christians who are in direct contact with their Lord. Strange then, that few present evidence of setting apart the entire day to him. It's a good job that in the West, if not under Taliban rule elsewhere, we have done away with those troublesome public stonings.

What though of Jesus' get-out-of-stoning-free card, when, flouting Sabbath laws, he declares himself Lord of the Sabbath and says that the Sabbath was made for man and not man for the Sabbath (Mark 2.23-24). It seems not to trouble him one iota that he contradicts not only the fourth commandment - where the day is designated not for man at all but for God - but also his own claim in Matthew 5.18 that 'until heaven and earth pass away, not one letter, not one stroke of a letter, will pass from the law until all is accomplished'. What are Christians to make of it? As 'all' is still not accomplished, heaven and earth being where they've always been, does the law about the Sabbath stand or not? Or are any and all activities permitted on the Sabbath? Christians have evidently decided they are, thus rendering the fourth commandment redundant. Jesus rewrites it, Christians don't keep it: shopping trips and barbecues it is.

Number 5. Honour your father and your mother, so that your days may be long in the land that the Lord your God is giving you. (Exodus 20.12)

In view of Leviticus 20.9, where the penalty for dishonouring or cursing father and mother and father is - yes, you guessed it - death, this commandment makes perfect sense. Of course you've a better chance of living - the 'long in the land' bit is entirely superfluous - if you avoid giving the folks a reason to have the neighbours round to help them stone you.

So what does 'dishonouring' mean? Could it be telling your mother to mind her own business? Jesus tells his to do just that in John 2.4 and disowns her entirely in Mark 3.33. In spite of all the wondrous things she is supposed to have experienced at the time of his birth, she doesn't seem to understand what Jesus is about and that really ticks him off. He tells her his followers are now his mother, brother and family, which, as Tom Wright points out, would have been 'shocking in the extreme' in the Jewish peasant culture of the time.

Perhaps, though, this is still not enough to qualify as *bona fide* dishonouring. What about hating parents? Maybe that would do it. Jesus says in Luke 14.26 that anyone who would follow him but does not 'hate' mother and father is not worthy of him, and in Matthew 10.34-35 he declares that he has not come to bring peace to the world (he wasn't wrong there) but to set a man against his father, and a daughter against her mother. He seems in all of these instances to advocate dishonouring parents and in so doing serves as the model for his believers to similarly disregard it, if that's what they want to do. God's eternal values: don't you just love 'em?

Number 6. You shall not murder. (Exodus 20.13)

Picture the scene: the Israelites have witnessed Yahweh's might in freeing them from slavery in Egypt. He's inflicted six plagues on the Egyptians, culminating in the massacre of all Egyptian firstborn sons (who says he doesn't believe in child sacrifice?), while passing over the Israelites' with a clever trick; he's led them out of Egypt as a pillar of cloud during the day and as a pillar of fire at night; he has parted the sea for them and drowned the Pharaoh; he has miraculously fed them in the wilderness with manna from heaven; he has done all manner of other amazing feats right before their eyes. And the Israelites are suitably impressed: 'Israel saw the great work that the Lord did against the Egyptians. So the people feared the Lord and believed in the Lord and in his servant Moses'. (Exodus 14.31).

But wouldn't you know it, the minute his back is turned, they forget all about him and make a golden calf to worship instead. They really are a difficult lot to impress, though you have to admire their artistic flair. Still, a graven image is a graven image, and there's a heavy price to be paid. Of course, they don't know this yet as Moses is still up Mount Sinai talking to shrubs, with the freshly-minted commandment designed to inform them, rather belatedly as it turns out, that graven images are verboten. Ignorance is no defence in the Lord's eyes, however, and so, as soon as he's descended the mountain with all ten commandments (plus a few extras), Moses erupts. He smashes the tablets that Yahweh has personally written and takes radical action. Exodus 32.26-29 takes up the story:

> *Moses stood in the gate of the camp, and said, 'Who is on the Lord's side? Come to me!' And all the sons of Levi gathered around him. He said to them, Thus says the Lord, the God of Israel, "Put your sword on your side, each of you! Go back and forth from gate to gate throughout the camp, and each of you kill your brother, your friend, and your neighbour." The sons of*

> *Levi did as Moses commanded, and about three thousand of the people fell on that day. Moses said, 'Today you have ordained yourselves for the service of the Lord, each one at the cost of a son or a brother, and so have brought a blessing on yourselves this day.*
> (Exodus 32.26-29)

Moses demands this mass slaughter of his own people in spite of the newly supplied commandment prohibiting murder. There is no evidence in the text that when he has his bully boys destroy their unarmed brothers and neighbours, that Yahweh sanctions the killing. He simply isn't mentioned; Moses unleashes the brutality, not God (though he makes up for lost time later on, as we shall see). To the sceptic, this text and all other similar ones, illustrate how primitive, barbaric tribesmen justified killing those they disagreed with by supposing that the Lord wanted them to do it. The religious fanatic is not averse to using the same justification even today.

The Israelites don't just limit mass murder to their own tribes and families, though there are several other occasions when again they indulge in fratricide (see Numbers 25.3-5, for example). The Old Testament is full of the murder and slaughter of men, women, children and livestock of other tribes who are unfortunate enough to cross the Israelites' path. When they do, their bloody obliteration is sanctioned time and time again by either Israelite leaders who seem instinctively to know what their God is like, or by direct command from Yahweh himself. Here are a few representative samples of divinely-sanctioned butchery:

1) Numbers 31.9-10, 14-15, 17-18:

> *They did battle against Midian, as the Lord had commanded Moses, and killed every male... The Israelites took the women of Midian and their little ones captive; and they took all their cattle, their flocks, and all their goods as booty. All their towns where they had settled, and all their encampments, they burned... Moses became angry with the officers of the army, the commanders of thousands and the*

commanders of hundreds, who had come from service in the war. Moses said to them, 'Have you allowed all the women to live?... Now therefore, kill every male among the little ones, and kill every woman who has known a man by sleeping with him. But all the young girls who have not known a man by sleeping with him, keep alive for yourselves.

2) Deuteronomy 13.12-15

If you hear it said about one of the towns that the Lord your God is giving you to live in, that scoundrels from among you have gone out and led the inhabitants of the town astray, saying, 'Let us go and worship other gods', whom you have not known, then you shall inquire and make a thorough investigation. If the charge is established that such an abhorrent thing has been done among you, you shall put the inhabitants of that town to the sword, utterly destroying it and everything in it - even putting its livestock to the sword.

3) Isaiah 13.15-18

Whoever is found will be thrust through, and whoever is caught will fall by the sword. Their infants will be dashed to pieces before their eyes; their houses will be plundered, and their wives ravished. See, I am stirring up the Medes against them, who have no regard for silver and do not delight in gold. Their bows will slaughter the young men; they will have no mercy on the fruit of the womb; their eyes will not pity children.

4) Joshua 6.20-21

As soon as the people heard the sound of the trumpets, they raised a great shout, and the wall fell down flat; so the people charged straight ahead into the city and captured it. Then they devoted to destruction by the edge of the sword all in the city, both men and women, young and old, oxen, sheep, and donkeys.

If you are feeling particularly masochistic, you might want to read more of these dreadful accounts for yourself; there are many others to choose from. You'll be interested to discover if you do, that each time the Israelites commit genocide, they help themselves to the gold and silver left behind, adding to the Lord's treasures in their own sanctuary. 'Do not steal' be damned - those priests were on to a good thing! My point, however, is that in spite of issuing the sixth commandment – 'you shall not murder', lest you've forgotten amidst all the slaughter - the Lord proceeds to instruct his followers to murder all and sundry, usually because they have the audacity not to believe in him. It is entirely coincidental that the tribes they are instructed to wipe from the face of the earth very often occupy land that the Israelites want for themselves. You will search in vain for a prophet who comes clean and says: 'God is calling us to wipe out the people we see before us, which is rather fortuitous as they're living exactly where we need to pitch our tents'.

Completely irrationally, modern Christians argue that none of the slaughter of the Old Testament contravenes the sixth commandment. That's because killing and genocide are not the same as murder, you see, though the difference might have been academic to those on the receiving end of an Israelite sword. Christians also argue that if God commands his people to kill, then *ipso facto*, it cannot be murder because God commands it. *Good News* magazine employs just such a tautology: 'the Sixth Commandment reminds us that God is the giver of life, and He alone has the authority to take it or to grant humans permission to take it'.

Really? The number of Israelites slaughtered by their own brothers and friends in Exodus 32, was, we are told, 'about three thousand'. This is a similar number to those killed in the 9/11 attacks, the perpetrators of which also claimed to have been directed by *their* God to kill unbelievers. Were the people in New York's Twin Towers, and the unfortunate passengers in all of the planes involved on that day, killed or were they murdered? Certainly, their lives were brutally and forcibly taken from them by individuals acting in Allah's name, and we would be right in saying, as we do, that they were murdered. Were their murders any different from those in the Old Testament, committed in Yahweh's name? We would be right in saying they were different neither in kind nor quantity. Christians are being disingenuous when they claim that divinely sanctioned killing, whether by ancient tribes or modern extremists, is not murder.

Like the Third Reich, murder is Yahweh's final solution, but often first resort, in his dealing with his creation. Imagine him in human form: a volatile, tyrant sanctioning murder not only as the means of managing inter-tribal relations, but for any infringement of his arbitrary rules, for the heresy his priestly S.S. find everywhere, for declining to engage in the murder of others and even for the behaviour of earlier generations that this psychopath finds offensive. Would he merit our respect, loyalty and love? Hardly, though we might fear, hate and despise him, while the obsequious among us attempt to garner his favour by carrying out his murderous wishes.

So it was that in May 2009, George Tiller, a doctor who carried out late term abortions, joined the growing list of those from his profession murdered by Christians acting under divine ordinance. This time the perpetrator was pro-life activist *(sic)*, Scott Roeder, who shot Tiller at point bank range in the face as he served as an usher in his church in Kansas. It was not the first time an attempt had been made on the doctor's life, as he had previously survived being shot in 1993, and had also had his clinic bombed in 1985. A number of Christian groups were quick to distance themselves from the killing, offering - rather belatedly one would have thought - prayers to the bereaved family. Others, however, acclaimed Roeder an 'American hero', with Dave Leach of *Prayer and Action News* arguing in a legal brief for Roeder that the murder was – you guessed it - justifiable on biblical principles. Roeder was eventually convicted of Tiller's murder and given a 50 year jail sentence.

Of course, the doctor's murderer was, and apparently still is, an extremist, and few Christians would resort to carrying out such a crime for their ideals. Nonetheless some do, with their actions inadvertently supported by more moderate believers who accept unquestioningly that the murder and slaughter in the Bible is justifiable because it is sanctioned by God and is part of his nature.

Given this is the case, can Christians support the death penalty and is capital punishment murder or just common-or-garden killing? Albert Mohler, president of Southern Baptist Theological Seminary, thinks the death penalty 'is first of all about underlining the importance of every single human life' and is therefore, in the same way that black is really white, 'pro-life'. *Good News* magazine justifies it rather differently:

> *'For certain offences, God's law permits constituted government authorities to impose capital punishment. When the state abides by God's principles, this action does not violate the Sixth Commandment... He has revealed, in advance, which offences deserve the sentence of death.*

Committing murder comes under this heading of course, but as you'll recall, according to the Old Testament so do numerous other, much more insignificant offences - working on the Sabbath, sex at the wrong time of month, being an awkward teen. There are, as we shall see later, some Christians who, given the chance, would bring back the death sentence for all the 'offences' that displease God (especially homosexuality) but as ever, many, like *Good News* magazine, simply fudge the issue. What other 'offences' merit execution? Perhaps all of those God 'reveals', perhaps only murder; the Bible really isn't a lot of use in helping us decide. In the end, Christians are free either to support the death penalty, as Yahweh most certainly does, or to oppose it because Jesus doesn't seem like the kind of chap who would approve.

Indeed he doesn't. He expresses his thoughts on the sixth commandment in Matthew 5:21-24, though it is difficult to see what he actually adds to it:

> *You have heard that it was said to those of old, 'You shall not murder, and whoever murders will be in danger of the judgement.' "But I say to you that whoever is angry with his brother without a cause shall be in danger of the judgement. And whoever says to his brother, 'Raca!' shall be in danger of the council. But*

whoever says, 'You fool!' shall be in danger of hell fire.

Being angry with a 'brother' - women and non-Jews don't seem to be included here - is sometimes a step on the road to committing murder. However, not every angry outburst - in fact very few indeed - leads to murder. Being angry and even abusive is not, by any standard, the equivalent of taking a life, though the punishment Jesus proposes appears identical. Do Christians never get angry without cause? Do they never call someone a fool? I know from experience they are fond of quoting the King James' version of Psalm 14.1 to atheists: 'the fool hath said in his heart, there is no God', which amounts to the same thing. And doesn't Jesus himself resort to anger and call others 'blind fools' when he disagrees with them? (Yes, in Matthew 23.17). And what is being angry 'without a cause' like anyway? Everyone has a cause when they're angry. All the same, we'd all better watch who we're calling 'Raca' next time, just to be on the safe side.

The sixth commandment then is compromised by the many Bible-based provisos and exceptions that believers want to include under its rubric. It has been so from the beginning and as a result the commandment's authority is reduced to: 'You shall not commit murder, though even this is okay if it is divinely sanctioned or maybe even state approved. Or maybe not'. This is the same sort of moral relativism that Christians are so eager to condemn in others.

Number 7. You shall not commit adultery. (Exodus 20.14)

Christians commit adultery. Not all of them, to be sure, but sufficient numbers are no better at up-holding this commandment than non-believers. Yet this commandment is one which makes it through to the New Testament intact, with both Paul and Jesus speaking at length about it.

Related to adultery is divorce, and while not every divorce arises from adultery, Jesus is particularly exacting in his expectations of his followers in this area, demanding even more rigorous observance of Jewish law than that found in the Old Testament:

He said to them, 'Whoever divorces his wife and

marries another commits adultery against her; and if she divorces her husband and marries another, she commits adultery.' (Mark 10.11,12)

Jesus is very clear here that whether or not adultery is the cause of divorce, it becomes the *result* once the partners remarry. Even the innocent party, should they remarry, is made into an adulterer, according to Matthew 28.32. (Jesus speaks here from within the confines of his patristic culture, and refers only to the woman as the potential innocent in a divorce; the principle nonetheless applies to wronged husbands).

We might expect that as a result of Jesus' teaching about divorce, Christian men and women avoid both it and the consequent adultery that remarrying entails. And we'd be wrong. According to the Christian *Barna Research Group*, which carried out an extensive field study in the USA in 1999, 'born again Christians are more likely than others to experience a divorce', (and) that pattern has been in place for quite some time'. George Barna, himself a Christian, goes on to say that 'We would love to be able to report that Christians are living very distinct lives and impacting the community, but ... in the area of divorce rates they continue to be the same (as everyone else)... We rarely find substantial differences'.

An update of the research in 2008 revealed similar results, with the group reporting that 'the divorce figure (for born-again Christians) is statistically identical to that of non-born again adults: 32% versus 33%, respectively'. While figures for the number of divorced Christians who remarry are not available, it seems likely that a significant number will do so, as evidently they did in Jesus' time. Take, for example, 2012 Presidential hopeful and Roman Catholic, Newt Gingrich who, while opposing gay marriage on the grounds it shows 'outrageous disrespect... for the majority of people of the United States who believe marriage is the union of husband and wife', 'respects' the sanctity of the institution by signing up to it as often as he can. He's now on sacred union number three with two divorces under his belt.

If we take American Christians as representative of believers as a whole, with a third of them divorcing and many undoubtedly remarrying, it looks once again as if Christians, collectively, fail to uphold another of God's commandments. Not only that, they also disregard the related teaching of the one they call their Master.

But, wait, it gets worse. You don't need to have been married and divorced to have committed adultery. You don't need even to have had sex with someone who is not your spouse. For a man to look at a woman lustfully is, according to Jesus in Matthew 5.28, just as bad. Perhaps too a woman looking at a man in the same way is similarly sinful, but Jesus neglects to say, seeing the issue through his culture's male-dominated perspective once again.

Overlooking the fact that lusting after someone else is definitely not the same as actually having sex with them, Jesus has the remedy for wandering eyes, which follows in the very next verse: 'if your right eye causes you to sin, tear it out and throw it away; it is better for you to lose one of your members than for your whole body to be thrown into hell'. A bit drastic perhaps, but there it is; the Son of God is clear about how to avoid the sin of checking out a member of the opposite sex. That's why you see so many one-eyed Christians around the place because they all take his admonition very seriously. (He is the Son of God after all).

Except... you don't. Either Christians ignore him entirely on this one or they never look at the opposite sex with an eye to sexual congress. We all know they're like the rest of us in this respect – some, as Jimmy Carter once famously did, are honest enough to admit it – and some even act on it; the divorce rate among Christians is not the same as it is for everyone else just because they get tired of being married.

Perhaps though Jesus is being metaphorical when he proposes that gouging out one's eyes is the best way to deal with lust. Not surprisingly, Christians prefer this possibility. In *The Method and Message of Jesus' Teachings,* Robert Stein argues that:

> *what Jesus was seeking to convey to his listeners by this use of overstatement was the need to remove from their lives anything that might cause them to sin. There is no sin in life worth perishing over. Better to repent*

of that sin, even if it is as painful as tearing out an eye or cutting off a hand, and as a result enter the Kingdom of God than to cherish that sin and be thrown into hell. Jesus is saying in effect, "Tear out anything in your life that is causing you to sin and keeping you from God".

If that was his intention, Jesus might have actually used these words. If he wants to say 'in effect' that the believer should jettison anything from his life that causes him to sin then why doesn't he? His sayings in Matthew 28 are compatible with his view elsewhere that it is not that which is outside a person that causes him to sin, but that which is within. Jesus' words here are consistent with this notion; Stein ignores both the context of Jesus' pronouncement – it is specifically sexual – and dilutes the seriousness that he imputes to 'sins' in this context.

To ensure his listeners understand his instructions on this matter, Jesus goes on to use a doublet (or rather Matthew does; doublets are far more common in Matthew's gospel than in any other), to emphasise his point by repeating it in slightly different form. Matthew 5.30 reads: 'And if your right hand causes you to sin, cut it off and throw it away; it is better for you to lose one of your members than for your whole body to go into hell'. If you ever wondered if God opposes masturbation, along with any other sexual pleasure, here's your answer. Which is why we see so many one-handed Christians...

The difficulty with interpreting these and other verses metaphorically is that Christians want to claim that the Bible is the literal 'word of God' and then want select parts of it to be metaphorical – and guess who they think should do the selecting. Once again - and isn't it becoming irksome that they think they can? - Christians can't have it both ways. Even if they could, how would they know which parts to interpret literally and which symbolically? Perhaps the Holy Spirit tells them, or maybe, and more likely, it's just their personal preferences. After all, who wants to lose eyes and hands just for being human? If that's not enough, Jesus encourages other mutilations for the sake of his Kingdom when he reveals in Matthew 19.12 that 'there are eunuchs who have made themselves eunuchs for the sake of the Kingdom of heaven. Let anyone accept this who can'. No Christians today seem able to 'accept' this recommendation, either; what a truly feeble bunch they are, putting their testicles before the Kingdom!

If, on the other remaining hand, Stein is right and Jesus does not intend his comments to be taken literally, then they are remarkably irresponsible. It seems likely that, given that he believed the end of the age was fast approaching, Jesus may well have meant what he said, counting on the probability (as he saw it) that anyone who followed his ridiculous suggestions would not be eyeless or handless for long. They would, at the resurrection, be fully restored to live in the Kingdom where, according to Matthew 22.30, they would not be troubled by either impure thoughts or marriage itself (and so wouldn't need those testicles anyway).

For now though, the evidence suggests that significant numbers of Christians are unable to keep the seventh commandment, find divorce acceptable, do the odd bit of lusting and happily ignore Jesus' injunction to cut off body parts that cause sexual offence. It would seem that these Christians at least are not in the least 'offended' by lascivious thoughts and even the occasional playing away from home.

Number 8. You shall not steal. (Exodus 20.15)

The Israelites really must have been a disreputable lot if they need Yahweh to tell them not to steal. Had they not, by this time in their history, arrived at this moral precept for themselves as other cultures had before them? Tim McHyde who offers 'revolutionary explanations for Bible prophecy, mysteries and difficult verses' thinks so: 'None of us need God to tell us not to steal, commit adultery or bear false witness because other people, society and government will quickly object to that behaviour as immoral or unethical'. This rather puts paid to the idea that atheists and other non-believers cannot be moral without God looking over their shoulder; McHyde acknowledges that morality is societally based.

This commandment is not, then, great revelation and is hardly needed at all, except for morally impoverished iron aged tribes, who fail, as usual, to obey it. After massacring neighbouring tribes the Israelites plunder their treasures - for Yahweh and his priests, which makes it all right - and help themselves to any virgins, which they are at liberty to deflower (see, for example, Numbers 31). If this isn't stealing what is?

Do today's Christians do any better? Let's consider whether they contravene this commandment along with the previous six:

Is the church that demands adherents to work for nothing or for very little stealing from them? You bet. Do such churches exist? Terry Jones, energetic Qur'an burner, expects his flock to work for little or nothing, and when they do make money to hand over a percentage of it to him.

Do Christian businesses treat their employees fairly and honestly, or do they expect that, because they are all Christians together, it is perfectly in order to cut back on what they pay their workers? Deuteronomy 24.14 reminds them it isn't.

Do Christians steal people's ability to think for themselves? Isn't the conformity enforced by the church on the converted just this?

Do they steal individuals' sexuality, setting conditions on how this might be expressed once they become members of the church?

Do priests and pastors who sexually abuse or rape children rob them of their innocence and sense of well-being, while violating their bodies? An independent commission in Belgium reported in 2010 that 'no congregation escapes sexual abuse of minors by one or several of its members... We are talking here about anal and oral abuse, forced and mutual masturbation... None of us was prepared for the severity of some of the accounts of abuse that we were given'.

Do evangelists steal from the gullible when they take their money from them to support their own lavish lifestyles?

Do Christians rob gay people when they prevent them from having the same rights as others? Christian groups in America, together with the Church of England's former Archbishop of Canterbury, George Carey, and its current Archbishop of York, John Sentamu, campaign vociferously to prevent same-sex couples, most of whom are not Christians themselves, from marrying.

Do they steal from the collection plate? A 2007 survey by the Loiusville Institute found that over a five year period, 85% of Roman Catholic dioceses had church money stolen by those responsible for collecting it, with 11% experiencing the embezzlement of sums greater than $500,000.

Do they defraud supporters of their own missionary work? In January 2011 the *International Bulletin of Missionary Research*, 'the reliable source for Christian mission history and analysis', estimated that Christian leaders would commit around 34 billion dollars worth of fraud during the year. And in case you think that's a one-off, researchers from the *Center for the Study of Global Christianity* calculate that senior Christians commit 90 million dollars in financial crimes daily, with this kind of fraud growing at a rate of 5.97% each year.

Do they steal from their God when they cherry-pick which parts of 'his word' they will follow and which they abandon?

Do they steal from him when they withhold what they own instead of giving all in his service? Some commentators, like the *Word Of Truth Radio Network*, think so:

> *God's work goes begging today because church members have spent their money on pleasure... spent it on self rather than having honoured God with the first fruits of their increase, their tithes and offerings. My friend, are you stealing from God that which honours Him as the Giver of all things?*

Do Christians steal? I'll leave it to you, dear reader, to decide.

Number 9. You shall not bear false witness against your neighbour. (Exodus 20.16)

That is, don't lie, slander or misrepresent others (God makes himself a little clearer in Leviticus 19.11). But who is 'your neighbour'? Undoubtedly when these laws were created the term referred exclusively to other Israelites. After all, Yahweh sanctions all sorts of brutalities against other tribes, so niceties of not telling fibs about them would hardly matter. Witnesses were important in the punishment of infringements of God's essential laws, like not wearing garments of mixed fabrics and sowing your field with two kinds of seed (Leviticus 19.19). We might ask why, if, as the Exodus account would have us believe, Moses trip up Mount Sinai is the first time anyone has cast eyes on these laws, there is one - this one - about the procedures surrounding the execution of existing laws, and indeed, of people who infringe them.

All of the laws, from the ten commandments to the tedious lists of regulations in Leviticus, evolved over time as the social rules of a tribal people and many of these depended on witnesses for their implementation. The story of the woman caught in adultery in John's gospel illustrates how important it was that the appropriate number of witnesses be present before any law-breaker could be stoned to death, the invariable penalty for transgressing the law.

With such severe penalties, it was crucial that individuals were not falsely accused of crimes by vindictive neighbours and fellow tribes-people (if only the Christians in Salem during the witch hunts there had read up on this commandment). In its original form, then, this commandment is about not making false accusations against your neighbour, in view of the severity of the potential consequences.

Jesus expands the definition of who is a neighbour, so that it encompasses not just other tribe members as it did originally, but anyone and everyone. We might also recognise though that Jesus himself is quite prepared to bear false witness when, in John 7.8, he tells his disciples he won't be going to the Jewish festival of Booths, only to do so two verses later 'in secret as it were'. Be that as it may, with Jesus' refinement this commandment comes to mean, 'don't lie about, accuse or misrepresent anyone else'. Not a bad idea – but do Christians believe it? Do they comply with it?

You can no doubt guess the answer by now. So prone are some Christians to bearing false witness, they bear it against themselves. A recent report by the University of Michigan about church attendance concludes that American Christians 'stretch the truth' about how frequently they attend worship. Naturally, they claim that they go much more often than they do and there are, no doubt, a range of reasons why they might do this – social pressure and the need to appear to be holier than they are, for example, but no such reasons justify what the report describes as American Christians' 'consistent failure to match self-reported rates'. In less euphemistic terms, what we're talking about is yet another big, fat, Christian lie.

Christians are quite happy too to falsify recent history: step forward, once again, that Stranger to the Truth, Pope Benedict XVI! Raping children he tells us, was quite the norm - the rage even – up until a few years ago, and we shouldn't, as a result, make too much of his church's predilection for a spot of recreational child-molesting:

> *In the 1970s, paedophilia was theorised as something fully in conformity with man and even with children... It was maintained — even within the realm of Catholic theology — that there is no such thing as evil in itself or good in itself. There is only a 'better than' and a 'worse than'. Nothing is good or bad in itself.*

I'm not sure which 1970s Ratzinger is referring to here - perhaps it's the alternate reality of Philip Pullman's *Dark Materials* trilogy in which the Catholic church maintains its stranglehold on society – but it is not the seventies I, or anyone else, grew up in. The Pope cannot fail to know that this terrible excuse for deplorable behaviour is nothing more than a fiction; false witness in other words, designed, but failing, to get his church off the hook.

So, if mendacious Christians cannot be honest about themselves, or even the recent past, what hope is there that they will represent their 'neighbours' fairly? The reverend Martin Ssempa, leading light in the Ugandan anti-gay movement, shows videos in his church of some bizarre and extreme homosexual behaviour, practised by a tiny minority of consenting adults behind closed doors. Ssempa, however, claims that this activity is representative of all homosexual behaviour, carried out by all gay people everywhere. Lest you think I'm misrepresenting Brother Martin, you can find him online bearing false witness in this way - or, if we're to be more accurate, lying shamelessly.

What these few individuals do is not what most gay people do. His disregard for the ninth commandment would be deplorable enough if it stopped there, but Ssempa goes on to argue that because of this extreme behaviour - practised, remember, by very few - all homosexuality and all gay people in Uganda should be criminalised, that homosexuals should be severely punished and, in some cases, executed, simply because they are gay.

Not only is Martin Ssempa's premise seriously flawed, but he draws a conclusion from it that it does not support: more bearing of false witness. His argument is akin to saying that because some Christians (priests in the Roman Catholic church and, evidence is emerging, in Southern Baptist churches in the USA) have raped and otherwise sexually abused young children, Christianity and Christians should be criminalised. Merely being a Christian should then result in the severest of penalties. The parallel is applicable, except of course the gay men in Ssempa's video are adults and, presumably, mutually consented to do what they are doing; the choir boys, orphans and deaf children molested by Christians had no such choice.

Ssempa, who was charged in late 2010 with attempting to blackmail a fellow pastor, is not alone in misrepresenting gay people and not the only Christian to bear false witness against his neighbours. *Christian Voice*'s Stephen Green claims that gay people are not marginalised but are themselves oppressors, while *Focus on The Family* suggests that attempts in the American school system to eliminate bullying are all part of a sinister 'gay agenda', which, it would seem, only they know anything about (perhaps because they invented it). Though this ubiquitous organisation knows the difference between homosexuals and paedophiles, it alleges nonetheless that it is the former who are 'out to recruit your children' through anti-bullying campaigns. This wilful confusion serves *Focus On The Family's* own alarmist agenda – expressed on their ironically named 'True Tolerance' website - and epitomises the kind of false witness that the ninth commandment forbids.

Christians also persistently misrepresent a second group, that of non-believers, and atheists in particular. The first speech made by

Pope Benedict XVI on his arrival in the UK in 2010 falsely equated atheists with Hitler. Hitler was, like the Pope, a Catholic: 'I am now as before a Catholic and will always remain so', he confessed in 1941. Pope Benedict, like Hitler, was a Nazi in his younger days, a member of the Hitler Youth Movement. Quite how atheists are like Hitler, Ratzinger did not make clear - but then that is the effect mud-slinging has.

Other Christians point to the supposed misery and emptiness of being an atheist:

> *If we try to live consistently within the atheistic world view, we shall find ourselves profoundly unhappy... For one cannot live happily and consistently on an atheistic world view.* (William Lane Craig: *The Absurdity of Life Without God*)

> *A world without God is a world filled with hopelessness and despair. Man cannot find in himself the answer to "Why should I keep on?" Life without God has no purpose that gives hope.* (Kansas Expressway Church of Christ)

There is no evidence at all that atheists are any more hope-less or unhappy than Christians. Those who live life without reference to any god are just as capable as those who profess belief in the Christian version of living happy, fulfilled, moral lives. They don't worry, for a start about whether they're pleasing or offending a deity, whether they reach his supposed standards or subscribe to doctrines sufficiently correct to guarantee eternal life (because they know there isn't one). Most atheists I know, and others, such as those who operate atheist websites, appear well-balanced, happy and able to live life to the full. To see this for yourself have a look for yourself at the *Friendly Atheist, Pharyngula, Daylight Atheism, The Thinking Atheist* and *40 Year Old Atheist* blogs or read Dan Barker's *Godless*.

Christians also claim that without God, there is no basis for morality, accusing non-believers of being either immoral or moral relativists who adapt their morals to suit circumstances. Objective standards or moral absolutism, they say, can only be derived from God. However, picking and choosing which of God's supposed commandments should be followed and which to dispense with, either because they have been superseded (how can an absolute be superseded?) or because they are not compatible with modern culture (infanticide or slavery anyone?) is moral relativism *par excellence*. Christians do not derive their morals, as they like to claim they do, from the illusory absolute standards of the Bible. As we have already seen and will continue to see throughout this book, the Bible, with all its stoning and smiting, provides little basis for moral living.

Even the Bible's more reasonable admonitions, like caring for others, are not the product of Christianity having arisen independently throughout human history: C. S. Lewis devotes the appendix of *The Abolition of Man* to instances of intuitive morality in non-Christian cultures past and present. In any case, polls in the USA - even those by evangelical pollsters - have repeatedly shown that there is little 'little measurable difference between the moral behaviour of churchgoers and the rest of American society', atheists being just as capable of behaving morally (and, no doubt, immorally) as Christians. Many of those who first provided help after the earthquake and tsunami that hit Japan in March 2011 belonged to groups of no religious affiliation. Many who gave to those groups were also non-believers. Like Hemant Mehta, writer of the *Friendly Atheist* blog, they embrace the Golden Rule - treat others as you would like to be treated - as the guiding principle of morality.

Available to all, and with no god required, the Golden Rule pre-dates Jesus, appearing in non-religious philosophies of Ancient Egypt and Greece hundreds of years before his birth. Christianity, whatever its adherents might falsely claim, has no monopoly of the idea; as Lewis, Paul Kurtz, Sam Harris and others demonstrate, God is not needed for people to behave honourably.

Christians must claim that he is, of course. If atheism represents the opposite of Christian belief then apologists for the faith must denigrate the competition - rather like those McDonalds' ads that trash Burger King - to make their own product seem superior and hence more attractive. While I can't speak for burger companies, Christians, those custodians of higher morality, bear false witness when they claim atheists are hopeless, unhappy and living in despair. Perhaps they trash the opposition because their own product really isn't that great and they know it.

Number 10. You shall not covet your neighbour's house; you shall not covet your neighbour's wife, or male or female slave, or ox, or donkey, or anything that belongs to your neighbour. (Exodus 20.17)

Evidently Yahweh was really thinking ahead with this one and came up with a commandment designed to apply across all times and cultures. Not really; not only is it of its time - and bottom of the list for a reason - but who even knows what coveting means? If it means 'desire', then capitalism has had it, given that it depends entirely on the desire for more. So does so much human striving, ambition and development; if ancient people had managed to avoid coveting, we would all still be living in tribes, chasing antelope on the plain and eking out an existence with stone tools (don't even think of wanting bronze ones). In his book *The Rational Optimist: How Prosperity Evolves*, Matt Ridley makes the point that trade, relying as it does on covetousness, is directly responsible for the peculiarly human trait of approaching, trusting and communicating with strangers when they have something we need (and covet). 'Where commerce thrives', he says, 'creativity and compassion both flourish'. This commandment and Jesus' later warnings about covetousness condemn us to a primitive, isolated life indeed.

It could be, however, that to covet means to desire to an obsessive degree, without regard for the rights of others - perhaps in the way the Israelites coveted the lands of their neighbours, eventually taking them by force from their rightful occupants. If this is what is being prohibited then of course the commandment is to be commended, but in the end this is a thought-crime injunction; it isn't actually about *doing,* or not doing, anything. The stealing, murdering and adultery that coveting might lead to among the more unstable are covered elsewhere in this wearisome list. So how is coveting policed? Who is the victim of an infringement of this commandment, assuming most instances do not lead to murder or theft of property, livestock or wife, all of which appear to be of equal value in this commandment? Does the tenth commandment make any real sense?

It is possible, as a sermon of my own Christian days suggested, that what the commandment warns against is a frame of mind that does not stop at wanting what our neighbour has, but, if desire is thwarted, would gladly see him (and it is a 'him') deprived of the object of desire: a sort of 'if I can't have it, there's no reason why you should either' mentality. This is mean-spirited to be sure, but isn't what the commandment specifies. Even if it were, we are brought back to how such base thinking might be policed and the fact that any act intended to deprive the owner of an object of desire is covered by other commandments. God seems to have such a down on humankind: might the commandment have been phrased more positively? Something like, 'Be glad for your neighbour when he or she is successful, when he or she gains possessions that you yourself don't have. Be content with what you have'. But, no. As ever, he's got to accentuate the negative.

In Luke 12.15, Jesus associates covetousness with greed and the acquisition of possessions: 'Take heed and beware of covetousness, for one's life does not consist in the abundance of the things he possesses' (KJV). For Jesus, covetousness is synonymous with acquisitiveness, the 'storing up' of worldly goods instead of 'treasures in heaven'. This takes us back to his teaching on riches, of putting mammon ahead of serving God. As we have already established, Christians are as prone to this as anyone else. A few years ago showman evangelist Benny Hinn coveted a new jet. He coveted it so much he went out and bought it even though he didn't want to use his own money to pay for it. Consequently, he wrote to his followers that he had:

> *taken delivery on our Gulfstream G4SP plane, which we call Dove One. I have enclosed a beautiful photo-filled brochure to explain more about this incredible ministry tool that will increase the scope of our*

> *abilities to preach the Gospel around the globe. Now we must pay the remainder of the down payment, and I am asking the Lord Jesus to speak to 6,000 of my precious partners to sow a seed of $1,000 in the next ninety days. And I am praying, even as I write this letter, that you will be one of them!*

No news on whether he received the $6,000,000 in time, but Hinn is now able to take the gospel to the poor in spirit using the $35 million 'Dove One'.

Do other more run-of-the-mill Christians covet? Given that Christians' lifestyles are indistinguishable from anyone else's, we can be sure they do. They, like us all, covet comfortable lifestyles and the attractive accoutrements of the western world. Do they also covet things from which the rest of us are immune? Others' greater spirituality or status within the church? Who can blame them if they do? They're only human after all.

If only their God saw it that way.

The evidence would suggest that as a body (and that is what they see themselves as) most Christians don't believe Jesus when he says the way to eternal life is to keep the commandments. Or, if they do, they don't do a very good job of keeping them, except for those they particularly like or try to inflict on others. Stephen Green of the UK's *Christian Voice*, laments the fact that modern Christians neither adhere to nor do enough to promote these primitive laws: 'Christians need to say loudly and clearly that these laws of God that look so harsh to modern eyes were given by God because He loves us and wants our societies to thrive and enjoy His blessing'. Any civilised society needs to be grateful they don't, as, thanks to the efforts of more enlightened individuals, we in the west no longer live in a theocracy of death penalties and amputations.

Yet still some Christians persist in declaring the moral significance of the ten commandments. As I write, another group in the United States seeks to erect a monument to them on public property in

Illinois, a school board in Virginia is about to install the ten commandments in its classrooms, in spite of a legal ruling instructing it not to, and Republican Dan Flynn proposes a bill that would protect teachers who display the ten commandments in their Texan classrooms. Flynn believes this 'patriotic' breach of the law that in America keeps religion out of public life will teach children morals; we can only wonder what sort. Before Christians try to inflict their dubious ten-commandment-based morality on others, perhaps they could give some thought (I know, too much to ask) to the following:

i) they don't actually follow the commandments themselves (see above). While they claim to derive their morality from the Bible, Christians are no better than non-believers at obeying the ten commandments.

ii) the commandments are from the Jewish law which most of the time Christians say is not relevant any more (even though their Saviour says it is);

iii) the first four commandments are not about morality at all, but the worship of an ancient, despotic desert deity, who, surprisingly, not everyone believes in or even wants to;

iv) the few decent injunctions that remain, once those about not offending God and the other useless ones are removed, are intrinsic to all human morality and existed long before Moses' imaginary trip up Sinai.

Perhaps when Christians talk about deriving their morality from the Bible they don't really mean the ten commandments and the other strange, often downright immoral prescriptions of the Old Testament. Although the precepts laid down by Jesus are based on these older rules, perhaps Christians actually derive their morals from Jesus himself and are better at doing what he tells them to. In the next chapter we'll see if they do.

Chapter 4

On Being Perfect

Let's take a look to start with at Jesus' summary of the morality he expects followers to demonstrate. You'll notice that along the way he proposes changes to the old Jewish law, which, as we've seen, he insists cannot be altered by the tiniest amount (Matthew 5.17-19). How's that for a consistent perspective?

> *You have heard that it was said, "An eye for an eye and a tooth for a tooth." But I say to you, Do not resist an evildoer. But if anyone strikes you on the right cheek, turn the other also; and if anyone wants to sue you and take your coat, give your cloak as well; and if anyone forces you to go one mile, go also the second mile. Give to everyone who begs from you, and do not refuse anyone who wants to borrow from you. You have heard that it was said, "You shall love your neighbour and hate your enemy." But I say to you, Love your enemies and pray for those who persecute you... For if you love those who love you, what reward do you have? Do not even the tax-collectors do the same? And if you greet only your brothers and sisters, what more are you doing than others? Do not even the Gentiles do the same? Be perfect, therefore, as your heavenly Father is perfect.* (Matthew 5.38-48)

This is Jesus' prescription for moral perfection. He concludes his sermon with the injunction to 'be perfect' because it is the end result of behaving in the way he describes: 'do these things', he is saying, 'and you will be perfect'. Jesus and his synoptic scriptwriters do not to subscribe to Paul's view that perfection is achieved by supernatural means; as we shall see, Jesus is emphatic both here and in many other places, that a person's own efforts and changed behaviour determine their status before God and their suitability for his Kingdom. You might already be wondering where all the absolutely perfect people are in today's world, because seek as much as you like, you won't find them. Why might that be? Let's analyse each of Jesus' requirements in turn to discover why:

Jesus' followers are called to be pacifists: 'do not resist an evildoer' he tells them in Matthew 5.39, 'but if anyone strikes you on the right cheek, turn the other also'. More than pacifists, they are commanded to be completely and utterly passive when confronted by 'evil-doers'. This is an absurd requirement as it stands, and Christians know it, which is why the majority of them are not pacifists, let alone passive. They're not prepared to take what others dish out, as Jesus insists they should. So what do they do? They do what they usually do when Jesus is being too exacting; they change what he says, reinterpret it ('he doesn't intend this to be taken literally!') and dilute it.

According to *Revelife* ('Christian Community for Heart, Mind and Soul'), what Jesus 'really' means here - even if it's not what he says - is that Christians 'shouldn't respond in kind', and similarly the *Provocative Christian Living* group also emphasises non-retaliation. But these interpretations fail to take into account the distinctly *responsive* nature of the passivity Jesus expects. He says categorically that when slapped or insulted (the back-handed slap he implies would have been intended as an insult) one should not merely *avoid* retaliating, but respond by offering oneself up for more of the same treatment. This is why, instead of opting for a metaphor that suggests 'do not respond in kind', Jesus insists the other cheek must be offered *as well*. In fact, he has a metaphor at his disposal to convey a non-responsive walking away, which he uses in Matthew 10.14 - 'shake the dust from your feet' - but he doesn't use it here, where his meaning is much more radical.

There is something peculiarly active about the passivity Jesus proposes – it is the same enthusiastic, self-abnegation exhibited by Jesus at his trial and by early Christian martyrs. They were all evidently made of sterner stuff than today's believers, who rightly don't like the sound of where 'turning the other cheek' leads. Incredibly, some Christians in the USA use these same pacifist verses to justify their 'God-given right' to bear arms, in order to defend themselves.

Who says Americans don't do irony?

With that in mind, it is time for a little experiment: some data gathering for ourselves that will demonstrate the extent to which Christians are willing to comply, without cynicism or irony, with their Saviour's peculiar requirements. While the Bible assures us it is wrong to put the Lord God to the test (Deuteronomy 6.16, etc), rest assured the same does not apply to believers themselves.

Our experiment is a cruel one to be sure, but given Jesus' command in Matthew 5.42, that believers should 'give to everyone who begs from you, and do not refuse anyone who wants to borrow from you', we would be within our rights to test their adherence to the principle. After all, Jesus specifies that his followers must oblige 'everyone' and 'anyone' who asks, which is accommodating enough to include any sceptics conducting an experiment. He doesn't stipulate either that those doing the asking have to have genuine need; indeed the entire thrust of his teaching in this section of Matthew is about responding sacrificially to unreasonable demands. We won't be unreasonable – so no slapping of cheeks – and we will do our best to ensure our request is designed to meet as genuine a need as we can create.

For any experiment we need a hypothesis, so I propose that for this particular one we go with something like 'Christians will not give to those who beg from them nor lend to those who ask to borrow'. If you want to amend this to suit your own circumstances, by all means do. You can choose too whether you're going to beg, which means you get to keep anything you are given, or to borrow, in which case you won't and you'll need to pay it back at a later date.

Next, you'll need to select your subject: you can choose an individual - they must of course be a card-carding, Spirit-filled Christian – or an institution: a church, say, or Christian organisation like *Focus on the Family* or *Christian Voice*. Whichever you opt for, you'll need to ensure they are capable of meeting your request - we're not going to pick on Christians of more modest means - and decide what you will ask for. I suggest that if your subject is a renowned evangelist or the pastor of a so-called mega-church you could reasonably ask him or her to lend you the money to pay off your mortgage, for example, or to meet medical expenses. I'm sure he or she will agree that these qualify as truly genuine needs, though you don't necessarily have to tell them why you want the money, given there's no mention of the beggars in Jesus' instructions explaining themselves. On the other hand, if you think it will go some way to help disprove the hypothesis, you can and perhaps should be clear about why you want the cash.

Right. You should be all set. Be sure to let me know how you get on and whether your Christian subject demonstrates the hypothesis or refutes it. I'll collate the data.

What's that you say? You're not going to bother because it's a foregone conclusion that most Christians, whether prominent individuals, churches, organisations or ordinary believers won't give to anyone and everyone who asks?

You could well be right, because, although Christians do give generously to causes close to their hearts, they baulk at the idea of giving to just anybody, in spite of what Jesus says. Take the case of the two women who arrived with their children at the *House of Mercy* shelter for the homeless in Georgia, USA. The two women, and their children were denied both shelter and mercy because Elder Bobby Harris suspected they were gay. This should not have made any difference to Elder Bobby's obligation to obey his saviour's injunction to give to those in need, but it did.

As it happens, the women were not gay, but Elder Bobby's suspicions, together with his self-righteousness, were enough to have him turn them away. After all, Jesus specifically excludes homosexuals from his command to give to others and as a Christian one can't be too careful - maybe he rules out people who *look* like they might be gay too. At least this is how it must read in some Bibles, including that of Harris Himes, pastor of the ridiculously named *Big Sky Christian Center* in Montana. His Bible tells him not only to ensure that he doesn't help gay people, but that he do all in his power to ensure no-one else does either. Pastor Himes campaigns for landlords to have the right to discriminate against gay people looking to rent housing in the state. To do otherwise, claims the pastor, with the same sense of justice and command of grammar demonstrated by those who oppose others' rights, 'actually discriminates against me and those who believe as I do that homosexuality and transgender and all of these things is an abomination to God'. That's Leviticus 20:13 again - how it always trumps anything Jesus had to say.

The next part of the recipe for perfection - 'if anyone wants to sue you and take your coat, give your cloak as well' – is mentioned before the give-to-all business but takes that particular injunction a stage further. Where there is a social basis to the proposal that his followers give to anyone who asks, there are legal connotations to this new expectation, suing being then, as now, a legal procedure. Jesus is saying that if you are sued you should not just hand over what the court decrees, but more besides, the cloak being a more valuable asset than a shirt. But that's not all; Jesus doesn't say that you need to be sued successfully to have to do this, nor indeed sued at all. No, he says that if anyone so much as *wants* to sue you, you should hand over your goods. They don't have to go through with the legal proceedings – the very intent of suing should prompt you to hand over your clothing. To Jesus' first century audience, who didn't have entire wardrobes of clothes to offer would-be plaintiffs, a shirt and cloak were essential, valuable items. This is another completely preposterous idea, and I defy anyone to produce a contemporary Christian anywhere in the world who complies with it.

Even with the Holy Spirit purifying them, believers fall seriously short of Jesus' expectations of perfection – and we're not even half way through his list of impossible expectations. Surely they stand some chance with his next one, his famous line that 'if anyone forces you to go one mile, go also the second mile'. Let's set it in context to see.

Living in an occupied territory, a member of the occupying forces, a Roman soldier, could compel you to carry his back pack for him for the next mile of his march. You would have no choice in the matter, not unless you wanted to be brutalised, though the soldier could not ask you to go beyond the initial mile; he could find himself disciplined if he did. Having carried his pack, you would then have to walk the mile back to where you started. And yet Jesus says that you should not just oblige with the mile the soldier insists you walk with his heavy possessions on your back, but should walk the next mile too, and then trek back two.

It's possible that Jesus is suggesting that going the extra mile is one way in which the oppressed can take back control of the situation, leaving the oppressor confused and potentially in trouble for seeming to take his conscript more than the single mile he was allowed to demand. If so, it is a radical means by which to highlight the injustice of the situation and unsurprisingly today's Christians seem not to care for the principle of cutting their noses to spite their face that underpins it. Jesus is not talking about doing that extra bit of service for the church, nor of giving a friend a lift nor of doing the household chores cheerfully, as various web-sermons suggest. He is talking about serving an enemy, one of the hated occupying forces and of going well beyond what is asked by them. Contemporary equivalents might be paying twice the taxes demanded of you; opting, when wrongfully arrested, for two nights in police custody instead of one; working not just the single extra hour your boss asks of you but two - and both for nothing.

You think any of this will make any difference to the underlying unreasonableness of the expectations? You think your demonstrating a lack of self-respect will impress the authorities or your boss? You're right, it won't; it's more likely that your stupidity will be taken advantage of and you'll be exploited still further. Christians know this too, which is why they rarely do as they're told by going 'the extra mile'.

But Jesus isn't finished just yet with his impractical suggestions for responding to others' unreasonable expectations. In fact, as he warms to his theme he becomes even more exacting: it's a good idea, he decides, to 'love your enemies and pray for those who persecute you'.

Let's get this straight - Jesus isn't speculating about respecting others, being kind to them or treating them nicely. He's talking about *loving* them. There's no merit, he says, in merely loving family and friends; people who are likely to reciprocate. As he acknowledges condescendingly, even sinners and heathens manage to do that. He expects far more from his followers. They are called not just to show love to random 'others', but to their *enemies.* And how is this love defined? According to Paul in his paean to love in 1 Corinthians 13, Christian love is sacrificial, freely-given and all-embracing. It is this kind of love that Christians must demonstrate towards those who dislike them, mistreat them and wish them ill; they must have their enemies' best interests at heart, praying for their well-being. Paul goes so far as to say that without such love the believer amounts to 'nothing'.

Then Jesus goes and spoils it all by saying something stupid (as if everything up this point hasn't been): 'for if you love those who love you, what reward do you have?'. Suddenly, unexpectedly, he's talking about rewards. What happened to unconditional love for others, for one's enemies? Of love that does not seek reward? Aren't Jesus' followers capable of loving others because they share a common humanity? It would seem that even though sinners and heathens are capable of loving others unaided, Christians need the stick and carrot of punishment and reward to manage it. Love, it would seem, is not its own reward. So let's see how Christians exhibit this love-for-enemies in practice, knowing their chance of reward rests on how they go about it:

Dale Mcalpine is a street preacher in the north of England. He was arrested in early 2010 when he declared to a gay community police officer that 'the Bible says homosexuality is a crime against the Creator', adding, correctly, that it was not against the law to say so. While there is no doubt his arrest was unlawful, Mcalpine forgave his persecutors and then, calling on Jesus' words in Matthew 5.44 to 'sue those who persecute you', proclaimed that that was precisely what he would be doing. Except... this is not what Jesus says. He is quite clear that the believer's response to unfair treatment should be, firstly, to 'go also the second mile' - which should have prompted Mcalpine to ask for extra time in the cells – and, secondly, to 'love your enemies, bless them that curse you, do good to them that hate you, and pray for them which despitefully use you, and persecute you' (KJV). Paul too instructs Christians to 'bless those who persecute you; bless and do not curse them' (Romans 12:14). Sadly, there's no mention from either of the suing option. Mcalpine may not have known this, but *The Christian Institute*, which sprang to his defence and financed his ultimately successful legal action, surely does. It has a history of supporting litigations by Christians who have been slighted in some way or, as the Institute puts it, 'discriminated against', and boasts of being 'a non-denominational Christian charity committed to upholding the truths of the Bible'. This is with the exception, obviously, of 'truths' about blessing persecutors and turning the other cheek.

Finally, Jesus issues the injunction to be perfect; 'be perfect, therefore, as your heavenly Father is perfect' is how he puts it. It is not difficult to see how, with the moral standards he expects, no-one is. And doesn't he, in any case, have a mighty peculiar idea of perfection? If he thinks the murderous old despot of the Old Testament is 'perfect', then he has little grasp of what constitutes perfection. Perhaps, though, his 'Heavenly Father' is a different concept altogether, as heretical groups of believers down the ages have claimed, often with fatal consequences for themselves. It is true that orthodox Christians have been known to approach the 'perfection' shown by Yahweh – they too have slaughtered, murdered, plundered and suppressed, but this isn't perhaps what Jesus has in mind.

It is often claimed, even by those who don't believe in him as their saviour, that Jesus offered great moral teaching: C. S. Lewis even cautions against seeing Jesus as simply 'a great human teacher' when, in Lewis's eyes, he was far more besides. I would, however, invite any believers who are still reading to consider whether the moral guidance Jesus provides here in Matthew's gospel is in any sense 'great'. If you think that it is, because Jesus is Lord, a perfect being and possibly God himself, then you need to explain why it is never followed by Christians, and never has been. You need to explain why you yourself do not apply it in your life, because as sure as poached eggs is poached eggs, you do not. You do not give to all who ask; you do not invite insult after insult and violence on top of violence; you do not give away valuable and essential possessions when threatened with legal action – you are actually more likely to do the suing. And lest you think I am advocating a far more exacting morality for Christians than I would from anyone else, you will bear in mind, won't you, that is not I who insists on it, but your Saviour. It's not unreasonable under the circumstances to expect to see you obeying him.

As it is fairly safe to assume you don't, I would further invite you to consider whether instead of being 'great', Jesus' teaching is in fact unreasonable, unrealistic and impractical. If you are honest, you will acknowledge that it is all of these things, not great or timeless at all, and that is why you, and all other Christians worldwide, disregard it. Jesus' moral teaching is no more than a series of reckless suggestions, a formula that applied can lead only to poverty and abuse, not perfection. You are probably wise to ignore it and to spend your time instead impeding gay marriage and judging the rest of us.

Still, if perfection is not for you, Christian, then maybe some of Jesus' other recommendations, scattered throughout the gospels, hold greater appeal. Luke's gospel also includes the impossible expectations we have just looked at in Matthew, and embellishes them further. In 6.35, for example Luke's Jesus tells anyone daft enough to listen to him to lend and expect nothing in return and on the surface this seems to be the same as an instruction to give things away. But the key word here is 'expect'; lend without the expectation that you will get anything back – meaning that you shouldn't do people favours with the expectation that they will reciprocate: do things for others freely. This shouldn't be difficult – even the enlightened heathen could manage this one - so why is it that some Christians look for financial return on what they do for others? Why do faith-healers expect those they help to 'sow a seed' by donating a large amount to their 'ministry' *in return*?

Part of the law Jesus subscribes to forbids the charging of interest on loans, so his teaching here is, as we might expect, in line with that. But as usual he goes further in insisting that the lender should not even look for the return of the sum lent. It is, he suggests, a bonus if it comes back, but it's not essential that it does. He is trying to create a frame of mind here that is content to let things go once they have been lent to others: why worry about hanging on to material things when the world as we know it is going to end soon? He makes no provisos about who those we lend to might be. Conceivably they could be your enemy or your neighbour - both of whom he is quite keen that you love - or a member of your family (whom he is less enamoured with). Nor is he specific about what it is these people might borrow from you, so while money certainly qualifies (we've already seen what he recommends in terms of giving it away), so too does any other item you happen to own.

We now pause while Christians try to refute that this is what Jesus 'really' means.

Now that they've realised he cannot mean anything other than this, we'll continue:

So, when you, heathen reader, ask to borrow your Christian neighbour's lawn-mower, he should lend it you without expecting that you return it. Or his car. Or, indeed, his house. He won't of course be disappointed when you don't return any of these things, because he will have a Christ-like frame of mind that comes from following this command of Jesus'. He will say to himself, rather: 'it doesn't matter, I wasn't expecting my belongings back anyway. I lent them expecting nothing in return'.

And for the Christian who can't decide who to invite to his latest party or soiree, Jesus has the answer! Here's his perfect solution:

> *When you give a luncheon or a dinner, do not invite your friends or your brothers or your relatives or rich neighbours, in case they may invite you in return, and you would be repaid. But when you give a banquet, invite the poor, the crippled, the lame, and the blind. And you will be blessed, because they cannot repay you, for you will be repaid at the resurrection of the*

> *righteous.* (Luke 14.24-26)

He doesn't mean it literally, you say? But isn't everything in the Bible the literal word of God? And what could he possibly mean otherwise? Don't go looking for explanations of these verses, or 'get-out' clauses from them, on Christian websites because there aren't any. That's because Jesus can only mean exactly what he says here, which has nothing to do with feeding the hungry in soup kitchens or with food parcels. In what is another of his social-reversal commandments, he impresses on his followers that he expects them to wine and dine complete strangers in their own homes (check out the context in Luke 14) without any expectation of reward or returned favour. That's why at the sumptuous banquets in the Vatican, the parties thrown by the Archbishop of Canterbury and the dinners given by each and every 'righteous' Christian you know, it's only ever the poor and the disabled who are invited. Just as Jesus says it should be.

He also advises his followers how to pray, saying 'when you pray, pray in private', which, even though it really ought not to be, turns out to be another bit of morality Christians find impossible to adhere to. Given its demonstrable ineffectiveness – its utter uselessness – it could be argued that prayer doesn't qualify as 'morality' at all. However, as it is usually intended at least in part to invoke God's help for the supplicant and others, we'll concede that it might be. Here then are Jesus' instructions on how to go about it:

> *And whenever you pray, do not be like the hypocrites; for they love to stand and pray in the synagogues and at the street corners, so that they may be seen by others. Truly I tell you, they have received their reward. But whenever you pray, go into your room and shut the door and pray to your Father who is in secret; and your Father who sees in secret will reward you.*
> (Matthew 6.5-6)

Decades before these words were recorded, Paul was having to take the church in Corinth to task for its ostentatious use of 'praying in tongues' (1 Corinthians 14). This phenomenon is when believers make unintelligible noises that they claim the Holy Spirit instigates and only the Holy Spirit can understand. In reality, of course, no-one understands them, because they are just unintelligible noises, as Paul himself admits in 1 Corinthians 14.2. Jesus, however, who seems to know nothing at all about praying in tongues, is not only speaking out against over-the-top displays of spirituality. He is providing instructions for how his followers should act 'whenever' they pray. He is clear that they should not do so in public but should be secretive about it, praying behind closed doors, alone and in private.

There is no room for symbolic interpretation of what he says, yet, since the early Christian community in Corinth, Christians have systematically flouted this stipulation. Today, there is public prayer in churches, schools and council chambers, at coronations, inaugurations and graduations and at any other gathering where believers think they can make their presence felt. Evidently Jesus was wrong to say that prayer is a private matter between the deluded and their God. Otherwise these Christians would be doing as he said, instead of the exact opposite.

And so, in this consideration of Jesus' moral teaching, to the famous 'let he who is without sin cast the first stone' from John's gospel. This aphorism and the circumstances that prompt it are universally acknowledged to be a very late addition to the text; as a result, it is unlikely to be an authentic saying of Jesus'. At first glance this would seem to be rather a pity when it conveys a compassion so often lacking in Christians' dealings with non-believers and those whose sexual behaviour they find objectionable. Told in John 8.2-11, this quite complex story relates how a woman has been caught in adultery – 'in the very act' according to the KJV. We might wonder by whom, but evidently there were, just as today, voyeuristic busy-bodies in the ancient world, ever eager to tell tales on those who didn't share their own upstanding morals. Jewish law, like Shar'ia law in the hands of extremists today, decreed that those who committed adultery should be stoned to death. Through his considered retort, Jesus appears to side-step the execution of both the law and the unfortunate woman, though, as Christians point out, he doesn't let her off entirely scot-free. He sends her on her way with a warning to avoid sinning again, as if her narrow escape weren't enough to convince her to mend her ways.

It might seem that what we should take from this story is that Jesus is intent on rescuing the woman from a terrible fate, and that he does so in a way that is both compassionate and clever. But we'd be wrong, because this is not what this story is about and not the point its creator wants to make. What he has Jesus do is refuse to consider the case because it has not been brought to him in strict accordance with the law. The 'law of Moses' that the Pharisees refer to is found in Leviticus 20.10 and Deuteronomy 22.23-24 where it stipulates that an adulteress and her colluding partner, the adulterer, must be brought to trial together and that *both* should be stoned. We mustn't forget that Jesus positively approves of this law - he says so in Matthew 5.19 - and consequently his reaction is not intended to suggest that stoning is a marginally excessive penalty for extra-marital sex.

Instead, he demonstrates his superior knowledge of the law and uses it against the woman's accusers. Those eye-witnesses are important too; even though they are mentioned, they don't seem to be present and without them, no stoning can take place. In Jewish law it is the accusing witnesses who are required to cast the first stones (Deuteronomy 17.6-7). Jesus is fully aware of this (as surely the Pharisees are too) and it is to the absence of witnesses that he refers when he asks the woman, 'has no one condemned you?'. He acknowledges that he too is not a witness to her alleged adultery when he adds, 'neither do I condemn you' (John 8.10-11), but this isn't necessarily the compassionate response it appears to be: it is Jesus adhering to the law.

The woman cannot be stoned on technical grounds. In what is really a set-to with the Pharisees about the law (John 8.6), it is as if her rescue is incidental. Her life is saved but nothing else changes: if her co-accused and eye-witnesses had been present, what would have been Jesus' way out then? With no technicality to fall back on, would he have endorsed the execution? As a supporter of the law he would have had to.

In the episode as we have it, he does not propose the bending of the law, let alone its abolition. Neither does he object to its severe penalties for adultery. This woman's rescue is a one-off: others unfortunate enough to be caught while having sex with another's spouse, provided the technicalities of the law are met, would still fall under its prescription. They would be pelted with rocks hurled by witnesses and holy men untroubled by whether or not they themselves were without sin.

The whole of this miserable incident, then, is lacking in any real moral teaching. The woman's alleged transgressions seem slight when compared with everyone else's: she is used by both parties – principally by the Pharisees, but also by Jesus - to score points off one another. What the story's creator wants to convey, ultimately, is Jesus' adherence to the letter of the law, and his demonstration of that adherence. It is this that saves the woman, not a show of mercy, forgiveness or love.

Atheist comedian Ricky Gervais has said that he would like to see the 'little gem' that is 'let he who is without sin cast the first stone' adhered to by everyone, so that no more stones would ever be thrown. The original context of the saying, sadly, doesn't lend itself to such universal application. This perhaps explains why Christians today feel under little obligation not to hurl their metaphorical rocks at others, especially those with sex lives of which they don't approve. Or, indeed, those with sex lives. We shall consider Christians' enthusiasm for stone-throwing more fully shortly.

In spite of this, what distinguishes Christianity from other belief systems for most people is its purported emphasis on love and forgiveness. These are the reputed hallmarks of the faith, its perceived essence (though you can be excused if you thought it was its rabid anti-gay stance that marked it out). We might suppose then that Jesus' teaching about forgiveness would be clear and straight forward. Instead, it's muddled and contradictory.

In Matthew 18, he offers his disciples three different perspectives on forgiveness, three disparate and incompatible strands. In the first, which can be found in verses 15-17, Jesus is made to address issues of the early church about which he would have known nothing. It was not his intention to establish a church but to preach the imminent end of the age and coming of the Kingdom. So this part of his teaching is anachronistic, added, as is much in the gospels, by later believers keen to see their Lord address their particular concerns, even when he hadn't. Here are the words that are put into his mouth:

> *If another member of the church sins against you, go and point out the fault when the two of you are alone. If the member listens to you, you have regained that one. But if you are not listened to, take one or two others along with you, so that every word may be confirmed by the evidence of two or three witnesses. If the member refuses to listen to them, tell it to the church; and if the offender refuses to listen even to the church, let such a one be to you as a Gentile and a tax-collector.*

In other words, the church member who offends another (and how easily that is achieved!) and who refuses to be coerced into compliance, should be named and shamed and then ousted from the church. Which is fair enough; the early church was entitled to have whatever rules it wanted, even if they did contradict what their Lord appears to have thought about the matter. Evidently the community who added this church-related teaching to Matthew's gospel could not manage to forgive in the way Jesus said they should – freely and repeatedly according to the second strand of his teaching - and needed some other way to deal with members of the congregation who sinned against others.

Retrospective approval of their strategy then became necessary, so when they eventually got their hands on Matthew's gospel in some form, they made Jesus endorse their way of doing things. They do this even though their ideas bear no relation to what Jesus himself probably said about forgiveness. This tells us quite lot. Either the early community that added to Matthew was, until the gospel eventually came their way, unaware of Jesus' teaching on the subject, or they did know of it but found it impossible to put into practice. It's possible too that this particular teaching is the earliest of the strands that appear in this chapter of Matthew, given that the early church needed to establish practical systems for dealing with those who strayed, decades before the gospels came to be written.

The second perspective of forgiveness Jesus offers is far less practical, though considerably more charitable. As impracticality is a hallmark of much of Jesus' moral teaching, it seems likely that this alternative, contradictory teaching emanates from him:

> *Then Peter came and said to him, 'Lord, if (a brother) sins against me, how often should I forgive? As many as seven times?' Jesus said to him, 'Not seven times, but, I tell you, seventy-seven times.* (Matthew 18.21-22)

Jesus wants forgiveness to be endlessly and freely given. This is the significance of the seventy-seven times, or 'seventy times seven' as the KJV puts it. This sounds simple enough but is fraught with problems:

1. Peter's question and Jesus' answer relate specifically to forgiving fellow-believers. In context, this probably meant only fellow-Jews but we'll generously assume that both had later, non-Jewish followers in mind too. This doesn't alter the fact, however, that Jesus' teaching here is strictly 'in-house': believers are not being called upon to forgive those outside the fold at all, nor do women appear to be covered by his edict.

2. He is unclear about whether forgiveness should be given whether it is asked for or not. Does the Christian go on forgiving his brother (or sister) even when they're not remotely sorry for what they have done? Or is penitence a requirement on their part? There are hints in the parable that follows that some pleading from the offender might not go amiss, while Luke, evidently unhappy with Jesus' vagueness, tries to clarify the situation: 'If another disciple sins, you must rebuke the offender, and if there is repentance, you must forgive' (Luke 17.3). Unfortunately, this

amendment raises further questions, not least whether it's okay to withhold forgiveness if the perpetrator expresses no regret.

3. Matthew's Jesus doesn't indicate whether he's talking about one offence that needs to be forgiven repeatedly, whenever it comes to mind, or countless offences each requiring its own forgiveness. He could mean both. The early church was clearly having difficulty with the lack of specifics in Jesus' teaching, so Luke, once again, comes to the rescue: 'if the same person sins against you seven times a day, and turns back to you seven times and says, "I repent", you must forgive' (Luke 17.4). While we can be fairly certain these are not the words of Jesus - Matthew, using the same sources as Luke, is unaware of them - they do go some way to answering the question of whether *every* offence must be forgiven. Yes, according to Luke, provided there's repentance. But no, presumably, if there isn't.

4. Jesus doesn't consider the implications of all this endless forgiving. While the psychological effects of forgiving can be beneficial to the forgiver (I'm sure Jesus was aware of the studies that indicate this to be the case), the individual who forgives ceaselessly is setting him or herself up as some sort of human doormat. And as Christians are fond of pointing out Jesus doesn't call them to be anybody's patsy: in the words of the admirable Desmond Tutu, 'forgiving doesn't mean turning yourself into a doormat for people to wipe their boots on'.

No, Jesus doesn't ask for that at all... except here. (So best ignore what he says).

Jesus follows his poorly thought through advice about constantly forgiving with a parable that introduces the third, dissonant strand of his teaching on the subject. In it, a king forgives one of his slaves, who then refuses to forgive a fellow slave (Matthew 18.23-35). As a result, the king withdraws his earlier forgiveness, saying:

> *"I forgave you all that debt because you pleaded with me. Should you not have had mercy on your fellow-slave, as I had mercy on you?"* And in anger his lord

> *handed him over to be tortured until he should pay his entire debt. So my heavenly Father will also do to every one of you, if you do not forgive your brother or sister from your heart.* (Matthew 18. 32-35)

The story stresses how important it is we forgive others – or release them from their debt - if we want God to forgive us, even though this was not what the disciples originally asked about. Jesus seems to have drifted into making a theological point about how divine forgiveness is entirely dependent on the extent to which an individual forgives others. As we shall see, Paul finds himself unable to agree with such a silly notion, though it is consistent with the prayer Jesus teaches his disciples - 'forgive us our sins as we forgive those who sin against us'; that is, may God forgive us in direct proportion to the forgiveness we give to others.

Jesus appears oblivious to the fact that, although the positioning of the parable suggests it is intended to illustrate the seventy-times-seven principle, it really doesn't. What it reveals is that God himself is not the type of guy who is prepared to forgive innumerable times. To forgive repeatedly, it turns out, is not divine. If, however, the preceding verses are to be believed, it is something this inconsistent God expects of mere sinful humans. The irony of this 'do as I say, not as I do' scenario seems to be lost on Jesus, as it is on his disciples and his followers today. The forgiveness modelled in the parable by a supposed loving Father is limited, turns to anger when it isn't emulated and leads to eternal torture.

Just as the first and second perspectives of forgiveness that Jesus offers contradict each other, this third is similarly incompatible. It is as if the compiler of Matthew's gospel has collected all of the teaching about forgiveness circulating in his early church community and grouped it together without any thought for consistency. While Christians might resist such an idea (this is 'God's Word' after all), the alternative is that it is Jesus himself who is confused.

Undoubtedly there are Christians who are capable of remarkable feats of forgiveness, forgiving those who have murdered loved-ones; terrorists who have destroyed life and property; emotional and sexual tormentors; people who have wronged them in more mundane ways. Equally there are non-Christians who forgive in like measure, and Christians who find themselves unable to forgive, which all suggests that the capacity for forgiveness is human and not divine. It doesn't come from Jesus' ring-fenced teaching nor from a capricious God.

So what's a Christian to do when it comes to forgiving a fellow-believer? Do they take a deputation and try to extract a plea of forgiveness from an offending brother? Do they forgive him endlessly, but only if he's sorry? Or do they do what God does and give him one chance only, risking their salvation in the process?

It's a difficult call. If only there were some clear teaching about it somewhere.

Being a Christian and following Jesus is entire. In addition to doing everything he commands in his teaching about perfection, it entails putting others first, meeting their unreasonable demands, always giving and forgiving. More than this, it involves constantly saying 'no' to yourself, putting to death your own wants, needs, desires, feelings, rights, concerns, ambitions, well-being, comfort, security and safety. As Jesus summarises it,

> *If any want to become my followers, let them deny themselves and take up their cross and follow me.*
> (Mark 8.34, Matthew 16.24 & Luke 9.23)

Looking at the majority of believers today, you would hardly know that being a Christian involved the denial of one's entire being, but nonetheless it is what Jesus demands of them in all three synoptic gospels. (There is a faint echo of the same idea in John 12.26, but Jesus' exacting demands are considerably softened in the fourth gospel's love-in).

Does such self-abnegation qualify as morality? When it results in putting others' interests before one's own, yes; but this isn't quite what these 'take-up-your-cross' pronouncements are about. He calls in them for complete commitment to himself and his cause, which, as we know, is to announce and usher in God's Kingdom on Earth. He demands his followers put aside their entire lives to assist him in achieving this – it is a small, short-term price to pay to gain eternal life in a Kingdom that is just around the corner. This is what he means when he insists in Matthew 11.30 that what he's asking is easy; giving one's entire life to a cause is not at all easy, but doing so for a short time is manageable.

Of course, modern Christians don't accept that their Lord and Saviour is addressing his immediate circumstances in most of what he says. Thanks to Paul's corruption of what Jesus was about - more about this soon - they unthinkingly assume his mission was to die to redeem mankind, instead of announcing the arrival of the Kingdom in his own time. As result, they marginalise much of Jesus' teaching, either because it doesn't make sense in its new context, doesn't fit Paul's salvation formula or is just too damned demanding next to the effort-free spirituality they prefer. They still insist, of course, that Jesus' words have eternal value and an application throughout all time - how could they not when they see him as God incarnate? - with most unaware of what those words are and what they mean.

In so doing they extend the shelf-life of sayings like 'if any want to become my followers, let them deny themselves and take up their cross and follow me' far beyond that which they were intended to have. They make a universal morality out of them – which believers themselves generally disregard - when they were not moral injunctions to begin with. Consequently, statements like these become still more impossible morality. With very few exceptions, Christians do not deny their self-interest, crucifying their own needs and desires daily to follow Jesus in every detail. It isn't possible to do this in any case, as we have seen, but it isn't I who insists they should: it is Jesus, though this time Jesus as reinterpreted through the lens of Pauline theology and that very same self-interest that Jesus insists should be regularly put to death.

For Jesus the imminent Kingdom is all. He finds it difficult to tolerate those who don't share his vision for his people, his followers and himself. In case we've forgotten, this sees Jesus and his twelve best mates (Judas included) ruling a restored Jewish nation on behalf of God, with the rest of the world subjugated and subject to this great Kingdom (Matthew 19:28 etc). As the Romans would mockingly remind him, he did indeed envisage himself as 'King of the Jews'. With such illusions of grandeur it is inevitable that his paranoia would occasionally surface, preserved for us in the later, massaged gospel accounts.

We see it, for example, when he declares, like all beleaguered messiah-figures before and since, that 'he who is not for us is against us'. Alternatively, he might have said, 'he who is not against us is for us' because he's made to make both of these statements: the first in Luke 11.23, the second in Mark 9:40. But they mean different things. Mark's version is inclusive, while Luke excludes and rejects with its 'he who is not for us is against us'. It is likely that Jesus uttered only one of the remarks and the alternate version exists because those creating his story 40 and 50 years after his death couldn't remember quite what it was he said: 'was it we're all included if we don't oppose him or we're all against him if we don't go along with him? What the hell (we can imagine them thinking) it hardly matters'.

Except, of course, it does matter: one of the sayings embraces others, and therefore might be regarded as moral, while the other is smugly elitist, bullying and immoral. Neither, though, is true; just because I'm not 'for' my local football team - as in I don't actively support it and attend its fixtures - does not mean I am against it. It is possible to be indifferent or to think the matter sufficiently inconsequential to have to take sides. Equally, if I am not opposed to, say, vegetarianism, it does not mean, as Mark's Jesus seems to think it does, that I actively promote it or am 'for' it. Neutrality is permissible on any issue.

The fallacy of for-and-against extremism can be seen more clearly in President George W. Bush's take on it, when in 2001 he claimed that 'either you are with us, or you are with the terrorists'. It was divisive nonsense to suggest that those who opposed his position, post 9/11, of reviving a completely unconnected war were on the side of hijackers. Jesus' attempt to create a similar dichotomy is equally absurd.

Both of his supposed statements show a profound lack of understanding of human decision making and commitment, reflecting instead something of his arrogance and paranoia. He presumes to determine where the people of his day should stand in relation to his far-from-convincing Kingdom message, and polarises their position on an issue of importance primarily only to him.

For all that, Christians today are prone to subscribe to Luke's harsher saying than Mark's more inclusive version. Perhaps if Christian groups heeded the saying as recorded in Mark, they would recognise that those with different doctrinal positions from themselves nonetheless work towards much the same goals, whatever these might be in today's distorted Christianity. As it is, the church seems to prefer Jesus in negative, excluding mode: 'whoever is not for us is against us'. The result, sanctioned by his divisive words, is a fractured Christianity of exclusive sects and denominations.

Jesus is nothing if not versatile: when not expressing his paranoia, he likes to engage in a spot of morbidity. With his own death in mind, he announces in John 15.13 that 'no one has greater love than this (than) to lay down one's life for one's friends'. Sounding very much like a later gloss supplied by a particular community of believers on what their leader's death meant to them, this is similar to the idea more fully worked out in Paul's writings that Jesus' death was in some way redemptive. The authors of the fourth gospel see it as being peculiarly for them and other 'friends', explaining in the following verse that to be a friend of Jesus means doing as he commands. The saying also serves as a salve for members of that same community who might be called upon to die for their faith.

But is martyrdom really the greatest expression of love it is possible to imagine? Can love even be measured so that martyrdom comes out on top as the greatest there is? Situations where love is best expressed by the laying down one's own life are few or non-existent in the lives of most people; yes, the verse is used, usually by politicians, to interpret and justify the often needless deaths of those in the military, but this is to remove it from its exclusive, and excluding, friends-of-Jesus context. The love that most of us are called to deliver is more mundane and an expectation in life, not death, and is no less costly for all that. It is love that is, at the very least, as sacrificial, giving and caring as throwing one's life away for the sake of fellow-believers. There are expressions of love that are conceivably *more* loving than this: the love that gives itself to raising children or is spent in living service to others; the life-time love that cares for the sick, the elderly, the infirm. No-one is able to say these are lesser forms of love.

Even so, it is rare these days to see Jesus' greater love demonstrated by mainstream Christians. I'm not advocating Christians should martyr themselves for their fellow-believers but it wouldn't be unreasonable for one or two of them to lay down their lives as demonstration of the veracity of their Saviour's words: perhaps Westboro Baptist Church would be prepared to lead the way on this one? There is less facetiousness in this suggestion than you might suppose. Jesus has it in mind when he commands those wanting to follow him to 'take up their cross' (Mark 8.34). Anyone carrying a cross under Roman occupation was doing it for one purpose only - to be nailed to it, there slowly to die, just as Jesus himself was to do. Again, this is likely to be an anachronistic saying placed in Jesus' mouth after his own death by crucifixion, but the principle remains: expect as a follower to die for the cause.

As we might expect, modern day Christians spiritualise the challenge, because Jesus can't possibly mean what he says here in any literal sense! They argue instead that what he is really talking about is putting to death one's human nature with its 'self-indulgent passions and desires', as Galatians 5.24 puts it... and then fall short of doing even that. But where the mainstream fails to demonstrate Jesus' radical call to lay down one's life, fringe movements excel, with members of cults like Jim Jones's 'People's Temple Christian Church' and David Karesh's Branch Davidians committing mass-suicide in his name, inspired by his peculiar, poisonous view of love.

Jesus' morality is, then, as difficult to apply as the Old Testament variety, even by born-again believers with the Holy Spirit living inside them. I have some sympathy with them, I must confess. Much of what Jesus expects is impossible; it is intended for the short-term, for a world not expected to last much longer but to be replaced by a new world order where God reigns and whose inhabitants live with each other in love. This is not the world he left behind, nor is it that in which we find ourselves today. Jesus' ideas are woefully impractical, which is why the early church experienced such trouble with them (see 1 Corinthians, for example) and why Christians today continue largely to ignore them.

So what is it of Jesus' message, as opposed to Paul's, that they do believe and act upon in their lives? Much of what Christians speak and write about is to do with personal forgiveness and salvation; maybe here they are much better at adhering to their Lord's teaching in this particular area. In the next chapter, we'll discover if they are.

Chapter 5

Morality and Salvation

Paul talks of 'grace', that is, of being 'saved' through God's loving kindness. The Law, good works and one's own efforts play no part in salvation as Paul conceives of it:

Since all have sinned and fallen short of the glory of God, they are justified by his grace as a gift, through the redemption which is in Christ Jesus. (Romans 3. 23-24)

Or, as the author of Ephesians puts it:

For by grace you have been saved through faith; and this is not your own doing, it is the gift of God - not because of your works, lest any man should boast. (Ephesians 2.8)

Jesus, on the other hand, promotes personal righteousness in all of his pronouncements. More than this, he relates personal morality directly to the degree to which one can expect God to reciprocate. He makes the point repeatedly that what the believer receives from God is meted out in exact proportion to what the believer himself does.

You want God's forgiveness? Then you must first forgive those who have wronged you:

For if you forgive men their trespasses your heavenly Father also will forgive you; but if you do not forgive neither will your Father forgive your trespasses. (Matthew 6.14)

As we have already noted, Jesus also includes this principle in the prayer he teaches his disciples in Matthew 6.12, as well as in Matthew 18.23-35, when he tells his rather severe story about how God withholds his forgiveness from those who don't forgive others.

You want to experience God's riches and blessings? Then first be generous yourself:

> *Give and it will be given to you; good measure, pressed down, shaken together, running over, put into your lap. For the measure you give will be the measure you get back.* (Luke 6.38)

You want to avoid God's judgement? Then don't judge others:

> *Judge not that you be not judged. For with the judgement you pronounce you will be judged, and the measure you give will be the measure you get.* (Matthew 7.1,2)

You want God to show you mercy? Then you must first show mercy yourself:

> *Blessed are the merciful, for they shall obtain mercy.* (Matthew 5.7)

You want God to show you compassion? Then be compassionate yourself:

> *The King will say to those at his right hand... I was hungry and you gave me food, I was thirsty and you gave me drink, I was a stranger and you welcomed me... Then the righteous will answer him, 'Lord when did we see the hungry and feed thee or thirsty and give thee drink? And when did we see thee a stranger and welcome thee?... And the King will answer them, Truly I say to you, as you did it to one of the least of these my brethren, you did it to me'.*

> *Then he will say to those at his left hand, 'Depart from me, you cursed, into the eternal fire prepared for the devil and his angels, for I was hungry and you gave me no food, I was thirsty and you gave me no drink, I was a stranger and you did not welcome me... Truly I say to*

you, as you did it not to one of the least of these my brethren, you did it not to me'. (Matthew 25.34-46)

Do Christians believe that the degree to which they demonstrate mercy and forgiveness to others is the degree to which God will demonstrate it towards them, both in this life and the next?

Generally, no. Here's a press release from Christian radio station, Q90fm, when they found out a speaker, Jim Wallis, at a Christian convention, was promoting the stuff and nonsense that Jesus refers to in the final quotation above:

...we heed Jesus' warning to care for "the least of these" in Matthew 25:35-46. We recognize that individually and as the Body of Christ we are not doing all we could as Jesus taught us to. But we do not believe the solution is the church partnering with the government in this endeavour. Feeding the poor with no ability to share the gospel message is at best an incomplete solution. And we fear this is what will happen as the government controls the purse strings. Doing so might indeed help them in this life, at least while the food and water lasts, but what about their eternal souls? While we are commanded by Jesus to help the poor, Jesus said our greatest calling is in Matthew 28:19: Therefore go and make disciples of all nations, baptising them in the name of the Father and of the Son and of the Holy Spirit.

This is a company that knows what Christianity is about, much more than Jesus ever did. While he commands that, unconditionally, the hungry should be fed, the thirsty given drink and the naked clothed, he forgets this can only be done if it provides an opportunity to 'share the gospel' and save souls.

If only Q90FM had read a little further in Matthew 28 because Jesus goes on to say that his followers should 'observe all that I have commanded you' – which must necessarily include feeding the hungry, clothing the naked and welcoming strangers. What it doesn't say is that 'the great commission', as Matthew 28.19 is called in Christian circles, is the Christian's *greatest* calling', particularly if all it means is spreading orthodox 'faith', as the reference to Father, Son and Holy Spirit suggests. (We might also note that the doctrine of the Trinity evolved long after Matthew's gospel was written and its inclusion here is likely to be a much later addition).

The point is not that Christians don't help the needy. Evidently some do, as do some atheists, Jews, Muslims and all manner of others. The point is that Christians have lost sight of the fact that for Jesus such behaviour directly equates with righteousness, which in turn determines one's ultimate fate. There really is no getting away from the correlation that Jesus is at pains to underscore, particularly in Matthew and Luke's gospels. The only recourse seems to be to disregard it, which orthodox Christians are content to do. They are much happier with the self-centred faith that Paul offers in Romans 5.17, 'the free gift of righteousness'. This makes far fewer demands, carrying only the minimal expectation that one's treatment of others has any bearing on one's own spiritual well-being. God will forgive the failure to meet others' needs anyway, because that is what he does: 'if we confess our sins he is faithful and just and will forgive us our sins and cleanse us from all unrighteousness' (1 John 1.9).

Except this isn't how it works, not according to Jesus; God's forgiveness, blessing, compassion and removal of judgement are entirely conditional. To Jesus, a 'measure for measure' arrangement is how one attains righteousness, which is not God-given, but is worked at in the practicalities of daily life, in relation to others.

To illustrate the point, Jesus tells a parable about a master who goes away on business, leaving his servants to take care of his household. The story can be found in Matthew 25.14-29, with an alternative version in Luke 19:12-28. The so-called 'parable of the talents' is part of a collection of stories that illustrate Jesus' thinking about the judgement that he insists will be the inaugural event of God's Kingdom on Earth. There will be, he tells us, a weeding out (Matthew 13. 24-40) and a separating of the bad from the good, in the same way that sheep and goats are separated by a herder (Matthew 25. 32-33). The parable of the talents incorporates all the trademark elements of his teaching - predictions of the second coming, judgement, inverted morality and an implicit acceptance of slavery – and has Jesus conclude that 'to all those who have, more will be given, and they will have an abundance; but from those who have nothing, even what they have will be taken away'.

We might wonder what sort of morality this is. Back in the 1980s, British Prime Minister, Margaret Thatcher, used it to justify a particularly avaricious form of capitalism and it is used still to exploit the poor, in the name of Christ, the world over. The tale does not, of course, involve any modern understanding of 'talents' - our natural or God given abilities – with a 'use them or lose them' tag-line. The similarity between the word in the parable and the modern notion of talent is entirely coincidental. Jesus' story refers to a significant amount of money determined by weight, so perhaps Margaret Thatcher's interpretation is nearer the mark than we might like to concede.

The talents in the story, however, are metaphors for personal righteousness, as Jesus makes clear when nearing the punch-line. His narrative stresses how important it is to be prepared for the coming of the 'Master', who appears to be Jesus himself in his Son of Man identity, bringing the Kingdom of Heaven in his wake. The unwise servant is the equivalent of all the other losers in Jesus' stories about the final judgement: goats, weeds, foolish bridesmaids, the rich and so on. The servant in the parable is 'unprepared' for his Master's return because he hasn't exercised his already limited righteousness, symbolised by the single talent he's been given. It's no excuse that his capricious, unjust Master, so like the God of the Old Testament, didn't endow him with much in the first place. Instead, so the story tells us, he buries his righteousness so that it isn't able to grow and bear the fruit required for entry into the Kingdom. (It's no wonder he's confused when Jesus says elsewhere, in Mark 4.8, that burying is exactly what should be done with the seeds of righteousness).

Nonetheless, like the weeds and the goats, the unfortunate servant and all like him are to be separated at Jesus' return from those who have cultivated righteousness by serving others, and are sent away to eternal punishment (Matthew 25.30 and 46). The righteous, with hair restored, will then live on the Earth under God's rule, and, according to Matthew 25.23, be 'in charge of many things', whatever that means.

The parable is as interesting for what it does not say as for what it does: it does not teach a formula for salvation, other than the requirement to be righteous (which, as we have seen, Jesus defines as caring for others); it does not promise that those saved from destruction will be raptured to Heaven or even taken there after death and offers little description of life in the new Kingdom of the new Earth. Jesus evidently thought this would be much the same as life in the old, but without all the bad people.

The point of the parable then is, as David Wenham summarises it, that:

> *In the future the servants will give account to their master for their good and evil actions and will be judged accordingly (e.g., Matt 25.14-30/Luke 19.11-27. Jesus emphasises that it will not be those who claim to be his followers who will enter the feast of the Kingdom, but those who live in practical love and obedience (Matt 7.21- 27/Luke 6.46-49; Matt 25.31-46).*

'Practical love and obedience' earn you your place in the Kingdom and the feast that follows the winnowing that takes place as it arrives. I am compelled to point out here that although Christians have effectively dumped this aspect of their Saviour's teaching, they still cherish the parts that, like all of Jesus' predictions of the end time and judgement, failed spectacularly to came to pass when he said they would. Righteousness did not win out, the Son of Man (or some facsimile thereof) failed to return; the Kingdom didn't materialise; the meek did not inherit the Earth and the unrighteous are with us still, managing the world's banks.

The rot set in even before the words of Jesus were recorded. The effect of Paul's writing, and that of those who follow him, is to spiritualise and anaesthetise the very practical connection Jesus makes between personal behaviour and God's response. It isn't possible to follow Jesus *and* later writers in this - what Jesus and they say is diametrically opposed. The two are, in this respect as in others, promoting different religions.

This is why the early Jewish followers of Jesus had so much trouble with Paul's theology, the Bible itself documenting their disputes (in Galatians 2.11-14, for example). While there is some evidence that Jesus saw his message as being exclusively for the children of Israel (Matthew 15.24 etc), Paul took it into the wider world and stripped away from it almost all of the requirements Jesus placed on those who wanted to survive the end of the age that he predicted. While he preaches about *becoming* righteous, saying 'my brothers are those who hear the word of God and do it' (Luke 8.21), Paul speaks about righteousness being given by God 'through faith in Jesus Christ for all who believe' (Romans 3.21). Paul devises a salvation formula of justification through faith, while Jesus talks about practicalities - selling one's possessions, feeding the hungry, forgiving others - and they both cannot be right.

The writer of the letter from James recognises the problem as he tries to direct later followers back to a righteousness cultivated through helping others:

> *If a brother or sister is ill-clad and in lack of daily food, and one of you says to them, "Go in peace, be warmed and filled", without giving them the things needed for the body, what does it profit? So faith by itself, if it has no works, is dead.* (James 2.15-17)

However, instead of following Jesus and James, whom many believers think was Jesus' brother (though he wasn't and doesn't overtly claim to be) Christians are much more prone to subscribe to Paul's spiritualised salvation, with its emphasis on taking ('sanctify me, Lord!') not giving. It is easier to judge and withhold forgiveness from others, to exalt oneself and dismiss the needs of others when one's own salvation doesn't depend, as Jesus says it does, on doing the opposite of such things. It is remarkable that the set of beliefs proposed by Paul - a man who never met Jesus but derived his theology from an inconsistently reported vision of some sort - is repeatedly chosen by Christians over and above the teaching of the man they hold to be God in human form.

Woe betide anyone, then, who suggests, as Tom Wright does in *Surprised by Hope* and Steve Chalke in *The Lost Message of Jesus*, that the coming of the Kingdom involves social action. The two have been castigated for having the temerity to remind fellow-Christians of Jesus' exhortations to feed the hungry, clothe the naked, visit the imprisoned and the rest. Spiritualised Christians know better, of course, and dismiss Wright as 'heterodox' and someone who 'gets it quite wrong when it comes to the gospel', because his reading of it, and Chalke's even more so, threatens their self-serving ideas about salvation. As Tom Wright notes in *Surprised by Hope*, the abandonment of this crucial part of Jesus' teaching has precipitated 'among some would-be orthodox Christians a reaction against any social or political dimension to the gospel, and against Kingdom language altogether'. How right he is: the 'orthodox' view is expressed by Gary Gilley, pastor of Southern View Chapel in Illinois, who writes on the church's web-site:

> *when we turn to the New Testament, we find that, while Christians are to be loving and generous to all people, they are never told to attempt to remedy the consequences of the sin of unbelieving humanity through social action. Instead they are instructed to meet the needs of brothers and sisters in Christ... In fact, the church is never commissioned to rectify injustices by dealing with the symptoms of sins but to "radically" uproot sin itself through the gospel.*

Gilley's assertion that believers are 'never commissioned to rectify injustices' is true enough provided the teachings of Jesus are ignored completely. This sort of slippery manoeuvring makes the Christian's life so much easier, even if it is a million miles from what Jesus actually teaches. As for the clear connection Jesus draws between social action and the individual's place in the future

Kingdom - well, that's not really important in the super-spirituality that is today's orthodoxy. What did Jesus know anyway?

PART FOUR: RE-BRANDING THE MESSAGE
Chapter 6
Bible Worship

It requires only careful scrutiny and consideration to realize that the teachings of Jesus and those of Christianity are not the same. There are a number of practices and special beliefs in Christianity that are not founded on anything that Jesus actually taught or said.

So says Christian mystic John Davidson in *Gospel of Jesus: In Search of His Original Teachings*. Too right, John! Rejecting a good deal of what Jesus tells them to do, Christians, sensing the vacuum perhaps, have replaced his commands, impossible as many of them are, with a repertoire of superfluous and non-biblical beliefs. This in itself runs contrary to the Bible's warning that believers should subscribe to 'nothing beyond what is written' (1 Corinthians 4.6), but since when has 'God's Word' deterred Christians from doing what they want? In this section, we'll take a closer look at the beliefs Christians uphold in place of all that spurious nonsense of Jesus'.

Let's bring on fallacious belief number one, on which so much else hinges: the Bible is the literal, inerrant Word of God.

As *The Way of Life* Christian website puts it:

'The Bible, with its 66 books, is the very Word of God. The Bible is verbally and plenarily inspired as originally given and it is divinely preserved in the Hebrew Masoretic Text and the Greek Received Text. The Bible is our sole authority in all matters of faith and practice. The King James Version in English is an example of an accurate translation of the preserved

Hebrew and Greek texts; we believe it can be used with confidence'.

Try as you might, you will not find the Bible claiming it is the Word of God, capitalised or otherwise. The phrase does appear in English translations of the Bible, almost always without a capital 'W' (the one exception being Revelation 19.13, where the capital does appear). On none of these occasions is the Bible referring to itself and we will see soon why it cannot possibly be doing so.

Instead, the phrase 'the word of God' is used to give a character's pronouncements added clout in the *immediate context* in which he finds himself. One of its earliest occurrences is 1 Samuel 9.27, in the Old Testament, and quite clearly it cannot there be referring to the various versions of the gospel message, nor Paul's plan of salvation, all of which lie many years in the future. In fact, the 'word' on this occasion has to do with Samuel's impromptu appointing of Saul as king of Israel - and a pretty disastrous one he turns out to be.

Christians usually base their conviction that the Bible is 'the Word of God' on a verse in 2 Timothy (3.16): 'all scripture is inspired by God and profitable for teaching, for reproof, for correction, and for training in righteousness'. There are some serious problems with this claim, however.

Firstly, 'inspired by God' does not mean the same as dictated by God. The book you are now reading is inspired, as I explained in the introduction, by my born-again friend, Simon. Yet Simon has written not one word of it, nor is it likely he would approve of anything it contains. Yet he did indeed inspire everything you read in it. Another way of expressing his inspiration would be to say that, unknowingly, he 'prompted' or 'motivated' me to write the book, so removing the idea that he somehow exercised control over the writing. So it is with the Bible's 'inspiration'.

Most people experience some form of inspiration of the prompting sort in their lives, and even Christians do not necessarily claim that this comes in the form of a precise verbal message from God.

Significantly, the word 'inspiration' simply means 'breathed in', so there's no reason to think that the Bible authors' inspiration, even allowing for prompting of a divine sort, is verbal either. At most, God might have 'warmed up' the Bible's writers in the same way you and I breathe on our hands on a cold winter's morning. Alternatively, it could be that their religious fervour was self-generated and that God had nothing to do with it.

There are, moreover, parts of the New Testament where the author, usually Paul, states categorically that what he is saying is entirely his own judgement rather than being 'from of the Lord'. In 1 Corinthians 7.25, for example, he sets himself up as an expert on young women, when he says, 'now concerning virgins, I have no command of the Lord, but I give my opinion as one who by the Lord's mercy is trustworthy'. A few verses later he again makes clear he is expressing his *own* ideas, this time about widows remaining unmarried. We could, of course, make a case that none of his words are 'the Lord's', but I'm arguing here against the widely-held Christian view that the Bible in its entirety is the Word of God. Paul's asides in which he makes clear he is expressing his own views, indicate that even he accepts not all he writes is 'inspired'.

Secondly, the 'scripture' to which 2 Timothy 3.16 refers cannot be the Bible as we know it today. This was not compiled until about 260 years after these very words were written. At best, the author of 2 Timothy is referring to the first five books of the Bible - the Pentateuch - and maybe, possibly, though we cannot know for certain (you see how tentative it is?) some of the writing he had encountered that was eventually included in the New Testament. By the same reckoning though, he could equally be referring to books that at one time were considered to be inspired but did not make it into the final 27 books of today's New Testament. This is also why the use of the term 'the word of God' in other places in the Bible cannot be referring to the Bible as a whole. No-one knew when using the words in their original context that there was going to be a Bible, let alone one divorced from its Jewish roots.

Thirdly, most scholars today are convinced that Paul did not write

2 Timothy, even though it claims that he is its author. There are very good reasons for saying the letter was written between 100-150CE, thirty-six years at the very least after Paul's death in 64CE. In other words, 2 Timothy is a fake, claiming to be written by one person - Paul - when it is in fact the creation of another, taking advantage of the reputation of the more well-known writer. How far can such a false witness be trusted? Most people in any other context would say not at all. And yet Christians take this forger's letter to be 'inspired by God', just because it says it is. In essence they are saying that God is happy to inspire forgery, and not just in this instance either: none of the 'pastoral' letters (1 and 2 Timothy, together with Titus) is written by Paul, even though all of them claim to be. The second letter to the Thessalonians and those to the Ephesians and Colossians are not by him either; 1 and 2 Peter are not by the (illiterate) apostle Peter and the letters of James and Jude, while wanting us to think that they are, are not by Jesus' brothers. In short, and as Bible scholar Bart Ehrman puts it:

> *many of the books of the New Testament were written by people who lied about their identity, claiming to be a famous apostle — Peter, Paul or James — knowing full well they were someone else. In modern parlance, that is a lie, and a book written by someone who lies about his identity is a forgery.*

Christians do not accept that the Qur'an is the word of God (Allah), nor the book of Mormon, even though both say they are, so why do they take it on trust, from a forged document that was lucky enough to find its way into the New Testament, that it and all other 'scripture' is inspired? 'Faith', they would tell you; but in this as in many other contexts, it is extremely misguided faith.

It's not just the forged parts of the New Testament that call into question its inspiration and reliability. Crucially, the accuracy of gospels is highly questionable and so too, as a result, are the sayings attributed to Jesus there. This is because, to begin with, nothing he said was written down at the time he said it. Jesus would have spoken an Aramaic dialect, and might possibly have known some Hebrew. All four gospels, however, were written in

Greek, with the earliest, Mark's, being composed about 40 years after Jesus' death by someone from an entirely different culture: Mark's knowledge of Palestinian geography and of Jewish customs is poor. Later still, Matthew and Luke used Mark's account to create their own versions of what Jesus said. They supplemented it with other written material they had available, none of which seems to have been written in Aramaic. Very few of Jesus' words, therefore, were recorded in his own language. With the exception of phrases such as 'Talitha Cumi' and 'Eli, Eli, Lama Shabachthani', the records we have of his reputed utterances are translations, originally into Greek, created between 40 and 85 years after he lived.

Christians will argue, and do, that none of this matters as the Holy Spirit preserved the essential meaning of Jesus' sayings, firstly as they were conveyed by word of mouth, then as they were recorded in an entirely different language, and then as the gospel writers (who almost certainly were not called Matthew, Mark, Luke and John) shaped them into their own accounts. The Holy Spirit continued to ensure their purity and accuracy, Christians insist, as they were altered both accidentally and intentionally by later Christian scribes with their own agendas.

You can decide for yourself how reliable all of this makes them: it helps if you believe that everything Jesus said was divinely inspired to begin with so that it emerges from this turbulent process untarnished as the inerrant Word of God. This though is circular reasoning that entails starting with your conclusion, only to ensure you end up with it again. It hardly matters, in any case, when Christians disregard most of Jesus 'inspired' teaching in favour of the mysticism of Paul and his emulators.

The most significant use of the idea, if not the exact phrase, of 'the Word of God' can be found at the start of John's gospel. Its writers use what is thought to be an early Christian hymn of praise to open their account, elevating Jesus to the status of the 'logos' (the Greek word usually translated as 'Word') or expression of God:

In the beginning was the Word and the Word was with

> *God and the Word was God. He was in the beginning with God; all things were made through him, and without him was not anything made that was made... And the Word became flesh and dwelt among us, full of grace and truth; we have beheld his glory, glory as of the only Son from the Father.* (John 1.1-3 and 14)

So, if we must have a 'Word of God', it is not the Bible but the Christ, which, by the time the fourth gospel was written is what Jesus had evolved into. The same grand idea is also found in Revelation 19.13, which is the only place in the Bible where the full, capitalised phrase is used of Jesus. However, the pre-existent logos is not a title Jesus claims for himself in any of the gospels and, being a concept far more at home in Greek mythology, would have been alien to him. To usurp the term and apply it to the Bible, therefore, as Christians do, is to elevate the Bible to the same level as the Christ whom they profess to worship as God. This is, in Christians' own terms, a form of idolatry.

Believing in the Bible's inspiration as 'the Word of God' leads too to other insupportable claims about it, chief of which is that, firstly, it is the *literal* word of God and, secondly, that as a result, it is inerrant – free from error and entirely accurate in all of what it reports and claims. We have seen many times already in this book how it is far from inerrant – in this section alone we have noted how it asserts three New Testament books are from the hand of Paul when in fact they were written by an anonymous forger. There are not only the well-documented inconsistencies and contradictions in details but also significant and irreconcilable differences of doctrine between Paul, Mark, James, Matthew, Luke and John, as they interpret Jesus' ministry, life and death. These differences have given rise, from the beginning of the Christian faith to the present day, to innumerable conflicting interpretations of the Bible and ways of being a Christian, in spite of Jesus' prayer in John gospel that his followers be one just as he and the Father are one.

You have only to read Christian web-sites, like those of *The Christian Research Network, Apprising Ministries, Possessing The*

Treasure, Sola Scripture and *Herescope* to gain a sense of how minute differences in biblical understanding lead to Christians condemning as unscriptural and 'of the devil' the beliefs of other Christians. According to these web-sites, current movements within mainstream Christianity, all of which claim their doctrines are derived from the Bible, such as the 'Dominion Movement', 'Emergent Christianity', the 'Purpose Driven Church', the 'Alpha Course' and the 'Apostolic-Prophetic Movement', all misunderstand the Bible, having been misled by Satan and false prophets to an entirely mistaken interpretation of it. (You don't, incidentally, need to know the specific details of what these groups believe and do, but if you feel you must, you can always Google them). Like these movements, as well as the web-sites that point out often without a modicum of humility where each has gone wrong, different groups of Christians throughout history have claimed that they and only they have the correct interpretation of scripture. This must be why, as we've already noted, there are currently over 34,000 Christian groups and denominations, most of whom insist that theirs is the only true interpretation of 'scripture', arrived at with the Holy Spirit's guidance.

None of this would be possible if the Bible were inerrant; it is precisely because it contains so many conflicting doctrines and ideas that any and all interpretations find support within its pages. If 'God is not the God of confusion' as Paul asserts in 1 Corinthians 14.33, then he can't possibly be the author of the Bible, which is thoroughly confused in itself and leaves nothing but confusion in its wake. Paul's claim, then, is yet one more point on which the Bible is completely mistaken.

The great mass of interpretations also points up the fallacy that the Bible is the 'literal' word of God. If it were, there would be no need for interpretation; it's plain, literal meaning would be transparently clear. There are, however, significant parts of it, including the gospels, that even Christians admit need to be interpreted because on face value, the literal or apparent meaning is, at least to the modern ear, complete nonsense. What is Jesus talking about in Matthew 11.12, for example, when he says, 'the Kingdom of heaven has suffered violence, and the violent take it by force'?

Does Matthew 16.19, where Jesus tells Peter 'whatever you bind on earth will be bound in heaven, and whatever you loose on earth will be loosed in heaven' make any real sense? In *The Reason for God*, Pastor Tim Keller proposes that the solution to understanding offensive or nonsensical parts of the Bible is to have the 'historical context' of such verses explained by a 'decent commentary'. But this is not taking the Bible literally, nor is it a technique that Christians apply consistently. Instead it confronts Christians with a raft of difficult questions that only cognitive dissonance - sorry, the Holy Spirit – protects them from: If Christians need a commentary to help them discover the 'true' meaning of some verses, then why not all? How do they know which they need help with and which can they take as they stand? Why are some parts context bound while others are meaningful in all times and all places?

As it is, the Bible does not claim it is literal, and indeed in numerous places patently isn't -

i) Jesus does not intend that we believe the Good Samaritan and the Prodigal Son, for example, actually existed. The stories he tells about them do not relate events that happened to individuals he could put a name to. Even Christians understand that he tells such stories to illustrate, or obscure, a point. They are intended to contain and perhaps to convey a truth, but the parables themselves are not literal events;

ii) Jesus did not try, nor does he advocate others should, threading a camel through the eye of a needle. Similarly, he is not attempting in Luke 5.37 to give advice to wine-merchants about the best ways to store their product. He is, rather, speaking metaphorically, again to make a point. Metaphor, particularly when exaggerated to the point of hyperbole as Jesus' frequently is, cannot be, by definition, literal.

Many Christians are reluctant to admit that many parts of the Bible are metaphorical or context bound, because doing so might also mean that one has to acknowledge that other parts of the Bible are also far from being literal. Perhaps the story of Adam and Eve is a parable too, a myth designed to account for the fallibility of human beings? No, says Doctor John MacArthur, because if you concede that, then Bible truth is like a house of cards and the whole inerrant edifice is likely to come tumbling down. But, as more liberal Christians are prepared to consider, it could be that Adam and Eve, like the Good Samaritan, never actually existed. The same might be true of Moses (many scholars think so). And perhaps it's also the case that the resurrection is simply a beautiful metaphor for... well, anything you like really: becoming spiritually alive is one possibility, suggested by Timothy Freke and Peter Gandy in *The Jesus Mysteries*. In fact, there's no end to the possibilities once you concede that at least some of the Bible is metaphorical and symbolic. Safer to assert, contrary to the evidence, that the Bible in its entirety is the authoritative, literal Word of God and, as the *Christian Research Network* proclaims, 'the one inerrant, reliable and objective source of Truth'.

Albert Mohler, president of The Southern Baptist Theological Seminary warns Christians that they are 'entering a new phase in the battle over the Bible's truthfulness and authority' and that 'the rejection of biblical inerrancy is bound up with a view of God that is, in the end, fatal for Christian orthodoxy'. He advises believers to 'be thankful for undisguised arguments coming from the opponents of biblical inerrancy, even as we are ready, once again, to make clear where their arguments lead'. If this sounds nothing like a commitment to truth, that's because it isn't. It's an appeal to consequences that can be paraphrased as 'we don't want to admit that the Bible is riddled with errors and inconsistencies because we don't like what the implications might be'. (Compare with the Christian response to evolution: 'we don't like the implications of the theory so we reject the facts it explains'). Such Christians keep the Bible 'inerrant and inspired' only by pretending there is no evidence to the contrary.

Perhaps then the claim will hold up that despite being written over long periods of time by different authors, the Bible presents an entirely consistent message. At least Christians say so with annoying persistence. Here's a representative statement from Professor Rob J. Hyndman:

> *One thing you will notice as you start to read the Bible regularly, is that its message is remarkably consistent. Despite being written by many different authors, from all walks of life, over a period of about 1600 years, the basic message is the same. Of course, this is what you would expect from a book inspired by God.*

Unfortunately, you won't notice anything of the sort because it isn't remotely consistent. Nor was it written over 1600 years, but we'll let that pass. To demonstrate that there is no thematic consistency to the Bible, let's take an absolutely crucial part of the Christian message, namely the means by which a person can be 'saved'.

Human beings, believers tell us, are estranged from God and need to re-establish their relationship with him. To make this possible, Jesus came into the world, proclaiming the good news that he was the means by which the rift between man and God was to be healed. Arguably, this is the most significant idea of the New Testament, the authors of which all lived within about a hundred years of each other: they should, as a result, have the least difficulty in presenting a coherent and consistent explanation of 'God's purpose in Jesus'.

Paul, the earliest of the New Testament writers, interprets this central idea as Jesus having paid the price for mankind's sins as God demands. This is known as the atonement: Christ paying our debt for us, the result of which is, as Christian church leaders of my youth liked to say, a restored 'at-one-ment' with God. According to Paul's theology, a person is saved when they accept Christ's atoning death, believing it pays off the debt owed to God because of sin. That's it - nothing more – all you have to do is claim the gift for yourself. This is what Paul means by faith, and he explains it thus to the church in Rome:

> *...the righteousness of God has been disclosed... the righteousness of God through faith in Jesus Christ for all who believe. For there is no distinction, since all have sinned and fall short of the glory of God; they are now justified by his grace as a gift, through the*

> *redemption that is in Christ Jesus, whom God put forward as a sacrifice of atonement by his blood, effective through faith. He did this to show his righteousness, because in his divine forbearance he had passed over the sins previously committed... he justifies the one who has faith in Jesus.*

The price of the atonement is Christ's blood. God accepts Jesus' sacrifice as payment for human sin, his life being, as it says in Mark's gospel (10.5), a ransom for many. All you need do, according to Paul, is accept that Christ has bought your redemption, so that God is able to overlook and 'pass over' your sins.

So far so good. Except in Matthew 25, as we have seen, the gospel writer has Jesus say that one is made righteous (i.e. right with God) not by a human sacrifice, but by serving others: the poor, the hungry and the imprisoned. No mention of 'propitiation' (acquittal), saving blood or even faith.

And Luke sees it differently again: his Jesus says that what is involved is denying oneself and taking on the demanding work of preparing for the Kingdom (Luke 9.23). Again, there's no mention of Christ's death as an atonement. This is because Luke has a rather different take on the matter, which he expresses in Acts 2.36-38 and elsewhere. He sees the sacrifice of Jesus as some sort of prompt for people to seek forgiveness from their sins, and as Bart Ehrman explains, this is not at all the same as atonement. If Jesus' atonement paid for humankind's sin, as Paul claims, then asking for forgiveness of those same sins becomes superfluous. To compound the issue, Luke, in Acts, puts his own explanation of Jesus' death – that it's about seeking forgiveness - into Paul's mouth, even though it is at odds with the real Paul's ideas of atonement that he expresses in his letters. Consequently, 'Paul' says in Acts 13.38-39 that 'through this man (Jesus) forgiveness of sins is proclaimed to you; by this Jesus everyone who believes is set free from all those sins', while in those letters that are genuinely his (1 Thessalonians, Galatians, 1 and 2 Corinthians, Romans, Philippians and Philemon), he doesn't mention forgiveness once.

Luke also implies that salvation is not necessarily only for the individual, but is also made possible when the head of a household converts. Then, the rest of his family, as well as his slaves, are likewise automatically saved. When Paul and Silas are miraculously freed from prison in an episode in Acts, their jailer asks them what he must do to be saved. They answer: *'Believe on the Lord Jesus, and you will be saved, you **and your household'**.* (Acts 16.30-31). Vicarious salvation is undoubtedly an interesting prospect - unless of course you don't want it - and Luke is the only one to mention it.

The writers of John's gospel, writing well after Jesus' death - the event that so many others see as the lynch-pin of salvation - explain that the way to gain eternal life is simply to 'hear' Jesus' words and believe in God: 'Anyone who hears my word and believes him who sent me has eternal life, and does not come under judgement, but has passed from death to life' (John 5.24). No mention, again, of Paul's complex theory of atonement. Had the authors of Matthew, Luke and John not heard of it? Were they part of communities separate and different from those established and indoctrinated by Paul? Did they know of Paul's ideas but disapprove of them? There is certainly doctrinal discordance between them, as there is also between John and the synoptic gospels..

Later in his letter to the Romans, Paul himself seems to offer alternatives to his atonement theory. In chapter 10, verses 9 and 10, he suggests that all that matters is *either* believing in the resurrection *or* declaring out loud that Jesus is Lord: 'if you confess with your lips that Jesus is Lord and believe in your heart that God raised him from the dead, you will be saved. For one believes with the heart and so is justified, and one confesses with the mouth and so is saved'. So which is it? Faith in Jesus' sacrifice? Belief in his resurrection? Simply declaring he is Lord? All three? It's hard to tell.

As it turns out you needn't worry about which is right if you're Jewish. This earns you a free Get-Out-Of-Hell card with no strings attached: 'all Israel will be saved; as it is written, "Out of Zion will come the Deliverer; he will banish ungodliness from Jacob. And this is my covenant with them, when I take away their sins".' (Romans 11.26-27). Paul is right that this is what is written, in Isaiah and Jeremiah to be precise, where Yahweh promises he will love his chosen people 'forever'.

You want another variation? The writer of Hebrews imposes a different meaning again on Jesus' death. He sees it as a master stroke in a cosmic battle between God and the devil, with the devil magically vanquished through the crucifixion. Jesus shared our flesh and blood, he tells us 'so that through death he might destroy the one who has the power of death, that is, the devil, and free those who all their lives were held in slavery by the fear of death'. (Hebrews 2.14-15). So now Jesus' death is to free us from the fear of death. This writer also sees Jesus as a high priest, appeasing God with a sacrifice of his own blood, just as Jewish priests offered that of goats and calves. (What is it with this God that he requires so much blood be spilt? If we weren't today so used to this kind of imagery as a result of a Christian heritage, we might not be quite so immune to the distasteful weirdness of all this bloody sacrifice).

What part does faith play in salvation? Paul evidently thinks it is crucial – belief in Jesus' atoning death - but James is adamant that faith on its own isn't enough. Echoing Matthew's sources he declares 'faith by itself, if it has no works, is dead... A person is justified by works and not by faith alone' (James 2.14-17,24).

So is it faith alone that saves, as Paul says, or is it, like James and Matthew claim, primarily good deeds? And what about Jewish law - what part does that play in redemption? Paul asserts that the law is finished, brought to an end by Christ's sacrifice (Romans 10.14), while Matthew's Jesus says that the law must be kept and the commandments followed (Matthew 5.17-19). So, is the Jewish law a dead end, as Paul argues (Galatians 2.16) or does it set believers free as James and Matthew's Jesus seem to think (James 1.25)? Paul's and James' theology is so utterly opposed that, once again, both cannot be right.

The writer of the first letter to Timothy, whom, you'll recall, was not Paul, has his own ideas about what really matters. He has, they will be pleased to learn, a special offer for the ladies, who can be 'saved through childbearing - if they continue in faith and love and holiness, with modesty' (2.15). Too bad though if you can't have kids. His fellow-forger writes in Titus 3.5 that God 'saved us, not because of any works of righteousness that we had done, but according to his mercy, through the water of rebirth and renewal by the Holy Spirit'. So now it's baptism and an infusion of the Holy Spirit that get the job done.

Confused? You should be. As another former minister, the late Ken Pulliam asks, 'if the Bible is really a revelation from God and if God really loves man and really wants to reconcile man to himself, would he not have made it much clearer how someone is to be saved?'. Instead, the New Testament is a muddle, with competing and conflicting formulae for salvation. Some, it is true, are reasonably compatible – claiming Jesus' blood sacrifice as one's own does not preclude being possessed by the Holy Spirit - but to try and force these disparate views together to create a consistent exposition of 'God's plan of salvation' simply will not work; they are not, and were never intended to be, a coherent package.

What we have in the books of the New Testament are the attempts of early believers and communities, from soon after Jesus' death through to the early second century, to find meaning in the life and death of their beloved leader - whom most of them had never met - and to account for the non-appearance of his predicted Kingdom of Heaven. Each did this in his own way, from Paul's fusion of dying god-men from Greek mystery and notions of Jewish atonement (he was, after all, both Jewish and Greek) to Matthew's and James' interpretation that it is in service to others that righteousness and salvation can be found.

It is little wonder that there is constant dispute between groups of Christians today about how to be saved. Some advocate that Paul's atonement formula is the only way, while others that it's repentance and forgiveness that are needed. In so doing they are compelled either to disregard, or pretend they are compatible when they are not, all of the other possibilities put forward in the New Testament, including those purportedly from Jesus himself. Such self-deception, however, does not miraculously give us a Bible that is consistent throughout.

Instead, it leads us to two conflicting claims about 'God's Word', namely that the Bible is straight forward and clear *and* that it needs interpreting. These two positions are expressed not only by doctrinally divergent Christian groups but are often held by individuals unable to see the dis-juncture.

When believers want to dictate others' morals with words from their holy book, it is, apparently, clear what it means; when they want to 'save' others from their sins, it is also perfectly straight-forward; when they want to impose their view of life, marriage and family on the rest of society it is, once more, transparent. It is seemingly not so clear, however, when it comes to the sacrificial demands it makes on Christians themselves. *Then* it needs interpreting. It is not clear either when Paul and his fellow New Testament writers expound their convoluted theologies: these also need interpreting. Nor is it straight-forward when its many contradictions need explaining and reconciling (an impossible task, to be sure, but just watch those Christians try).

Of course, Christians are right in this latter respect: there isn't a text anywhere, not least a religious one, that can be read without interpretation. A reader always contributes a significant amount of any meaning that the written word has to offer. As Jonathan Knight puts it in his book about, appropriately enough, Jesus: 'every human act or speech is mediated by interpretation. The act of interpretation constructs the meaning of an event for a new generation of interpreters'. Reading *is* interpreting. If it's not your own interpretation you apply to the text, it will be that of a so-called authority on it - a minister or Bible commentator or the official interpretation of your chosen sect. And that is on top of the interpretation that went into the writing of the text in the first place; Paul's interpretation of Jesus' mission that is very different from what the gospel writers interpret to be Jesus' own; the various fake Pauls' interpretations of the real Paul's interpretation; the scribes and copyists who knowingly amended the text to fit their particular interpretation.

There is no such thing as a pure reading of the Bible, written in various forms of ancient Hebrew and Greek and translated into modern languages – itself an interpretative act – over the millennia. So, yes, the Bible, already an interpreted book, requires interpretation. And this applies equally to all of those parts of it that Christians say are transparently straight-forward. When quoting these, they have already interpreted them with, they like to think, the help of the Holy Spirit, though in fact, it is through the prism of their own limited understanding, pre-existing prejudices and the influence of received perspectives that their 'definitive' meaning of the Word is arrived at. It is for this reason that no two Christian groups, sects or cults ever share the same interpretation of the Bible – not even those who profess to adhere to Martin Luther's dictum *Sola Scriptura*, meaning 'By Scripture Alone'. Scripture is never alone: it is always accompanied by its innumerable readers, 'authorities' and commentators, who add their own particular and peculiar interpretations to it.

Once again, believers cannot have it both ways: either the Bible says what it means and means what it says or it is in need of interpretation. In which case, why didn't God choose a better means of conveying his thoughts – he carved the first set of commandments directly onto stone, after all – rather than a muddled, fragmented book that requires great human ingenuity before it can be deciphered in anything like a coherent way? Couldn't he have been just a little bit clearer when dictating/inspiring it? Why *doesn't* it say precisely what he wanted it to say?

Some Christians, implicitly recognising the difficulties that the Bible gives believers, try to argue that it is secondary to an encounter or relationship with Jesus. But without the Bible there is no Jesus, and no Christianity. It is the only source of information about him, the only place the idea that he is somehow central to salvation is expounded. Christians differ in how they interpret the book, but they can only do that because it exists in the first place as the lynch-pin of Christianity. Until they can produce someone who has become a Christian solely through an encounter with Jesus, and not because of the Bible or its teaching, they cannot say the Bible is secondary. And while we're on the subject, if Jesus still exists in heaven and has a presence on Earth as the Holy Spirit, why don't we see conversions of this sort? Where are the individuals who, sheltered from Christian influences all of their lives, say in a remote province of China or in an uncharted Amazonian jungle, and never having seen a Bible or heard any of its doctrines, have spontaneously converted to Christianity solely through an encounter with Christ? It supposedly happened to Paul, so why are there no reported incidents of it happening in the ensuing two thousand years?

Because it doesn't happen, ever. The spiritual Jesus, principally because he doesn't exist, does not make himself known to people, unless the Bible is somewhere involved. Without it, no-one ever 'encounters' Jesus, becomes a Christian or comes to know what living the Christian life entails (even if ultimately they ignore this part of it). If the Bible ceased to exist - oh, that it were so - Christianity would, within a generation or two, also cease to be.

Chapter 7

The Christ Fantasy

In chapter 3 of *Mere Christianity*, C. S. Lewis proposes that Jesus was one of three things: he was either a lunatic on the same level as a man who thinks he's a poached egg, or a lying demon, or he was, and is, actually what he claimed to be: God incarnate. Christians are very fond of the 'Lunatic, Liar, Lord' conundrum - apologist William Lane Craig uses it on his website - which appears at first reading to have only one logical solution, namely the one that Lewis arrives at whereby Jesus is God. There are, however, insurmountable difficulties with the limited options Lewis presents.

The first is that Jesus does not proclaim himself to be God in any of the synoptic gospels. It is true he is made to make incredible claims about himself in the fourth gospel, but this only raises the question of why, if he did regard himself as divine, he fails to mention it in any of the other gospels and, perhaps more to the point, why the writers of those gospels fail to record his mentioning it. It would be a staggering omission on their part if Jesus had made such claims and they had neglected to include them. While Matthew indicates Jesus is miraculously related to God through the circumstances of his conception and birth, he does not say, or even imply, that Jesus is God incarnate. God's supposed impregnation of Mary with divine DNA produces what half of all impregnations by human males do – a son, not a clone of the father himself.

Not only do the synoptic gospels fail to represent Jesus as divine, they actually have him refute it: when an enquirer addresses him as 'good' teacher, he responds that no-one is good except God (Mark 10.17-18, Luke 18.18-19). Christians often claim, using convoluted logic, that this exchange demonstrates Jesus assuming both goodness and divinity; it is, they say, as if his response is actually, 'your calling me good shows you recognise me as God'. But this isn't what Jesus says and the response he does give, when taken at face value - and we are taking the Bible literally, after all - is not a commendation of the man's insight but a rebuke for blasphemously ascribing to him one of the qualities of God. It seems likely that the synoptic gospel writers do not have Jesus claim affinity with God, and instead have him refute it, because they are fully aware that he didn't make any such claim for himself. Even John's gospel, which presents a very different picture of Jesus from the synoptics, has him distinguish himself from God the father and acknowledge his subordinate position. 'The Father is greater than I' he says in John 14.28, an unlikely admission if he was God himself or if the writers of John's gospel and the creators of a much more mystical Jesus, regarded him as such.

There is also the problem of Jesus' baptism. Baptism was then, as now, about repentance and forgiveness of sin, as John the Baptist proclaims even before his encounter with Jesus. Here is how Mark's gospel records John's mission:

> *John the baptiser appeared in the wilderness, proclaiming **a baptism of repentance for the forgiveness of sins**. And people from the whole Judean countryside and all the people of Jerusalem were going out to him, and were baptised by him in the river Jordan, **confessing their sins**.* (Mark 1. 4-5, my emphases)

In *The Wrong Messiah*, Nick Page points out that Jesus' baptism by John must really have happened. It appears in all four gospels, but more importantly, it is something of an embarrassment for early Christians and the gospel writers; it implies that Jesus had sins he needed to repent of and be forgiven for. But what sins could a perfect being, God Incarnate, have committed? None - hence the embarrassment for early followers. The gospel writers can't omit the baptism - it is too well known – so they try hard to give it symbolic significance, with doves, heavenly voices and John the Baptist's sudden sycophancy (Mark 1.7-8). Nick Page too searches for symbolic meaning for Jesus' baptism, throwing up a number of unlikely possibilities all of which skirt or simply avoid the obvious: Jesus did not regard himself as a perfect being, let alone God Incarnate. This is what later followers decided he 'must' have been. In subjecting himself to John's baptism, Jesus publicly demonstrates the awareness of his own imperfection and need for forgiveness: further evidence that he is not a man who sees himself as God.

The second problem with Lewis' multiple-choice options is that he is not entirely honest in suggesting there are only three possibilities. It has been suggested, by Bart Ehrman, that 'Legend' is a fourth option; that the Jesus story as it came to be recorded in the gospels, together with Paul's expressed theology, represent an elaborate mythical encoding of Jewish, Greek and apocalyptic ideas, with perhaps some, but very little actual basis in reality. While there are undoubtedly significant elements of myth-making in the Jesus legend, I would suggest that there is a fifth option available to us that draws on some those already mentioned. Assuming, as Christians do, that Jesus existed, he was a man of his time, steeped in his religion, unquestioning in his commitment to Yahweh and empowered by his fervour for the Law. As such he believed he had a special relationship with his God, certainly seeing himself as one of his special sons (there are lots of sons of God in the Bible) and, probably, as his 'anointed one', or 'messiah'.

Even so, he would not have regarded himself as either perfect or divine, because there is nothing in the ancient Jewish scriptures, to which Jesus adhered, to suggest that the messiah, nor sons of God, are possessed of either of these characteristics. Indeed, the suggestion that a human being, however blessed, could, in some way, be divine would have been considered a blasphemy by all Jews, Jesus included.

More than this, Jesus' belief in himself as the anointed one, and his actual anointing in Mark 14.3, do not mean he was really the Messiah or, the Greek equivalent, the Christ. All it means is that he *thought* he was, subsequent events emphatically demonstrating that he was not. His belief that he was a special, anointed son of God, however, led him to the conviction that either he could be God's instrument in bringing about the Kingdom of Heaven on Earth, or that by his own actions he could compel God to initiate the new Kingdom. His actions, teaching and reputed miracles all point to one of these two possibilities. As recorded in the gospels and other New Testament writing, this was also the belief clung to hopefully, but inevitably forlornly, by subsequent devotees, for up to ninety years after his death. With our privileged hindsight, it would seem that in this respect, they, and Jesus too, did indeed enjoy a delusion of poached-egg standard. This does not make them lunatics, but shows how fervent religious belief, in a time and culture which knew of no other way of interpreting life, produces fanatical delusion. It is only when his God does not intervene, is not compelled to act and does not bring about the Kingdom (because, I would suggest, there is no God to do these things) that Jesus breaks free of his delusion. Mark retains his great cry of disillusionment, as dying on the cross he calls out the words of Psalm 22.1, 'my God, my God why have you forsaken me?'.

So, Jesus is, and was, none of the options Lewis suggests, but was an individual immersed, perhaps fanatically so, in the zeitgeist of his culture and age, believing himself to be appointed by God to usher in the new age. I do not have a word beginning with 'L' to add to Lewis's list that would alliteratively provide a fifth option of who Jesus was, but the evidence from the New Testament writings and the underlying disputes of the early church, reflect both Jesus' original conception of himself as 'anointed', preparing the way for God's intervention in Jewish history, and the subsequent aggrandisement of his nature by his later followers. They imbued him with mythical qualities, borrowed, in Paul's case, from Greek mystery religions and their dying god-men.

Soon after Jesus' life-time, Paul is arguing in Philippians that Jesus was 'in the form of God' but nonetheless 'did not count equality with God a thing to be grasped'. Later still the writer of John's gospel relates his belief that Jesus was the bodily incarnation of God's Word, in existence from 'the beginning'. But saying that the 'expression' or Logos of God became incarnate in the man we know as Jesus is a very long way from saying God in person assumed human form. Jesus, consequently, remains, even in the latest gospel, the Son of God (John 1.14) not God himself. Neither Paul nor John, nor *any* of the New Testament writers make the assertion that Jesus is God.

But they do surely insist that Jesus rose bodily from the tomb, don't they? And doesn't this prove beyond all reasonable doubt that Jesus was God himself, masquerading as a *bona fide* human being?

If it does - and Christians would very much like us to think that it does – where does it say these things? We have no first hand account of a post-resurrection appearance, not even from Paul who alludes obliquely, and without supplying any details, to his vision of the risen Lord in Galatians 1.11-12 and 1 Corinthians 9.1 & 15.45. By the time Acts came to be written – some forty years after Paul's conversion and at least twenty after his death - the event has evolved into Paul famously seeing-the-light on the road to Damascus. Acts relates the event three times, with significant differences in detail each time. What each has in common is that what Paul sees is a flash of light, which the later writer, 'Luke', interprets as the risen Christ. More than this, he creates a dialogue between the light and Saul (as Paul is known before his conversion) which Paul himself doesn't see fit to mention in any of his letters:

> *Now as (Saul) was going along and approaching Damascus, suddenly a light from heaven flashed around him. He fell to the ground and heard a voice saying to him, 'Saul, Saul, why do you persecute me?' He asked, 'Who are you, Lord?' The reply came, 'I am Jesus, whom you are persecuting.* (Acts 9.3-5)

Nonetheless, even in this later and heavily reworked version of events, what Paul sees, and allegedly hears, is not a physical Jesus but light from the sky and a disembodied voice, which, depending on which account from Acts you rely on, no-one else present either saw or heard. Paul himself doesn't even know what he is experiencing – certainly not a recognisable human figure – until the light tells him 'who' it is.

There is no difference between Paul's experience of a light purportedly from heaven and an event that occurred in its entirety -

as far as it occurred at all - in Paul's head. The original Greek of Galatians 1.15-16 makes absolutely clear that this is where it took place: while English translations say that the risen Christ revealed himself *to* Paul, the original Greek has Paul's initial experience of the Christ take place *in* him. Paul, then, admits only to an inner vision of 'a life-giving spirit' (1 Corinthians 15.45) and nowhere does he claim that he encountered an extrinsic, embodied Jesus. Nor does the writer of Acts, however much he embroiders Paul's experience, make the claim for him. The risen Lord, if he's become anything, is not a resurrected body but a spiritual being made of light.

Paul's sketchy mention in Galatians of his imagined encounter with a risen Christ, being the first account we have chronologically speaking of the resurrection, is only the start of problems we have with all the stories of Jesus' supposed resurrection. The gospels in which others occur were written at least between 15 and 50 years after Paul's own account. These later descriptions of the resurrected Jesus are similarly vague about Jesus' corporeality. Read them again without the presumption of two thousand years of Christian propaganda, and see for yourself how in those too, if the risen Christ features at all, his appearances are both utterly unconvincing and more involved the further they are from Paul's time:

Mark gets round the difficulty of representing the resurrected Jesus by not including him at all! There are no resurrection appearances in the oldest versions of Mark's gospel, itself the oldest of the four. Mark's account ends instead with 'a young man' simply telling Mary Magdalene that Jesus is risen. The alternate endings of the gospel, from Mark 16.19, are universally accepted as being later additions as most Bible translations indicate in their footnotes.

Mark's Jesus does, however, make a prediction about his resurrection during the Last Supper, where Mark 14.25 has him say: 'Truly I tell you, I will never again drink of the fruit of the vine until that day when I drink it new in the Kingdom of God'. There is not, in all the resurrection accounts - from the falsified endings of Mark, to those of the other gospels and the stories of

Paul's vision - any mention of Jesus celebrating his miraculous return, and the non-arrival of the Kingdom of God, by having a quick tipple with his old mates. The prediction is entirely forgotten about, as well it might be, when, according to Mark, Jesus doesn't have any earthly, post-mortem existence.

Matthew relates how, when the women visit the tomb, an angel informs them that Jesus has risen and then the Lord himself appears: 'And they came to him, took hold of his feet, and worshipped him. Then Jesus said to them, 'Do not be afraid; go and tell my brothers to go to Galilee; there they will see me.' At least he has feet, but is this not rather an odd encounter? Their leader whom they saw executed is alive once more and they worship... his feet? Don't they want to know how he comes to be alive again? What it all means? When a few verses later he appears to the disciples he issues them with instructions to make disciples of all men, in words that are evidently a much later formulation. His body, if he has one, isn't mentioned. He could just as easily be a disembodied voice.

In Luke, the self-same women don't see the risen Jesus at the tomb (does Matthew get this wrong or does Luke?). Instead, two men in dazzling robes - apparitions of light again – direct them to tell Peter that Jesus is gone. When Jesus does appear he joins two disciples who are walking to Emmaus; in spite of spending three years or more with him they fail to recognise him for the entire duration of this walk. When eventually they do, he simply vanishes, just like an apparition and not at all like a real person in a physical body. Later he joins the other disciples who are convinced he is a ghost.

Luke, however, is having none of it and it is in his gospel that we start to get the rather implausible accounts of Jesus directing witnesses to check out his wounds. The point Luke is making is that Jesus has returned in the same body in which he was killed, complete with nail holes and other injuries, together with the ability to disappear at will and project himself skyward, which is what he does at the end of the gospel. This is Luke, as ever, wanting it both ways - to persuade his readers that Jesus rose in the same body that he had prior to his death, but also that this same body now has super-powers. Significantly, it is the super-powered resurrected body that is the more plausible if the encounters with Jesus are, like Paul's, an invention of troubled human minds. We will return to this possibility in a moment.

John's gospel takes the resurrection appearances still further and we can see how they're evolving as beliefs about Jesus becomes increasingly formalised. He has the disciples and the women turn up at the tomb together (so does he get it wrong, or Matthew or Luke?) and find out for themselves that Jesus is not there. Mary remains behind, sees the obligatory angels (as the young man from Matthew's gospel has now become) and then encounters the risen Jesus. Remarkably, while she is confronted, supposedly, with someone she knows well, she fails to recognise him. This curiosity is becoming a recurrent theme: why is it that Jesus' intimate circle cannot recognise him when he looks the same - nail holes and all - as he did when they saw him last? Why do they need to have it explained to them that what they are seeing is Jesus himself? Does this not sound like a religious vision in need of explanation, exactly like those experienced in more recent years by impressionable young Catholic girls? Is it so different from those well-attested, but non-existent 'visitations' by abducting aliens? Figures who appear in dreams are often not instantly recognisable and require a level of interpretation; desperate true-believers are always only too ready to supply it.

The figure who appears in front of Mary then says something very peculiar: 'Do not hold on to me' he tells her, 'because I have not yet ascended to the Father'. This is very much like saying, 'don't try and touch me, because I'm not really here', as a vision without any substance might seem to say. John then has the usual kinky stuff about Jesus inviting his buddies to feel his wounds - just to demonstrate that the unrecognisable risen Christ has a real body, which, incongruously, can pass through walls.

The gospels also provide us with evidence that people of the early part of the first century took it for granted that individuals could be resurrected, either as apparitions or in reincarnated form. In

Matthew 17.13, for example, the disciples convince themselves they see the long-departed Moses and Old Testament prophet, Elijah, casually chatting with Jesus. Elsewhere, Mark records that many people, including Herod, regard Jesus as a resurrected John the Baptist (8.28 and 6.16) while others believe him to be Elijah, returned to Earth (again). Is this how the first 'witnesses' to Jesus' resurrection - the disciples on the road to Emmaus and Mary Magdalene – 'saw' him, and why they failed to recognise him? Did they encounter a different, inspirational figure, or perhaps more than one, who seemed to embody their master? Being capable of regarding him as a reincarnated John the Baptist or Elijah, they could be readily persuaded that Jesus was resurrected in another's body.

It is possible then that later accounts of Jesus' resurrected form displaying the wounds of his execution developed to dispel this possibility, once it began to prove troublesome. But whether by this means or by witnessing visions of their risen Lord, or both, those who first claimed he was alive were already prone to believing that the dead return; they had a mind-set that expected it, and, we can therefore safely conclude, created it.

The risen Jesus reprises his role at the start of Acts where the author records that, 'After his suffering he presented himself alive to them by many convincing proofs, appearing to them over the course of forty days and speaking about the Kingdom of God' (Acts 1.3). Luke's peculiar wording – 'presented himself', 'appearing', not to mention that Jesus supplied 'many convincing proofs' of who he was – is suspicious in itself. What are these proofs and why were they needed? Either what the disciples saw was their master returned from the dead in the flesh or it wasn't. 'Convincing proofs' means nothing more than 'persuasive interpretations' of mystical experiences, of visions and apparitions. Similarly, when Paul lists those who have seen the risen Christ in 1 Corinthians 15.5-8 his language taken at face value betrays the nature of these appearances:

> ...*he appeared to Cephas (Peter), then to the twelve.*
> *Then he appeared to more than five hundred brothers*

> *and sisters at one time, most of whom are still alive, though some have died. Then he appeared to James, then to all the apostles. Last of all, as to someone untimely born, he appeared also to me.*

Again, there is the emphasis on 'appeared'; not, 'he spent time with them' or 'he was physically present with five hundred believers', but that he was an 'appearance'. Paul couldn't be clearer about this. And indeed 'an appearance' is precisely what the risen Lord was for Paul in his own encounter, which he includes here as being identical with the others he notes. We have only Paul's word for the fact he appeared to the five hundred, incidentally; he doesn't say where or when this appearance occurred, but even so mass hallucinations are not unknown and it only takes a few avid visionaries to convince others of what they have all 'seen'. As Robert Wright points out in *The Evolution of God*, there is a 'conformist bias in human nature'. It would take only one or two influential individuals to convince themselves they'd seen a vision of the risen Christ for this conformist bias to persuade larger numbers of superstitious people that they had too.

There is nothing in what Paul says that suggests Jesus had been resurrected in bodily form, nor that early Christians believed he had. None of the gospels, nor Paul, nor Acts record the physical return of an executed man in a refurbished version of his original body. They talk almost exclusively about 'appearances' in need of interpretation. The mystical, visionary quality of Jesus' resurrection appearances is what came first in the early believers' experience of the risen Christ. Even the second century forger of 1 Timothy acknowledges the ethereal nature of the resurrected Jesus, who, he says, was 'vindicated *in spirit*' (3.16). Attempts to anchor such visions to reality, with the addition of the wounds that can be touched and the ability of his risen body to eat fish, are later, desperate developments. We know this because the further we move away in time from Jesus' death, the more of these attempts we see, while the luminary nature of the original experience remains. We know it too from Paul's vision of the risen Lord and from what Jesus himself is made to say about his post-mortem appearances:

> *For where two or three are gathered in my name, I am there among them.* (Matthew 18.20)
>
> *Remember, I am with you always, to the end of the age.* (Matthew 28.20)

Is he suggesting here that he will be physically present whenever a few believers meet together? That he'll be with them in the flesh as they wait for the end of the age? Evidently not: he is speaking metaphorically about a sense of presence, about the essence of his teaching, perhaps, or of feelings that the thought of him will elicit in his followers precisely when he is no longer available to them in a physical sense. And it's in this way that they experience him after his death, and Matthew is able write back into his gospel that this is exactly how Jesus predicted they would experience him. He would be with them in spirit, the intensity of religious feeling even allowing some to 'see' him. And so the idea of the spirit of the risen Christ develops, later to detach itself from its original role as little more than a vivid memory conjured up by believers, to become eventually the third party of the Godhead, the Holy Spirit: 'the Advocate, the Holy Spirit, whom the Father will send in my name, will teach you everything, and remind you of all that I have said to you' (John 14.25).

The Bible then does not preach the bodily resurrection of Jesus. It presents instead a series of visions that Jesus' anxious, zealous early followers experience after his death. It is only later, when Jesus fails to return to first century Earth, that the fate of believers who have died becomes an issue and bodily resurrection has to be given serious *(sic)* consideration.

Paul counters those who argue that those who have died must have sinned or lacked sufficient faith, by coming up with the idea in 1 Corinthians 15.35-54 that such individuals would be resurrected in an imperishable body when Christ did eventually return (yes, he really did make it up as he went along). But this unlikely proposition exists only for those unlucky enough to die before the main event, the establishment of the Kingdom on Earth.

Matthew gets carried away with this idea when he has hordes of the dead return to life as Jesus is crucified. He makes this remarkable assertion in Matthew 27.52-53, noting that 'the tombs also were opened, and many bodies of the saints who had fallen asleep were raised. After his resurrection they came out of the tombs and entered the holy city and appeared to many'. So, it wasn't just Jesus who was raised from the dead but hordes of 'saints' who were to be seen wandering about. Who were these 'saints' - an early Christian term for believers, indicating the anachronistic inclusion of this macabre event - and do they indicate a hitherto unrecorded mass-extinction of Jesus' followers within his lifetime? As no-one else in the New Testament thinks to mention such a significant occurrence, we can safely assume it has more to do with Matthew's enthusiasm for zombies than anything with a basis in reality. No-one comes close to suggesting Jesus himself numbered among the Undead. Even the over-excitable minds of the very earliest Christians knew that physical bodies could not revive after death; that ludicrous claim came from later fanatics.

Speaking of which, the further we move from Jesus' and Paul's times. the wackier the ideas become (not that Jesus' and Paul's aren't out of kilter to start with). One that is popular still today is the notion that God is a three-in-one type of guy. Otherwise known as the Trinity, this is one of those extra-curricular beliefs that no-one, not even Christians, understand. It has, moreover, no biblical basis whatsoever. The only place the Father, Son and Holy Spirit are mentioned together is Matthew 28:19, where Jesus is made to say, 'make disciples of all nations, baptising them in the name of the Father and of the Son and of the Holy Spirit'. A Christian reading the verse today, with an awareness of the doctrine of the Trinity, might easily assume that it is a reference to the idea that God is made up of three 'persons', but this is not the case. The verse carries no suggestion that the three entities are one, much less that they are all part of 'the Godhead'.

The notion that God is schizophrenically triune did not develop until three hundred and fifty years after Jesus' lifetime, in 381CE, with the Holy Spirit only just making it into the arrangement because no-one knew quite what to do with it otherwise. The term usually translated 'holy spirit', is *pneuma hagion*, which is not a proper noun in the original Greek of the New Testament. Even though ancient Greek frequently attributed gender to nouns, as do modern Greek and French, *penuma hagion* is neuter. The pronouns used of the spirit - 'it, 'which' and 'that'; not 'he' or 'who' - invariably reflect this. In other words, the original texts do not personify the holy spirit: it is a thing and not a person. This fits exactly with the idea that the spirit was simply a sense of Christ's presence generated by believers themselves with nothing miraculous or supernatural about it. Like Jesus himself, the spirit was eventually turned into something it was not originally meant to be by a succession of over-zealous believers. Once warm and fuzzy feelings mutated into a 'person', it was really only a matter of time before room could be made for them as part of God's inner circle. You might still wonder how this could happen; it is further illustration of what occurs when you live, as Christians did and still do, in a world of make-believe.

Today, the Catholic catechism describes the Trinity as 'a mystery of faith, one of those mysteries that are hidden in God, which can never be known unless they are revealed by God... God's inmost being as Holy Trinity is mystery that is inaccessible to reason alone'. The real mystery is how the idea got off the ground in the first place, when the Bible does not present Jesus as God and the Holy Spirit only made it into the cast by default. Accept it on faith if you must, but the Trinity makes a nonsense of the supposed Oneness of the Christian God and is a mystery only insofar as ideas that make no sense whatever can be said to be mysterious.

It's fortuitous then, as our Sunday school teachers used to tell us, that Jesus elected to use parables as a way of making spiritual truths clear to people. Unfortunately, this isn't how Jesus himself describes his little metaphorical tales. He explains to his little band of acolytes in Mark 4.11-12 that his parables are designed to *obscure* his meaning from the riff-raff:

And he said to them, 'to you has been given the secret

of the Kingdom of God, but for those outside, everything comes in parables; in order that they may indeed look, but not perceive, and may indeed listen, but not understand; so that they may not turn again and be forgiven'. (Mark 4.11-12)

Alluding here to Isaiah 6.10, where Yahweh commands the Old Testament prophet to mislead the people, Jesus clearly demonstrates that there are some he doesn't want in his exclusive Kingdom club, whom he doesn't want 'saved'. You may wonder, as I do, why the great preacher of love finds the need to speak to them at all, if all he's intent on doing is bamboozling them.

However mistaken Christians might be in regarding Jesus as God incarnate rising bodily from the grave, they can surely rest assured that their saviour's message was one of love and peace. To be sure, Jesus tells us to love God, our neighbour and our enemies and bestows peace, and healing, on some of those he encounters. Those 'outside', though, are excluded from his and his father's love, as are your parents, whom you must 'hate' if you choose to follow him, and those against whom you must take up your sword (Matthew 10.34).

Elsewhere, those who are not Jewish cannot be recipients of a love that is so conditional it hardly qualifies as love at all. In Matthew 15, when a Gentile woman asks Jesus to heal her child, he is insulting, ungracious and patronising – love doesn't get a look in: 'I was sent only to the lost sheep of the house of Israel', he tells her, '(and) it is not fair to take the children's food and throw it to the dogs'. He does eventually do as she asks, but only because he likes her smart answer to his supercilious put-down.

A man of his time, and certainly not one who existed outside of it, Jesus is complicit in slavery that exists all around him. He says nothing to condemn those who practise it or to support those who are subject to it. When he does mention it, which is often (there are fourteen events and stories in Matthew's gospel alone alluding to slaves), he accepts it as the norm. He condones the beating of slaves, for example, and their being hacked to pieces if that's what their owners feel like doing to them (Luke 12.46-48): it's all fine in the eyes of the Lord.

In Luke 7.2-10 he heals the young slave of a Roman centurion only because he is impressed by the authority the man wields over a large number of slaves. It is likely, given the centurion's fondness for this boy, described as being 'very dear to him', that the child was a catamite - a boy kept for sexual purposes. Where is Jesus' condemnation of the suffering he must have endured? Of the pederasty and cruelty, and of slavery itself? Where is Jesus' love for the boy, his freedom and his right to live unmolested? Here, from Matthew's version of the story, is the extent of it:

When Jesus heard (the centurion), he was amazed and said to those who followed him, 'Truly I tell you, in no one in Israel have I found such faith'.

Without any help from Jesus, the boy gets better but is no better off: he's a child sex-slave before his non-encounter with Jesus, and a child sex-slave after it.

Jesus regards entire swathes of people as pigs, telling his disciples in Matthew 7.5 not to cast their 'pearls before swine'. The swine he refers to are people whom he regards as ignorant, unsavoury and unworthy. He uses the insulting analogy deliberately, in full cognisance of the low regard in which Jewish custom held, and still holds, this ritually unclean animal (Leviticus 11.7). You can decide for yourself whether this represents an expression of love or arrogant disdain for those unconvinced by the news that the Kingdom of Heaven was just around the corner.

Finally, how does the man who advocates that his followers love their enemies go about it himself? He must, surely, provide a model of how to practise love towards such people. Judge for yourself how much love he reflects in his exchanges with those he makes his enemies, the scribes and Pharisees, with his constant 'rebuking' and criticism of their practices. They are, he lovingly tells them, vipers, white-washed graves, thieves, hypocrites, sons of the devil, blind guides, fools (oops - doesn't he expressly forbid this in Matthew 5.22?), greedy and wicked. It is no wonder these long established groups set themselves up in opposition to him. Perhaps if he'd been a little less arrogant and instead found it in himself to show the love to his enemies that he prescribes for everyone else, he might not have found himself in quite the pickle he ultimately did. Even his friend Peter gets it in the neck when he upsets this hyper-sensitive soul: 'Fuck off, you clueless bastard', he tells him in Matthew 16.23 (and, yes, his words do carry that strength of meaning) when Peter has the temerity to suggest the suicide mission Jesus has embarked on is maybe not such a good idea. All charmingly colourful of course but not what anyone could claim were loving responses to friend and enemies alike.

Love and peace or hatred and contempt? Jesus' message includes both. He is nothing if not inconsistent, like any other fallible human being.

Nonetheless, Paul sets him on a pedestal and Christians to this day are adamant that this flawed individual should be worshipped. Visit almost any Christian church of any denomination or flavour and you'll find its services consists of three components: Bible reading, teaching and 'worship'. Indeed, some groups refer to their services as 'worship' and attendees are widely referred to as 'worshippers'. Hymns and other songs of praise are addressed to and directed towards Jesus:

> *Praise Him! praise Him! Jesus, our blessed Redeemer!*
> *Sing, ye saints! His wonderful love proclaim!*
> *Hail Him! hail Him! mightiest angels in glory;*
> *Strength and honour give to His holy name!*

goes the classic hymn. And yet, where in the gospels do we find Jesus requesting, implying he is worthy of or needs worship like this? Where does the Bible as a whole suggest he needs songs sung to him? And what is he meant to do with them when they are? Listen in Heaven? Has he nothing better to do, no better source of entertainment than congregations that can't always hold a tune, intoning - if it's a modern 'hymn' they're singing - a single repeated line? Just how much can he get out of 'Lord Jesus come' repeated *ad nauseam*?

The answer can only be that he doesn't. Christians sing hymns and praise songs because it does *them* good, not because an individual who lived two thousand years ago gains any benefit. While believers started singing songs about and to him in the first century after he died, the man himself neither requested nor sought others' worship. On the contrary, he seemed positively to oppose it. When his buddy Peter suggests that he, Jesus, might be the Messiah, Jesus tells him not to make a song and dance about it (Matthew 16.16 & 20); when in Mark 14.3 a woman pours oil over Jesus, to show she thinks he's the messiah, he doesn't ask her for a quick rendition of 'Just A Closer Walk With Thee'; when he finds himself alone with his inner circle he doesn't suggest they sing a hymn of praise to him. Jesus and his disciples did sing (Mark 14:26) but it's a fairly safe bet he didn't lead them in a rousing chorus of 'How Great I Am' when they did. Their hymns were to their God, not to Jesus himself.

It wasn't until believers decided that Jesus had risen, somehow, from the dead and must therefore be a special divine envoy that hymns began to be addressed to him. The letter to the Colossians, written round about the time of Matthew and Luke's gospels by someone other than Paul, contains what may well be an early hymn about Jesus, as he forcibly morphed into something grander than an itinerant Jewish preacher (1.15-20). 'About', though, does not necessarily mean 'to', especially when the same letter points out in 3.16 that hymns are for showing gratitude to *God,* who evidently has more stomach for them. Almost all mentions in the New Testament of hymns of praise have God the Father as intended recipient, even when they are delivered 'through' or 'in the name of' Christ.

Full-blown hymns of praise to Jesus only come into their own when he finally becomes indistinguishable from God, some of these finding their way into the New Testament's later books (see Revelation 5.12, for example). But this is not what the gospels teach about him nor what he asked for for himself: nowhere does he see himself as a recipient of worship. Misguided human beings, desperate to believe, changed him into that, and continue to do so in our own time. If he hadn't died so long ago he'd be shocked at the attention, and maybe more than a little tired by now of 'Shine Jesus Shine'.

Jesus worship and the idea that 'the gospel' is the proclaiming of the salvation made possible by his death would seem to have developed hand-in-hand. The impulse to praise him grew out of the belief that somehow Jesus' death and resurrection restored our broken relationship with God. Undoubtedly, this interpretation of Jesus' purpose began with Paul whose creed, expressed only twenty years or so after Jesus' death, can be found in 1 Corinthians 15.13: 'Christ died for our sins in accordance with the scriptures... he was buried and was raised on the third day'. Expanded upon by generations of Christians since Paul's time, the doctrine now reads (in the words of the Reformed Baptists; might we ask what they are being reformed from?):

> *the gospel is the good news that Christ lived a perfect life, died on the cross, and rose from the dead to satisfy God's wrathful judgement on the world. Because of Jesus' payment in full for OUR debt, it is now possible for anyone to receive salvation through a living faith in Christ. This is the Gospel.*

Except it isn't. Jesus preached the 'gospel', Matthew 4.23 tells us, and this is definitely not what he preached. As Keith Ward concedes in the otherwise evangelical *The Word of God: The Bible After Modern Scholarship,* 'this was not Jesus' own message and could only have been preached after his death'. Indeed. So if this wasn't Jesus' gospel, what was his 'good news' and why didn't the synoptic gospel writers contrive to represent it as being the same as Paul's?

Jesus' good news, as you'll recall, was that the Kingdom of God on Earth was about to be established on earth, bringing with it a complete reversal of the social order and injustice, while sickness and oppression would be no more (Mark 10.31 and Luke 4.18-19). To be included in this Kingdom, one needed to be righteous, a state achieved by upholding Jewish law and showing compassion (Matthew 5.17-19). So the problem is not, as Ward hints, that

Jesus' gospel was different from Paul's because Jesus had yet to die. On the contrary, it is that he had been long dead when the gospels were written, yet the discord remains between Jesus' good news, as the synoptic writers report it, and Paul's very different interpretation, from which all later Christian doctrine, including that of the Reformed Baptists, is derived.

The two very different versions of the good news could easily have been harmonised retrospectively, had the synoptic writers wanted them to be. We can only assume they did not; perhaps they were unaware of Paul's 'gospel' (he was not quite as revered in the early church as we might suppose him to have been from his prominence in the New Testament), or perhaps they took exception to Paul's Greek mysticism, so much at odds with Jesus' concerns for the Kingdom here on Earth. Whichever it was, the good news of the synoptics' Jesus and Paul's 'gospel' were not reconciled, and it is difficult to see how they could have been without seriously compromising one or the other. (Such a compromise does exist, in the much later gospel of John, whose less principled writers eliminate almost all of Jesus' Kingdom teaching in order to bring him into line with the Pauline idea of a heavenly Christ). As it is, Paul's gospel and that of Mark, Luke and Matthew remain radically and irreconcilably different. When it comes to choosing which to follow, Christians invariably opt for Paul's spiritualised 'Christ', which is perhaps understandable, given that Jesus' good news, while not only the more morally demanding, came, in the end, to nothing.

Then again, perhaps salvation has nothing to do with *choosing* the right path from the many the Bible offers. Sure enough, within its pages is an entirely different explanation of salvation that would seem to override all the others. It is one that has no place for the much-loved Christian notion of free will. We need another chapter to consider why.

Chapter 8
Christians' Favourite Delusions

As they say on all the best talent shows, what a journey it's been: from Joshua Bar-Joseph to 'Jesus' to 'the Christ' to God Incarnate, Christians have manufactured a saviour from the most unpromising of beginnings. And they don't stop there – why should they? A host of other spurious ideas supplement their invented triune God. Indeed, his specialist act, the Great Salvation Plan, *necessitates* a whole range of additional beliefs to provide what is a very weak performance with minimal credibility. It goes without saying that these beliefs are largely unbiblical and entirely delusional.

Let's begin by looking at the notion which Christians insist underpins their God's Great Plan, that he has given us free will either to claim salvation or to reject it. But has he? Does the Bible tell us so? Try going online, finding an electronic Bible like the *Oremus Bible Browser* and entering 'free will' in Search. How many instances of the term will it turn up: Ten? Fifty? A hundred? I'll tell you to save you doing it (though please go ahead and try it yourself if you don't believe me). The answer is none at all; you will receive a message that says *'No verses found containing: free will..'*.

But perhaps that's because although the *phrase* 'free will' is not used, the *principle* is there, explained in different terms. No, that's not the case either, even though the idea that everyone is free to choose 'to follow God or sing the blues and who they're gonna sin with', as an old Christian rock song would have it, is central to modern evangelical thinking. 'Free will' is not what the Bible teaches, nor, science suggests, is it what people actually have. As Sam Harris demonstrates in *The Moral Landscape*, 'thoughts and intentions are caused by physical events and mental stirrings of which (we) are not aware'. Our genes, individual brain structure, hormones, bacteria levels in the body, the environment and our education all determine how we act and what we choose. 'We' have no say in the matter.

So what does the Bible teach instead? It tells us in Ephesians 3.1-6, written by someone claiming to be Paul but isn't, that God has an 'elect'; a group of people he chose to save 'before the foundation of the world'. He decided *then* whose 'hearts' he was going to change so that they could become part of his chosen few.

Pseudo-Paul is only echoing the real one who says in Roman 29-30:

> *For those whom (God) foreknew he also predestined to be conformed to the image of his Son, in order that he might be the first-born within a large family. And those whom he predestined he also called; and those whom he called he also justified; and those whom he justified he also glorified.*

Salvation is all God's doing: he calls people, he changes them so they conform to the image of Christ, he 'justifies' them. And he decided to do all of this long before any of them were born.

Jesus too is made to speak frequently of God's elect (in Mark 13.20 and throughout Matthew 24, for example) and as he notes in Matthew 22.14, 'many are called but few are chosen'. In other words, of the significant numbers drawn to his message, only a few have been selected by God beforehand for life in the new Kingdom. As he says to his followers in John 15.16, 'you did not choose me, but I chose you'. Looked at afresh, the salvation formula that had evolved by the time the fourth gospel came to be written, 'you must be born from above' (John 3.7), makes eminently clear the direction of salvation: God gives birth from *above*. As Calvinists know, human choice and 'free will' have no part to play in entering the Kingdom

So, unless God singled you out at the dawn of time, forget it. You can no more choose to be a Christian than you can choose not to be born into sin. And that's just the way it is; according to some parts of the Bible anyway.

Whether you choose to believe that you're one of the elect or you think you've made your own decision to follow Jesus what is important, Christians tells us, is that you share real intimacy with the Saviour. There are many permutations of this belief: having Jesus in your heart; walking daily with the Lord; enjoying a loving relationship with him; letting him speak to you, and all rely on the premise that the post-mortem Jesus is an eternal, supernatural being who is able, somehow, to stroll, chat and administer one-on-one therapy. The old spiritual, still much beloved in Christian circles, declares 'what a friend we have in Jesus', while Mary Stevenson's modern parable insists that his footprints are beside the believer's in the sand – except, that is, when he has to carry them.

However, like the notion of free will, the idea of Jesus as bosom buddy and occupier of right and left ventricles is nowhere to be found in 'God's word'. Yes, there's the possibility of feeling Jesus' presence when with other believers; the shared delusion of Matthew 18.20 that morphs, ultimately, into the Holy Spirit. And it's true too that Paul decides in 1 Corinthians 6.14 that believers' bodies are sanctuaries or temples of the same Holy Spirit. But these are both a long way from a Jesus who lives within the believer's heart and, as another old hymn has it, 'walks with me and talks with me along life's narrow way'. The Jesus of the gospels is not looking for people to be his friends; he calls them instead to be slaves and servants, working selflessly and sacrificially to bring about the Kingdom of heaven:

> *...whoever wishes to be great among you must be your servant, and whoever wishes to be first among you must be your slave; just as the Son of Man came not to be served but to serve...* (Matthew 20.26-28)

When they've turned themselves into lifetime servants of others, surely then Christians can expect God to reward them by taking them to heaven to live with him there. Like the disciples before them who wanted to be part of God's circle of favourites, they miss the point of what it was, and is, to be a slave; to work ceaselessly with no reward, no wages, no acknowledgement. The most any servant of God can expect, Jesus tells us, is that he will say 'Well done, good and trustworthy slave; you have been trustworthy in a few things, I will put you in charge of many things; enter into the joy of your master' (Matthew 25.23). That's it - that's the extent of the 'reward': more responsibility and the knowledge you've pleased the boss, and only then if you've given yourself tirelessly (albeit in the first century) to the inauguration of the Kingdom.

This also points up the futility of another grandiose Christian claim that God has a special plan for the individual believer's life, which he will use to direct them towards a specific career; guide them to the person they are to marry; tell them where they should live. Here, for example, is some 'guidance' provided by *Bible-Knowledge.com*: 'Remember – God already has your next new job all set up and planned out for you. All you have to do is simply wait for His timing to bring it to you!'. As we might by now expect, there's no biblical basis for this fantasy either - neither Jesus nor Paul (or any other New Testament writer) mention it, which is why Christian teaching promoting the idea fails, without exception, to reference either of them. Far from being an individually tailored life-plan, God's agenda, according to Jesus, is the same for everyone: it is to work tirelessly to bring about his Kingdom, loving your neighbour as yourself and God even more (Mark 12.28-34). And that, once again, is that. Or not quite because Jesus goes further. Nothing else, he insists, compares with God's Kingdom, the pearl of great price next to which everything else is without value or meaning (Matthew 13.45-46). So he demands over and over again that people abandon jobs, homes, spouses and family concerns to seek and work towards the Kingdom (Luke 12.27-37 etc). Why would he change - reverse even - these priorities, the central core of his 'earthly ministry', to direct the careers and prescribe the domestic arrangements of Christians today? Answer: he wouldn't, demonstrating just how much of a construct of their own imaginations is the Christ that Christians worship, profess to listen to and who, they maintain, guides the minutiae of their lives.

While they might not have Jesus as their intimate chum in this life, at least Heaven awaits those who are good and faithful slaves.

Christians will go to Heaven when they die, won't they?

Jesus didn't seem to think so, nor do the writers of the gospels. As former bishop of Durham, Tom Wright, puts it 'at no point do the resurrection narratives in the four Gospels say, "Jesus has been raised, therefore we are all going to heaven." It says that Christ is coming here, to join together the heavens and the Earth in an act of new creation'. Admittedly, in John 14, Jesus talks about his Father's house having many mansions (KJV), whatever that might look like architecturally, but already this is a changing perspective from the one expressed in the synoptic gospels. It is likely in any case that Jesus is referring to the idea which Paul and other New Testament writers invent, that the souls of deceased believers wait with God for bodily resurrection on the new earth in the new Kingdom.

Invariably the Bible's use of 'heaven' and 'the heavens' refers only to the expanse above our heads, which is how 'heaven', along with the earth, can 'pass away' (Matthew 24.35 etc). Similarly, when Jesus advises praying to our 'Father in heaven', he refers literally to a God in the sky. The 'vouchsafing' of souls, then, is not a permanent transition to the non-existent Heaven of later Christian tradition. Instead, it is a sleep-like state in an unspecified location, which may be what Jesus refers to as 'mansions' and later, at his crucifixion, as 'paradise'. From this state of sublime doziness, the dead will return to the new earth, with the triumphant Christ, to be given new, spiritual bodies. Paul explains the idea in 1 Thessalonians 4.13-16:

> *But we would not have you ignorant, brethren, concerning those who are asleep, that you may not grieve as others do who have no hope. For since we believe that Jesus died and rose again, even so, through Jesus, God will bring with him those who have fallen asleep. For this we declare to you by the word of the Lord, that we who are alive, we who are left until the coming of the Lord, shall not precede those who have fallen asleep. For the Lord himself will descend from heaven with a cry of command, with the archangel's call and with the sound of the trumpet of*

God. And the dead in Christ will rise first.

This doctrine, however, is not found in the synoptic gospels, where the Kingdom is imminent. It arose when believers began to die without the Kingdom having materialised, and early communities started to be concerned about whether and how the deceased would be part of God's new creation. Consequently, Paul and others concocted the idea - or were told by the Lord according to their own accounts - that the souls of the dead would somehow be kept safe until Christ's return. The Christian website, *Way of Life Literature*, represents this somewhat *ad hoc* doctrine accurately when it says:

> *We believe the Scriptures teach that at death the spirit of the believer passes instantly into the presence of Christ and dwells there in conscious joy until the resurrection of the body when Christ comes for His own (Mk. 9.4; 2 Cor. 5.8; Phil. 1.23; 2 Tim. 4.6; Rev. 6.9-11). At death, the spirit of the unbeliever descends immediately into Hell to await the resurrection of the wicked into judgement; there the conscious soul is tormented in fire (Mk. 9.43-49; Lk.16.22-31)'.*

Later believers still, second and third generation Christians, came to accept that they were, as Bart Ehrman puts it, 'in it for the long haul' and their theology had to change again. Jesus had already become a semi-divine being, supernaturally related to God with whom, according to Paul, he resided in the heavens. It was a short step to believing that that was where his suffering followers would go too. Consequently, in later Christian writing, God's (not so) imminent Kingdom on earth is in the process of being replaced with a promise of post-mortem eternal life in heaven. As Bart Ehrman says 'with the passage of time, the apocalyptic notion of the resurrection of the body becomes transformed into the doctrine of the immortality of the soul'. This belief is as different as it is possible to be from the gospels and Paul's letters, where bodily resurrection on a new earth is eagerly anticipated and prepared for.

So the choice for Christians ever since has been whether to believe Jesus and Paul, for once saying much the same thing, or later believers with their altogether different idea of what lies in store for those who 'die in the Lord'. Of course, today's Christians opt for the latter - even they have doubts that the Kingdom will come at this late stage.

What they don't consider is which of their ever-changing selves will be the one that makes it to 'the other side'. Does the Christian who passes away suffering from a dementia that has entirely dissolved his personality, his very self, find himself living for eternity in this condition? Does a deceased child convert find herself existing as a perpetual 8 year old? What about all of those aborted foetuses many Christians feel so strongly about, maintaining that they too have souls; do they remain embryos for their heavenly existence? Or does God change each arrival into the very best they could have been while on Earth? If he does, and everyone lives in their prime as a permanent 28 year old, how much of who they really were and are survives in Heaven? It doesn't sound like it can be very much. Perhaps that's why inviting dead believers to Heaven to live with him there has never been part of Jesus' and his Father's great plan.

Any Christian still reading this book will want to point out that Jesus does appear to talk about an after-life heaven - and hell - in one passage in Luke's gospel, mentioning the fires of hell in several other places as well. The passage in question, Luke 16.19-31, is the story of a poor man called Lazarus who on his death is taken by the angels to the bosom of Abraham, while the rich man who has ignored his earthly plight is condemned to hell. Of course, this is a parable, but in an effort to read the Bible literally, we need to consider that these words of Jesus seem to confirm the existence of heaven and hell as final destinations after death. If that is what Jesus is talking about, then we, and Christians who claim Jesus is demonstrating what the afterlife is like here, need to take note of the following features of the story:

1) Jesus does not refer to the place where Lazarus finds himself as 'heaven';

2) Even if it is, it is a particularly Jewish 'heaven', with Lazarus' resting on the bosom of Abraham;

3) This is a bodily resurrection: both Lazarus and the rich man have bodies - the finger of the former and the eyes and tongue of the latter are mentioned.

4) Lazarus does not go to this 'heaven' because he is 'saved', or because he has faith or because he subscribes to a particular set of doctrines. He is there because in life he was poor and an outcast from society (the 'evil things' of verse 25).

5) The rich man does not go to Hades (the place of the dead) because he lacks faith or because he failed to subscribe to a particular set of doctrines. He is there because in life he was rich and heedless of the plight of the poor;

This is not then the heaven of which Christians often speak, that exists on another plane and is accessed through being 'washed in the blood of the lamb'. This is about the Kingdom of Heaven that, from Jesus' perspective, is soon to be realised on earth. It exemplifies the radical social reversal that Jesus often speaks about as occurring when the Kingdom comes, and is an illustration of how the first will be last and the last first (Luke 14.11). Using characteristic hyperbole, Jesus demonstrates how the poor will inherit the Kingdom (Matthew 5.3); the hungry will be filled with good things, while the rich will be sent empty away (Luke 1.53).

We can assume that Lazarus has been resurrected into the new Kingdom on the new earth, together with Abraham with whom he shares a startling degree of physical intimacy. Interestingly, by the time John's gospel came to be written, some twenty to thirty years later, this parable has become an actual event in the life of Jesus, as he resurrects a real-life Lazarus three days after his death (John 11); so much for the reliability of the methods by which these stories were transmitted! In John's account there is no rich man, but back in Luke's story, the rich man appears to be in hell that is located... where exactly?

Jesus is quite clear that when the new Kingdom is inaugurated, there will be a judgement and that some will be found wanting: those who don't feed the hungry and clothe the naked, those who fail to forgive, the 'lawless' and the heedless rich, to name but a few. (Paul takes it upon himself to add a few more to the list in 1

Corinthians 6.9-10). At this judgement, the king - Jesus himself, presumably - will say to the condemned, ' "depart from me, you cursed, into everlasting fire prepared for the devil and his angels"... and they will go away into eternal punishment' (Matthew 25.41 and 46). Jesus seems to believe that this place of everlasting fire really exists, and certainly it bears resemblance to Gehenna, Jerusalem's perpetually smouldering dump where the bodies of executed criminals and dead animals were thrown. It is likely too he thought the location of the hell of 'everlasting fire' and 'eternal punishment' was below the ground, in keeping with the view at the time that creation consisted of heaven above, where the Lord dwelt, the earth itself and, below the earth, Hades or Sheol, the place of the dead. Hades, the word Luke uses in his story, is not called the 'under-world' for nothing, and certainly Jesus talks elsewhere about the dead being 'thrust down' into this place of outer darkness (Luke 10.15, KJV).

So, does Jesus promise the believers will experience eternal life in heaven when they die? No. Like Lazarus in the parable, they will be resurrected in the new Kingdom, currently running two thousand years late. Will the condemned spend eternity in hell? According to Jesus, yes; they too will be resurrected to be punished forever, deep in the bowels of the earth.

(If it all seems just a little bit fuzzy and more than unlikely, remember, it's in the Bible so it must be true).

You would think it would be a source of some anxiety among Christians that cherished beliefs about Heaven, Salvation and their 'walk with the Lord' are not to be found anywhere in their holy book. And you'd be wrong. They are unperturbed; they know what they have chosen to believe is true by virtue of the fact that they believe it. The creed, the arrogant insistence, of the modern Christian is 'I believe therefore it is true'.

Belief, however, is not evidence. It may be conviction and it may reflect deep feelings, but it does not, in any sense, make anything true. I might believe that I have the looks of Brad Pitt (or insert name of preferred hunk) but reality will quickly dispel any such belief. I may, similarly, believe I can fly, but leaping off the top of a tall building will demonstrate otherwise, as gravity behaves as gravity does. Evidence trumps belief every time. Christians are dimly aware of this and will tell you of the 'evidence' that they think underpins their belief. This evidence boils down to one of two things: the Bible and their own subjective experience.

The Bible, as we are seeing, rarely supports their convictions and is, in any case, an unsavoury concoction of brutality, impractical advice and mystery religion, written by primitive tribesmen and first century fanatics. In any other context it would constitute such poor evidence that it wouldn't be accepted as evidence at all. That it is seen as such by Christians is because of a cognitively dissonant mindset that disables their critical faculties and compels them to accept everything the Bible says, and many things it doesn't, as ultimate truth. They would not express it like this, of course, claiming instead that it is the Holy Spirit 'who' creates their inner conviction that the Bible, Christianity and personal fantasies are true. As William Craig Lane explains, Christianity is true because of the inner witness of the Holy Spirit, an argument that is beautifully circular saying, in effect, 'Christianity and its holy book are true. I know this because the Holy Spirit who lives in me tells me so. I know the Holy Spirit lives in me because the Bible says he does. Therefore, I know Christianity and the Bible are true because the Holy Spirit tells me so'.

Equally, Mormons claim that they 'know' a completely different set of improbable beliefs are true because they experience a 'burning in the bosom' that tells them they are. Roman Catholics say *their* faith is true because they experience Christ through the Eucharist, while Muslims know theirs is true because they have a real sense of Allah's presence.

All of these spiritual convictions are not, as a liberal theologian like Karen Armstrong might claim, evidence that there is Something Out There that loves and communicates with us, but more obviously that human beings' brains are adept at creating whatever 'inner witness' is required to support the beliefs and convictions they have arrived at. William Lane Craig concedes this when he acknowledges that '*anyone* (or, at least any sort of theist) can *claim* to have a self-authenticating witness of God to the truth of his religion. But the reason you argue with them is because they really don't: either they've just had some emotional experience or else they've misinterpreted their religious experience'. Any experience of 'self-authenticating witness' encountered by believers in faiths outside Craig's own brand of Christianity, is at best mistaken, at worst fake. But then, how can anyone know, Craig included, that his *own* conviction isn't just as much an emotional flush or mere subjective experience? Why is his conviction any more real than that of other kinds of believers? Ultimately, Craig can only say, "because it is": 'a person (possessed by the Holy Spirit) does not need supplementary arguments or evidence in order to know and to know with confidence that he is in fact experiencing the Spirit of God'.

In other words, the true believer knows his experience of the Holy Spirit is real because his experience of the Holy Spirit tells him it is. And round the argument goes again, though no amount of assertion makes a subjective experience an event in objective reality. It really is no good to add, as some Christians do (check out any of their websites), that they *firmly, strongly* or *sincerely* believe. Intensity of belief does not make it any more real or valid.

It is impossible for Craig, or any other Christian, to demonstrate that an entity he imagines inhabits his brain, no matter how convincing its presence may seem, has any existence anywhere other than in his brain. What the person who says 'I believe' is really saying is that they have no evidence at all for what they are claiming. If they had, they wouldn't need to *believe* it; they would know it. Of course, the Bible makes a virtue out of not knowing, of believing when there is no evidence. It calls this kind of wishful-thinking, 'faith', which, as the writer of Hebrews puts it, 'is the assurance of things hoped for, the conviction of things not seen'. So, maybe I do look like Brad Pitt, after all.

Christians counter the rationalist insistence on evidence with the assertion that faith and evidence-based reasoning are actually on an equal footing when it comes to knowing what is true. Knowing something wildly far-fetched - like the triune nature of God – is, they say, the same as knowing something that is scientifically demonstrable, like the fact that a molecule of water is comprised of two hydrogen atoms and one oxygen. But it isn't the same, and, as we've established, Christians who claim they know eight or more impossible things through faith don't *know* these things at all. They accept them on faith, which is another way of saying 'without evidence', because the Bible, their inner convictions or a pastor tells them to. This faith then colours their world-view to the extent that they see God even in those events that science explains without unnecessary recourse to the supernatural. Science offers evidence; rational thinking looks for evidence to inform its reasoning and shape its conclusions. 'Explanations' that stem from faith offer no evidence, but only supposition, unsubstantiated conjecture and wishful thinking.

Like the primitive people who wrote the Bible, many of today's believers attribute agency to weather conditions, earthquakes, eruptions, tsunamis and floods, seeing God's hand and malevolent intent behind the indifferent and indiscriminate forces of nature. Let's enjoy a few examples:

Hurricane Katrina struck New Orleans in 2006 because God needed to express his displeasure at legalised abortion (Pat Robertson);

The 2010 earthquake in Haiti, which killed almost a quarter of a million people, was punishment for an 18th century pact Haitians had forged with the devil (Robertson again);

The eruption of a volcano in Iceland in 2010, and the consequent disruption to air travel, was a 'menacing sign of God' because of Europe's continuing abandonment of its 'Christian heritage' (Association of Orthodox Experts in Moscow);

Floods in Queensland in 2011 were an attempt by God to 'humble Australia and bring her down on her knees. As she has taken pride in my blessing, and man has taken the glory and not given it to Me' (the ungrammatical *Catch the Fire Ministries);*

The earthquake which struck Christchurch in early 2011 was a punishment directly from God for New Zealanders' tolerance of gay people (US-based ChristchurchQuake.Net).

Flocks of birds that fell to the ground in Arkansas in 2011 were 'God's answer' to America's 'breaking restraints with scripture', whatever that might mean. (Seems to have something to do with those pesky homosexuals again but at least God's only taking it out on blackbirds this time. So says Christian 'prophet' Cindy Jacobs)

The Japanese earthquake and tsunami, in March 2011, were so that God could break 'the grip of idolatry' in that country (mad Cindy Jacobs again).

The arrested development of these Christians, and the subsequent immaturity of their 'reasoning', is a direct consequence of faith that, without the need for evidence, 'knows' the Lord's will and how he likes to act. As the sign outside the bizarrely named 'Victory Holiness Tabernacle Church' says: 'if your faith is big enough, facts don't count': in other words, believe what you want and, as long as you attribute it to God and believe it sincerely, it doesn't matter if it has no basis in reality. This is not a caricature of Christian faith but exactly how its early founders defined it. In John 20.29 they have Jesus say, 'blessed are those who have not seen and yet have come to believe', while the writer of the letter to the Hebrews, as we have just seen, insists that 'faith is... the conviction of things not seen' (Hebrews 11.1).

'Things' that are 'not seen' are, of course, no different from things that are non-existent, but remarkably, when faith and evidence collide, reality is made to concede. A positive virtue is made out of blindly adhering to superstitions that conflict with science and reason, so that the *Mountain Retreat* website can say with pride:

> *How do we know that the world was not created by evolution as it may seem? By faith! And we needed no scientist to convince us of that by their (supposed) scientific data. We had something far more reliable. The Word of God.*

But it isn't just in Christian perspectives on creation and evolution that the conflict between faith and science is revealed: the triumph of faith over evidence and reason is apparent in every tenet of

Christianity. To be a Christian you *must* accept through faith, and contrary to the evidence, that:
- there is a reality above and beyond nature wherein exist angels, archangels, devils, demons, principalities (whatever they are), spirits (holy and otherwise) and God himself;
- virgins can conceive and give birth;
- a man who died 2000 years ago is still alive;
- this man could, when he lived, defy gravity; control the weather; sweat blood; reanimate corpses (his own included); pass through solid objects and project himself into space;
- an intangible part of everyone survives death;
- people who have died will live again in an improved copy of the body they had when alive;
- God reversed the laws on which the universe operates to make all of this possible, because he wanted to sacrifice a part of himself to himself;
- he can do this because he is God;
- he prompted men to explain his plan in a special book;
- all you have to do to live forever is believe that every word of this book is true.

In addition to 'essential' beliefs like these, there are more still that Christians choose to accept on faith (as we are seeing in this section of this book), add-ons that Christians are invited to see as the underpinning of 'important' doctrines. While not absolutely crucial, they are recommended as a means of adhering to (uncorroborated) biblical truth. Consequently, we find Christians who believe that:
- God created the universe 6,000 years ago (because this is the time-scale that can be calculated from the Bible's genealogies);
- dinosaurs and humans co-existed (because this must be the

case if the creation stories in Genesis are literally true);

- reality can be changed by the simple expedient of asking God to change it (prayer);
- God directly controls the weather (omnipotence/divine irritability);
- Jesus is coming back - with a selection of scenarios available to true believers about what this will be like (the second coming);
- all unbelievers will be consigned to hell / oblivion / annihilation: again, take your pick (judgement).

There is not one scrap of evidence outside the special book that any of these items of faith are true. None is verifiable, and consequently none has ever been verified (accounts written interdependently fifty years after the alleged miracle-man lived don't count). There is, on the other hand, overwhelming evidence that virgins don't conceive; that there is no agency behind the weather and natural disasters; that nothing of an individual's self survives death and that dead bodies stay dead. This has always been the case and always will be. It was how nature operated two thousand years ago when all of the 'essential' items of faith, invented by the kinds of mind that believed earthquakes and floods were deliberate acts of God, were gaining currency.

Faith, then, is the capacity to believe any old mumbo-jumbo and to cling to it as truth for no other reason than a confused and very human book claims it is. As a way of knowing about the universe, life and the human condition, however, faith can never, has never and will never compete with science and evidential reasoning. If any real evidence existed for the incredible claims of Christianity there would be no need for faith; the evidence would be sufficient. But, as Sam Harris puts it, 'faith is generally nothing more than the permission religious people give one another to believe things strongly without evidence'. It is what is left when either there is no evidence or that which there is comprehensively refutes the claims of religion. Faith is the flimsy foundation of a house built on sand.

Reason, on the other hand, is regarded by many Christians as the path to self-delusion: they trust not, as Proverbs 3.5 tells them, in their own understanding. Presbyterian minister Tim Keller, who seems to imagine himself a latter-day C. S. Lewis, takes a different view of our rationality. While the Bible downplays human reasoning, Tim asserts that our cognitive faculties are God-given, telling us in the punnily titled *The Reason For God*, that human reasoning makes no sense if it is 'merely' the product of evolution. This is because a random and undirected process cannot produce a reliable rationality on its own. He is not entirely clear why this should be the case; evolution has, after all, led to other distinctly human characteristics on which we regularly depend, imperfect though they may be: language, memory, social bonding and creativity among them. However, having singled out reason, and having dismissed evolution as its cause, Keller jumps to the conclusion that the human capacity to think must come from God and is a 'clue', planted in every human being, to his existence. He marvels that

> *those who argue against the existence of God go right on using induction, language and their cognitive faculties, all of which make far more sense in a universe in which God has created and supports them all by his power.*

Evidently it is unreasonable of those who don't subscribe to a belief in God to continue to use his gifts of cognition and language (suddenly subpoenaed to appear in the case for the defence): they should abandon them immediately! And you'd be right if you think Keller's argument is entirely circular, one that presupposes its conclusion from the start: reason demonstrates that God exists, therefore God must have created reason, which demonstrates God exists, who must therefore have created reason... and so on, *ad infinitum*. If this the best our God-given critical faculties can manage then the case that they are the product of a undirected, random process (which, incidentally, evolution isn't) is entirely persuasive. Following Keller's argument to its logical conclusion, it has to be the case that the human capacity for unbounded *ir*rationality must be a 'clue' to the non-existence of the Christian God. What Keller demonstrates is that reason and induction, while superior in every way to faith, are only as secure as the premise from which they proceed. Get that wrong, by basing it on an insufficiency of evidence, and our cognitive faculties lead us further down the blind alleys of faith... or corridors if we're sticking to a house metaphor.

Once wandering confidently but blindly through these corridors, it's very easy for the believer to convince himself that the irrationality that's taken him there is the absolute truth and that this truth needs defending from the 'man-centred' philosophies and heresies that threaten his false security. He is compelled to declare to the ever-contracting walls of his make-shift reality, 'there's only one Truth: mine!'

You may not know it but there are 'false apostles and doctrines of demons' (1 Timothy 4.1) lurking everywhere, ready to delude gullible Christians (and aren't they all?) and lead them into heresy, jeopardising their eternal salvation. If you're an evangelical, the most demonically-inspired stumbling block is Roman Catholicism. If you're a Catholic, Pentecostals are likely to be your *bête noire*. Charismatic, Red Letter and Emergent Church Christians, meanwhile, think that each of the others hasn't got it quite right, or, indeed, has it completely wrong. In fact, Christians spend much of their time defaming variations of Christian doctrine that they don't themselves happen to believe in. To the outsider, all Christian groups, from evangelicals and Roman Catholics, to Dominionists and Baptists, differ very little. They all believe fantastic, unsubstantiated ideas so that their arguments between themselves are no different from disputes about whether the tooth-fairy wears a pink dress or a green one. They don't seem to realise that it's irrelevant what she wears when she doesn't exist. All of them, as we've seen, claim that their own preferred doctrines are based on 'inerrant' scripture, demonstrating just how imprecise and wide-open to interpretation 'God's Word' is.

The one thing that all dissenting groups do seem implicitly to agree on, however, is that the more demanding and unpalatable aspects of Jesus' teaching should be ignored. Instead of trashing each other, Christians might set about selling all they have and giving to the poor, just like their leader told them to. That, and not petty doctrinal squabbles loosely based on books of the Bible we know to be forged, would be real Christian living.

In 2010, when extremist American Pastor Terry Jones originally sought to burn copies of the Qur'an, Tony Blair, inter-faith advocate and UN envoy to the Middle East declared in an interview on the UK's Channel 4 news that Jones's proposal, 'is not something that represents any proper, true Christian thought'. But what does this mean? That Jones is not a true Christian? He believes, after all, that Jesus is his saviour, the Bible is the inerrant word of God and the Holy Spirit prompts him to live a radical lifestyle. And so does Blair. How, therefore, is Jones's Christian 'thought' any less representative of 'true' Christianity than Blair's, who was, after all, the Christian who, together with another high-powered true-believer, jointly instigated the Iraq war? Aren't Jones and Blair extremists in their own right, using their faith, as they both have, to support their own radical actions?

Believers who regard themselves as more liberal, less reactionary, frequently try to distance themselves from those of their own faith who embrace its more extreme ideology. However, as Sam Harris points out in *The End of Faith*, moderate belief is the medium in which extremist faith foments. If there were no 'respectable' Christianity, there would be no Terry Jones, no Westboro Baptist church (motto: 'God Hates Fags'), no Harold Camping, no Mormonism and no fundamentalist sects. All of these are a part of Christianity in exactly the same way that Episcopalians and Anglicans are; indeed Jones, Phelps and other extremists argue that they are *more* representative of Jesus' radicalism and 'Christian thought' than mainstream churches. They are, they would say, the only *true* believers. This because one man's essential beliefs are another's extremism, one believer's moderation another's apostasy. Faith allows any belief at all, without any substantiation or evidence, apart from 'God's word', which supports whatever and whichever absurdities innumerable Christian groups decide must be true.

Remarkably, given the tenuous nature of everything they believe, Christians insist they have a right to 'live according to conscience'.

What this usually means is that they see it as their God-given right to withdraw from serving or acknowledging the rights of fellow human-beings.

By the same principle, everyone else also has the right to live according to their own consciences. If we arrange society so that we don't have to help, provide a service or care for those whose lifestyles or beliefs are contrary to our own, we end up with a society that operates only on exclusion. The hotel owners who exclude homosexual couples will be matched by gay hotel owners who don't like Christians; Muslim shopkeepers who object to non-Muslims won't have to serve them; vegan restaurateurs will, on principle, bar meat-eaters; atheist surgeons will be able to deny treatment to the religious. Such a society could not function because we would all, at some point, be excluded, while at others we would be those doing the excluding. Conscience-based rejection of others, taken to its logical conclusion, could only lead to the breakdown of civilised living, with its reliance on interdependency and mutual cooperation. There is nothing biblical about living according to 'principles' that demand others be ostracised. On the contrary, Jesus demands that his followers give unconditionally to anyone and everyone who asks.

A comment posted on the UK *Guardian* newspaper's web-site following the case of the Relate counsellor who refused to help homosexual couples neatly summarises the issue:

> *Gay men and women have been giving good service to bigots for years. We've been nursing you through your illnesses, clipping your tickets, treating your diseases, teaching your kids, entertaining you on telly, delivering your mail, waiting on your table, shooting your enemies and cooking your dinner; all this time without ever claiming the "right" not to serve you if you don't happen to approve of us. It's time some straights grew up and stopped whining.*

Christians who claim they have a right to reject and exclude others 'according to conscience' would do well to consider how they would react if 'principled' gays, Muslims and atheists refused *them* the services they sometimes feel 'conscience bound' to refuse others. What cries of 'persecution' there would be then!

Oh wait! There already are...

In Western democracies Christians are regularly hauled from their beds in the middle of the night and put on trial for their faith. They are systematically rounded up at prayer meetings to be fed to wild beasts in arenas, with scoffing atheists looking on with relish (that little bit of pickle on the side). They are often forced to watch as their loved ones are torn limb from limb before being crucified themselves. Even when not subject to such atrocities, they are barred from worshipping publicly and from studying at the most respectable universities. They are frequently sacked from their jobs and deprived of their livelihoods, simply because they are Christians.

Hang on. This can't be right.

I interrupt this analysis of how difficult it is to be a Christian in the western world today with a much needed dose of reality. While Christians regularly claim persecution, there is no evidence whatsoever that in the civilised world they are subject to it. They misapply the term knowingly to the mild offence that they increasingly choose to take. In the distant past some Christians experienced persecution of the sort described (while some inflicted it on others), but today it seems that all that is needed is to irritate Christians - by questioning their views and practices or by challenging their prejudices and partialities - and they will immediately cry 'persecution!'. They are evidently not as resilient as those who preceded them.

The Bible tells them to endure persecutions, and more than this, to regard themselves as 'blessed' when persecutions come their way. So says Jesus in Matthew 5.11: 'blessed are you when people revile you and persecute you and utter all kinds of evil against you falsely on my account'. But today's Christians have no time for this kind of wishy-washy sentiment. Instead, they'll write to the newspapers about how badly they are treated and appear on TV bemoaning their lot. They also, naturally, reserve the right to 'persecute' others, and then to claim persecution themselves when anyone tries to stop them (it is their right, after all).

In the USA, Christians comprise 77% of the population. They have significant influence over both the policies of their country – all but one representative in the senate profess to be Christians - and the social standing of its citizens (you're nobody if you don't profess belief). Their churches enjoy tax-free status. Yet they cast themselves as the oppressed minority, delusionally lamenting the gradual stripping away of their 'religious liberties'. This is all hyper-sensitivity on their part: basing one's life on a book of myths and dubious morality is bound to make them insecure.

While they're behaving shamefully towards others, by denying them services or claiming oppression or abusing children, believers console themselves with the excuse that, when all is said and done, they are 'not perfect, just forgiven'. This decidedly unscriptural idea is endorsed on bumper stickers, in Christian songs and by preachers.

In one respect they are right: Christians are certainly not perfect; they are no better than the rest of us, which is what the slogan alludes to. It is an implicit admission from Christians that their chosen path is too hard, that even with Jesus' assistance, even with his Holy Spirit living in them, they are still unable to be what he commands them to be: 'perfect, as your heavenly Father is perfect' (Matthew 5.48). Disappointingly for those believers who would have it that what Jesus really means is that one day they will become perfect once the Holy Spirit has worked his wonders in them or when Christ returns or in the after-life, Jesus says nothing of the sort. In fact he spells out very clearly how to 'be perfect': don't resist evil-doers, go the extra mile, love your enemies, pray for those who persecute you (Matthew 5.38-48, previously quoted in full).

This recipe for perfection isn't difficult to understand, though it is, as we have seen, rather more difficult to act out. Jesus did not, however, regard it as impossible - 'my yoke is easy' he says in

Matthew 11.30 - and saw it as part of his radical agenda for ushering in the new Kingdom. By their own admission – 'not perfect, just forgiven', remember - most Christians choose not to act in the ways prescribed by their Lord that would make them perfect. Throughout this book we have considered instances where they have the opportunity to behave as Jesus instructs them, but don't. They sue instead of praying for enemies; they resist those they believe to be evil; they slander those who oppose them; they rarely turn the other cheek. These injunctions are, incidentally, why a 'Christian country' is an impossibility; to truly follow Jesus as a state and as an individual is never to defend oneself, never to retaliate, never to resist, but instead to love one's enemies. Jesus may not have regarded such ways of behaving as impossible, but they are, and Christians know it. Even though Paul repeats the command to be perfect (2 Corinthians 13:11) and a later New Testament writer suggests, somewhat preposterously, that 'those who have been born of God do not sin, because God's seed abides in them; they cannot sin, because they have been born of God' (1John 3.9), Christians prefer the easy, bumper-sticker spirituality of being forgiven, but decidedly imperfect.

With easy spirituality comes another self-generated belief with little basis in scripture: the assurance that God showers his blessings on his children. As far as its possible to tell with such a nebulous notion, Christians seem to see God's blessings as a kind of free-floating euphoria that he invariably bestows when their emotions are already worked up to excess.

As it happens, the New Testament uses the plural 'blessings' only once, in the letter to the Ephesians (1:3), forged in Paul's name. The Bible's idea of blessing, singular, is nothing like the feel-good factor that Christians covet, and while they may believe that their religion exists for the sole purpose of providing them with benefits and blessings, it doesn't. Not according to Jesus and not according to Paul. That's because being a follower of Jesus is not about absorbing all the wonderful feelings that God the Holy Spirit is prepared to infuse you with. It's not about your personal enjoyment of salvation, your individual holiness or even your entitlement to eternal life. It is about serving, sacrificing yourself, taking up the cross, adopting an extreme morality, forgiving to excess, all of which are directed outwards, not inwards. Being 'blessed', the term most commonly used by Jesus and other New Testament luminaries, is the acknowledgement God gives to those who serve others in the way Jesus says must be the hallmark of his followers. The best anyone can hope for, if Matthew 25.23 is to be believed, is that he'll say 'well done, good and trustworthy slave' on judgement day, which is hardly going to lead to being 'slain in the spirit'. The direction of Christian belief has changed since the writer of Acts decided that Jesus said, 'it is more blessed to give than to receive' (Acts 20.35). Christians now look in, not out; to the self, rather than to others: *bless me, Lord, bless me*.

There is, moreover, far more in the New Testament about Christ-followers meeting with suffering than with blessing. Paul warns the church in Rome, and by extension other believers, that God will expect them to suffer for their faith in exchange for the glory they're 'about' to receive on his return (Romans 8.18 etc). While God's children today feign suffering (see above), there is no evidence in the real world that he blesses them any more than the followers of other gods, or, indeed, the bastard offspring of this world: the followers of religions with no gods, agnostics, non-believers and atheists. They all experience the joys, pain, deprivations, rewards and eventual extinction of this life in equal measure. It could even be argued that those who originally fell into the hands of the 'living God', the Jewish people, have had a harder time of it than any other group aligned, or otherwise, with this particular capricious deity. The wanderings, dispersions, persecutions (often at the hands of Christians), pogroms and the holocaust exemplify the 'blessings' he has bestowed upon them. Perhaps Christians would be well advised to avoid their God's favour - he is the same God who used to bless the Jews, after all - if this is what it amounts to.

If not emotional euphoria, then perhaps the 'blessings' God bestows on his children are best seen as reassurance – faith as a comfort blanket for those who have it: 'blessed assurance, Jesus is mine' as Phoebe Knapp's hymn declares, 'I in my Savior am happy and blest'.

This is the line (without the Victorian sentimentality) taken by BBC journalist John Humphreys in his 2007 book *In God We Doubt*. He argues that those who experience calamity and tragedy in life, like the death of a child, need to be able to find solace in their faith. For that reason alone, he concludes, faith should be preserved and should enjoy immunity from criticism. There is much that is problematic with this argument, not least that it can serve as justification for anything that provides succour for troubled people, from astrology, healing crystals, homeopathy, recreational drug use and psychosis, to belief in any deity besides the Christian God. That we should protect and avoid criticising anything that feels nice, and might, if we shut off our critical faculties, be regarded as harmless, is patently absurd. Humphreys fails to make the case that Christian faith is different in kind, or even degree, from all of these other comfort blankets. One might expect that he would at least try to separate belief in Yahweh 2.0 (the New Testament version) from other gods – Allah, Krishna, Ahura Mazda, even the intolerant Yahweh 1.0 - but he doesn't, so perhaps the flavour of god is irrelevant so long as appeals to it provide reassurance.

Unfortunately, it is not quite so simple, as Humphreys also fails to take into account Christian doctrine; it isn't sufficient simply to call on God, Jesus or the Holy Spirit unless you are a fully-fledged born-from-above believer with the right doctrine under your belt. If you're not, the Christian God is of no comfort at all – he's going to send you to Hell because, whatever difficulties you are experiencing in this life, you are so corrupted with sin, he can't stand the sight of you (Psalm 5.5, John 3.36). I don't know about you, but I don't find that tremendously comforting.

It's a different matter, however, if you are one of his own. Then he'll expect that you give your life to him in its entirety, work tirelessly for his Kingdom, give away all you have, love your enemies and find him at work in all the deprivations of life (Mark 10.29-30). What he won't be, is sympathetic towards your bereavement: Jesus makes it perfectly clear, in Matthew 8.22, that all he is interested in is that you follow him; the dead, he says, can 'bury their own dead'.

Perhaps the special offer of eternal life is enough to tip the balance for you; maybe the comfort comes from believing that you and your loved ones will live again either in God's new Kingdom (long overdue) or in Heaven (not on offer). The evidence is so strongly against either of these scenarios – not to mention the fact that the dead always seem to stay dead - that the only comfort they provide is the result of wishful thinking. That being so, one placebo is as good as another, and if it's comfort you're after, you might be better off with the crystals.

Even as time-after-time they come away empty-handed, Christians remain undeterred in their manufactured thankfulness. More than this, with the sanctimonious smugness that only from religious possess, they see themselves as the only ones who are even capable of being thankful. In a pitifully unfunny cartoon on the *Answers In Genesis* web-site, a Christian replete in 'Ichthus' fish t-shirt (like the ones early Christians wore in the catacombs) raises his arms heavenward and declares 'God created me. I give thanks to God'. Next to him, wearing a Darwin fish with legs, his atheist counterpart can only whimper, 'I evolved from nothing. I give thanks to...'.

Coming from 'nothing', the cartoon implies, leaves the atheist with nothing to be thankful either for or to. Unsurprisingly, it is wrong on so many levels:

- thanking a non-existent being does not make that being real;
- even if it did, just what do Christians suppose their God created the physical universe from? (Clue: from nothing);
- not having a God to thank does not mean there is no-one to thank;
- the absence of a deity does not mean one can't be thankful *for* life and its benefits.

Because I've grown up, I don't thank Santa Claus for my Christmas presents. Rather, I thank those people who made and bought them for me. In the same way, I have no need to thank another figment of the imagination for the other gifts of life. I thank my parents, who did not create me from nothing, for my life. When I need to, I thank the other human beings who grow my food, contribute to my good health, treat me when I'm ill, make possible my comfortable life and love me. While perhaps I should, I don't spend all of my time expressing my gratitude to these others. Sometimes I am simply grateful *for* what life provides, without needing to direct that thanks to anyone in particular. When I slip between cool sheets on a hot summer's night, I don't make a point of getting up again to tweet my thanks to the manufacturer of my bed, to the companies that made the sheets and the detergent in which they're washed, nor to myself for doing such a splendid job of laundering them and putting them on the bed. Instead, I'm grateful *for* the wonderful cooling sensation they provide; my gratitude doesn't need to be directed *to* anyone, however much they've contributed to the experience. And so it is, for the non-believer, with the rest of life: there is much to be thankful for and our gratitude is no less authentic because it is not directed towards a God. Perhaps it is more real because it isn't.

Meanwhile, if Christians are so grateful to their God for making them, why are they so disparaging about this life: why do they claim with Paul that they count it as nothing?; why do they look on it with disdain, believing it is infected by sin? Why do they say it is merely a trial run for the supposed life to come? These are strange ways of expressing gratitude. As Richard Dawkins reminds believers: 'be thankful that you have a life, and forsake your vain and presumptuous desire for a second one'. This is the only life we have and that is reason enough to be grateful for it. Knowing this makes atheists among the most genuinely appreciative and grateful people on the planet.

Saving the best till (almost) last, we come to one of the most beloved of Christian delusions, that they should 'hate the sin but love the sinner'. Where in the Bible, we might ask them, can we find this popular sound-byte? Where do Jesus and Paul teach that Christians should love other people while demonstrating contempt for their behaviour? They don't, it won't surprise you to hear, anywhere. In the absence of any such directive from either their Lord or the creator of their spiritualised religion, Christians like to claim that the aphorism nonetheless encapsulates a principle central to the Bible's teaching. The difficulty with this idea, however, is that seeing a distinction between the individual and his or her behaviour is a strikingly modern and post-Freudian thing to do.

In the ancient world, a person *was* his behaviour. This view of humanity is the one that pervades the Bible because in the ancient world that is how humans viewed themselves: psychology hadn't been invented and people's motives were not a consideration. Individuals were what they did and were not detachable from their actions. Hence, the psalmist says of God: 'you hate all evildoers. You destroy those who speak lies; the Lord abhors the bloodthirsty and deceitful' (Psalms 5.5-6) without there being any distinction between the doing of evil and the doers thereof. Jesus' perspective is the same: people don't just *behave* well or badly, justly or unjustly, they *are* evil or good, just or unjust. So when he says in Matthew 5.45, '(God) makes his sun rise on the evil and on the good, and sends rain on the righteous and on the unrighteous', he makes no distinction between people and their behaviour but speaks of them as one and the same.

Paul's message too is not about isolating individuals' sin and pointing it out to them so that it can be excised, like a surgeon removes a malignant growth; he sees sin as an inherent part of human nature. Redemption, in Paul's theology, is not the result of dealing with one's sinful behaviour – let alone pointing out other people's - but by taking God up on his offer to overlook humanity's essential flaw in those who embrace the atonement (Romans 3.21-26). To be sure, Paul expected that the 'justified' believer would, because of their new standing with God, be 'a new creation' and no longer 'enslaved' to their inherent sinfulness (Romans 6.6 and 2 Corinthians 5.17-21). That his expectations were frequently dashed in this respect is evident in his surviving letters, particularly those to the Corinthians and the Galatians. You might think that this was clear enough demonstration his ideas were hopelessly adrift; but no, he presses on in the same vein in all of his letters and in so doing demonstrates consistently, though inadvertently, that 'loving the sinner while hating the sin' is not a biblical idea, not even in principle.

In practice, modern believers apply the maxim almost exclusively to homosexuals, whom they claim to love while hating their expression of their sexuality. That they apply it only to gay people is evident when you consider that Christians don't shout about their 'love' for those who gossip, while condemning their gossiping, nor, these days, for those who divorce, while demonising the principle of divorce. Some Christians don't accept the scientific consensus that homosexuality is likely to be the result of genetic factors and embryonic development, making homosexuality, as geneticist Matt Ridley puts it, 'an early, probably prenatal and irreversible preference".

Other Christians are of the opinion that whether homosexuality is predetermined or not is irrelevant; for these believers, being homosexual is a sin of the worst sort, regardless of cause, because it is 'a sin against the body' (1Corinthians 6:18). Even to marginally more liberal Christian groups, such as *Got Questions?Org* (tag-line - 'the Bible has the answers: we'll find them for you'), a homosexual disposition is the same as being congenitally prone to violence and rage. Still other Christian groups accept that homosexual people can't help being gay, but believe that they should resist acting on their sexual preference. This is the position assumed by *Exodus International*, a 'ministry' designed to rescue people from homosexuality, whose mission statement declares that it

> *...upholds heterosexuality as God's creative intent for humanity, and subsequently views homosexual expression as outside of God's will. As such, homosexual attraction and impulses – while not inherently sinful in themselves – are merely one of many human temptations reflective of our fallen nature. However, we affirm that choosing to resolve these tendencies through homosexual behaviour, taking on a homosexual identity, and involvement in the*

homosexual lifestyle is considered destructive, as it distorts God's intent for the individual and is thus sinful.

The Christian view is that gay people should forego all sexual fulfilment in their lives and deny themselves loving relationships, simply because these would, of necessity, be with a person of the same sex. While *Exodus* and those who subscribe to a similar philosophy might consider this to reflect the love of Christ, it is about as loving as an insistence that Christians may believe whatever they like but must never act upon it - church attendance, worship, hymn singing, prayer meetings and overt expressions of faith all disallowed. It is far more extreme, however, to deny individuals something as integral to their identity as their sexuality, than it is to suppress the expression of a set of beliefs. Being a Christian is, in spite of what Calvinists say, a choice, and perhaps something of an unnatural one at that.

The problem is that self-aggrandised believers see themselves as being called upon to uphold God's standards. They are, they are convinced, the only ones capable of challenging the oceans of immorality they see all around them. According to Lee Grady of *Charisma* magazine, Christians 'are called to confront sin in a spirit of love and honesty'.

In fact, this belief contains three errors:
   i) that Christians have a right to uphold God's standards by 'confronting' and judging the behaviour of others;
   ii) that God himself gives them this right;
   iii) that provided it is done in 'love and honesty', whether it actually is or not, Christians can say what they want about and to other people.

Let's have a look at each of these errors in turn:

Error number one: Christians have a right to uphold God's standards by 'confronting' and judging the behaviour of others.

If Christians are to be believed, the creator of heaven and earth - and the rest of the universe presumably - who knows all there is to know and is possessed of all power, needs flawed and feeble human beings, namely Christians themselves, to do his dirty work for him. Even those who claim that natural disasters are sent from God as warnings about or punishment for human sinfulness, maintain that he needs *them* to make this clear to humanity. As we shall see, these heralds of misfortune are particularly keen to show us just how hot and bothered the Almighty becomes about what human beings do without their clothes on. Still, if his obedient servants tell us that this is the way he's arranged it, then who are we to argue. We might, however, be just a little bit suspicious about how very human it all seems.

The only 'sin' Jesus confronts directly in the gospels is that of religious leaders. He is explicit otherwise about not judging others, saying 'do not judge, so that you may not be judged' (Matthew 7.1). Paul puts it even more strongly in Romans 2.1-3:

> *Therefore you have no excuse, whoever you are, when you judge others; for in passing judgement on another you condemn yourself, because you, the judge, are doing the very same things. You say, 'We know that God's judgement on those who do such things is in accordance with truth'. Do you imagine, whoever you are, that when you judge those who do such things and yet do them yourself, you will escape the judgement of God?*

And in 1 Corinthians 5.12-13 he asks :

> *For what have I to do with judging those outside (the church)? Is it not those who are inside that you are to judge? God will judge those outside.*

These warnings couldn't be clearer and yet Christians continue to see it as their duty to call out others' sins, failing to recognise that there is no difference between doing this and passing judgement. Naming and shaming is not a strategy Jesus used in calling people to him. The 'good news' he announced was about the coming of the Kingdom and the need to be ready for it. It was the encounter with Jesus himself and with this good news that prompted people to sign up to his movement, not the outright condemnation of their supposed shortcomings. As Tom Wright puts it in *Jesus and the Victory of God*, 'the point about Jesus' welcome to 'sinners' was that he was declaring, on his own authority, that anyone who trusted in him and his Kingdom-announcement was within the Kingdom'. Yet, in spite of his 'welcoming' of prostitutes, tax collectors, terrorists and other transgressors, the gospels record none of the confrontation and judgement that today's Christians feel it their right to exercise.

Error number two: God gives Christians the right to say what they want to others.

Without exception, Christian groups who rant and rave about others' behaviour, falling standards, false teaching and God's wrath claim that the Lord tells them do it and point to at least one Bible verse, often from the Old Testament, where he seems to do so. Westboro Baptist Church, for example, goes for half of Ezekiel 33.7: 'whenever you hear a word from my mouth, you shall give them warning from me', while *Christian Voice* goes for a KJV rendering of Psalm 94.16: 'who will rise up for me against the evil doers, or who will stand up for me against the workers of iniquity?'

You just can't argue with God - or your own interpretation of a verse of scripture taken out of context. This allows Christians to believe they 'stand for God' and are uniquely called to pronounce his judgement on others. Through Bible verses they align themselves with prophets of the Old Testament who, when the ancient Israelites were experiencing famine or defeat at the hands of their enemies, thundered that this could only be a punishment from the Lord, deserved because of sinful behaviour. Unfortunately for those still stuck in this kind of primitive mind-set today, the world does not work in this way. While human behaviour can and does affect our surroundings, the results are not punishments or warnings from God, but measurable cause-and-effect consequences. The universe, while indifferent to human needs and desires, is equally indifferent to human 'sin'. Christians' authority for what they say, therefore, comes from a seriously flawed understanding of a flawed book written, as we keep seeing, not by God, but by fallible human beings with an understanding of life and the universe even more primitive than their own.

Error number 3: provided it is done in 'love and honesty', whether it actually is or not, Christians can say what they want about and to other people.

According to their website, the Westboro Baptist Church is compelled by God to tell the world that he hates 'fags', Barrack Obama and America, while deserving praise for 9/11, dead soldiers and every natural disaster. The Bible warns, they say, of behaviour that will bring down God's wrath not only on individuals but on cities and entire nations (even Jesus likes this idea: see his rant in Luke 10:12-15). They therefore regard it as their Christian duty to make others aware of the danger they believe them to be in, by condemning their 'fag-enabler' country and picketing the funerals of soldiers who defend it, calling this their 'love crusade'.

Other Christian groups, while criticising Westboro's activities for being unpalatably un-Christian, are in no position either to condemn or distance themselves from the Westboro church. The Phelps clan do only what other Christian groups claim in principle, that because Bible says it, they are, in honesty and love, compelled to proclaim it. This same biblically-based fascism is an unmistakable component of *Apprising Ministries, Christian Voice* and any Christian who takes others to task for their beliefs, behaviour or lifestyle ('lifestyle' is always synonymous with sin in Christian-speak). Ken Silva of Connecticut River Baptist Church and the *Apprising Matters* website demonstrates how to use 'love' to bludgeon others:

> *...it's because I love LGBT people, for whom Christ died, that I will continue to tell them the truth. You need to understand that the truth is, unrepentant men and women continuing to openly commit sexual immorality as they live the sinful lifestyle of having sexual relations with another of the same sex, are still imprisoned by their sin. Those who affirm these dear souls in their sin are actually withholding the freeing power of God's Gospel from them. And by*

> *doing, despite all their pious blather about love, the fact remains they leave LGBT people locked away in the chains and darkness of their own personal prison cell of sin.*

Loved by Christians almost as much as LGBT people are atheists and 'Darwinists'. Richard Dawkins, as an atheist and evolutionist, receives a good deal of Christian love in response to his measured comments about evolution and religion. Some examples from his website sufficiently demonstrate, without much more comment from me, how Christians go about 'confronting' individuals with views they don't care for, in that famous 'spirit of love and honesty':

> *Dawkins, you atheist piece of trash. You will twist any truth into atheist propaganda. I am sure this is another distortion of the truth to satisfy your atheist agenda. You may think you are nothing more than just future wormfood but I have life everlasting thanks to the saving grace of Jesus Christ!*

> *you suck.. go burn in hell.. Satan Will Enjoy torturing you.. what happened mum didnt pay enough attention to you so you decided to rebel.. I hope for your own sake you see your grave mistake and repent.. God Dwells among as everyday.. you are the spawn of evil.*

> *I hope you die slowly and you fucking burn in hell! You dammed blasfemy!!! Right now you are rotting on the inside... But you must now (sic) that there is indeed a God! A great god! And he will forgive you if you regret from your fucking behavior. And you should realise thatyour entire life has been a delusion...and that right now your destiny is all fucked up! Fucking atheist!!!!!!!!!!!*

Evidently becoming 'a new creature in God' doesn't do anything for spelling, grammar or punctuation, nor for one's understanding of anatomy. As a final exhibit, here's Christian love being expressed towards the late Christopher Hitchens, after he was diagnosed with cancer of the oesophagus:

> *Who else feels Christopher Hitchens getting terminal throat cancer [sic] was God's revenge for him using his voice to blaspheme him? Atheists like to ignore FACTS. They like to act like everything is a "coincidence". Really? It's just a "coincidence" [that] out of any part of his body, Christopher Hitchens got cancer in the one part of his body he used for blasphemy? Yea, keep believing that Atheists. He's going to writhe in agony and pain and wither away to nothing and then die a horrible agonizing death, and THEN comes the real fun, when he's sent to HELLFIRE forever to be tortured and set afire.*

Christians have no right, God-given or otherwise, to berate others for their behaviour when their own behaviour is frequently indistinguishable from the worst of any heathen. Even if it were considerably better than that of non-believers, Christians would still have no grounds for judging their fellows: the Bible does not support their doing so, telling them unequivocally not to. Even when they disregard these warnings and engage in 'confrontation' of sin, they are as likely to do it in a 'spirit' of superciliousness, animosity and abuse, as in 'love and honesty'.

It all comes down to Christians' conviction that they, and they alone, know God's will and represent it on Earth. In a certain sense they are right because they share God's views on a range of issues only because the Bible is the product of prejudiced human beings, so, *ipso facto,* today's believers readily find their prejudices supported in his 'Word'. In their long and colourful history, Christians have reflected his will on slavery (he approves), women (he doesn't), Jews (he's gone off them), and heretics (he prefers them burnt).

Significantly, however, as western society has become generally more liberal and tolerant, so have Christian perspectives evolved to become more moderate. Most believers don't now subscribe to these former, abhorrent views, even though they claim that the

Bible and God's will remain constant. In spite of these significant and welcome changes in their outlook, Christians still claim they know what God thinks and that they represent his will in the world today: they know with certainty that he doesn't now support slavery; he's warming towards women and the idea they might become ministers in his church; he wants Jews to have another chance to find Jesus; he's a lot more tolerant of heretics, or at least has overcome his pyromania. Harvard law professor, Alan Dershowitz, captures the inconsistency of Christian understanding of the 'unchanging' nature of God's truths:

> *Organised religion is always having to say you're sorry for misunderstanding God's will in the past. That has been the history of organised religions. We're sorry for the Crusades. We're sorry that we slaughtered babies and children in the name of Jesus. We're sorry for the Inquisition. We're sorry for the pogroms. We were wrong then. God didn't speak to us clearly then. But he speaks to us clearly today!*

How curious it is too that it is the most fallible and uncharitable of human beings whom he chooses to speak to most clearly.

Chapter 9
Living In A World Of Make Believe

Having jettisoned the unreasonable demands of their self-styled messiah and replaced them with equally absurd beliefs of their own making, Christians, unsurprisingly, find themselves dislocated - 'in this world but not of it', as early Christians came close to expressing it. Blinded by faith in their adopted world-view, they are unable to recognised that it is they who are misaligned. Rather, they accuse the rest of the world of being out of step with what they've decided God's 'Word' declares to be the truth about life, the universe and human behaviour. The reality in which the rest of us live has, as a result, to be made to conform to their fairy-tale model. In the following two chapters, we'll take a look at how such a perspective spawns a further set of beliefs about the world and at the contortions Christians go through to compel reality to fit their mythology.

They will tell you, if you let them, that Jesus' return and God's judgement of the earth are near. They know this because of the rising levels of immorality in the modern world: the spread and acceptance of homosexuality (especially), adultery, greed, persecution of Christians, 'false' doctrine and contempt for spiritual matters. The problem is that Christians have been claiming this sort of thing since New Testament days:

> *All that is in the world - the desire of the flesh, the desire of the eyes, the pride in riches - comes not from the Father but from the world. And the world and its desire are passing away, but those who do the will of God live for ever.* (1 John 16-17)

For Christians in intervening years, the decline of civilisation has been marked by events that bear no relation to the behaviours that today so convince believers they are living in the end times. In 1909, for example, the New York Sabbath Committee was certain it was neglect of the Sabbath that would bring about the collapse of culture: 'liberty's only secure foundation is the Holy Sabbath... Where there is no Christian Sabbath, there is no Christian morality; and without this free institutions can no longer be sustained'. As we have seen, many of today's Christians don't give two hoots about the Sabbath, and yet civilisation manages to struggle on. Several online sources, including the *Religious Tolerance* web-site, have lists of end times predicted by Christians down the millennia, none of which has so far materialised. There are 113 for the years since 2000 alone, with a respectable number for the years up to 2020. Using his Bible in a way that can only be described as imaginative, Harold Camping, self-styled prophet of *Family Radio Worldwide,* 'calculated' the date of Jesus' return as May 21st 2011. Those persuaded by this particular wing-nut (to use Richard Dawkins's term of endearment) sold their belongings and campaigned across America, warning of Christ's 'guaranteed' return on that day. Referring to passages from the Bible about the so-called 'rapture', Camping and his disciples announced that Jesus would proceed to draw Christians up into the sky to be with him, and would begin the judgement of non-believers.

I'm writing this post-May 21st and also after the rain-check date of October 21st 2011, and, to the surprise of no-one except perhaps Harold Camping and his dupes, Jesus was a no-show on both occasions. Predictably, all mention of the predicted, 'guaranteed' date disappeared from the organisation's web-site the day after May 21st and Camping himself also vanished for a while with the considerable amounts of money he made from his manufactured non-event. Other Christians dismissed Camping as a crank and a fraud, but only because he predicted a specific date for the rapture, not because they have any doubts that Jesus will one day return.

Almost all Christians share his fantasy that their Lord will be back to bring about the end of the world. Many believe it will be soon, as many always have: Jesus' early followers were convinced it would be in their lifetime, because Jesus himself had apparently said so. The significant number of Christians who today believe that the end is nigh are only cranks to the same extent that Jesus and Paul were cranks. Like Harold Camping, Jesus and Paul encouraged their contemporaries to see themselves as living in the end times, and also like him, they were completely wrong. What Camping and all other modern-day, would-be prophets are doing is continuing this tradition of preaching impending doom, failing to appreciate the irony of a 'tradition' about imminence. We need not be too disappointed, however, that neither May 21st nor October 21st 2011 was the beginning of the end: Jesus has pencilled in December 21st 2012 as the next, absolutely guaranteed date of his return, according to the *God's Final Witness* web-site. Start selling your possessions now.

Perhaps one day in the far future, Christians will be right about the timing of end of the world. This will not be because they've correctly predicted it from their torturous and non-literal reading of the Bible, but because, sooner or later, the destruction of the planet and one of their excessive number of absurd predictions may just happen to coincide. Personally, I doubt it. Human behaviour is what it is, but what it is not is a barometer of cosmic calamity.

Meanwhile, the Antichrist waits in the wings, as Pastor Rod Parsley phrases this widely-held belief, waiting to deceive the world as part of an elaborate apocalyptic scenario. Christians see the Anti-Christ as a charismatic but secretly demonic figure who appears just prior to the end of time, promising to solve all of the world's problems. Gaining everyone's trust – everyone, that is, except Christians-in-the-know, whom he persecutes – he becomes leader of the world and once worshipped globally, reveals his true nature as (gasp) the devil himself! This hocum is at the heart of the lucrative *Left Behind* series by Tim LeHaye, while recent real-life candidates for the role have included the Pope (along with most of his predecessors), George W. Bush, Barrack Obama and Prince Charles (yes, really). Unfortunately for Christians preoccupied with this fictional character, the Bible does not mention a definite article Antichrist anywhere. The term 'antichrist' is used, without a capital, only four times in the Bible, on all four occasions by the writer of the first two letters of John. Usually known as Prester John, this is not the same John who is credited with the fourth gospel, nor 'John the Divine', the creator of the nightmare psychedelia that is Revelation. As Henry Ansgar Kelly shows in

Satan: A Biography, what Prester John talks about is a spirit of heresy that is, for him, quite literally, anti-Christ. Those who have adopted and who practise this heresy are therefore 'antichrists', because they stand in opposition to what had become, by John's time, crucial doctrines about the mythical Christ figure. Seeing himself as living in the last days, here is what he says in 1 John 3.8-12:

> *Children, it is the last hour! As you have heard that antichrist is coming, so now many antichrists have come. From this we know that it is the last hour. They went out from us, but they did not belong to us; for if they had belonged to us, they would have remained with us. But by going out they made it plain that none of them belongs to us.*

It is likely that John is railing against gnostic believers who had begun to dispute that Christ had ever appeared in bodily form. He takes pains in his letters to define as clearly as he can for his readers what these anti-Christ people are like:

> *Many deceivers have gone out into the world, those who do not confess that Jesus Christ has come in the flesh; any such person is the deceiver and the antichrist!* (2 John 1.7, see also 1 John 2.12)

An 'antichrist' then is not a future world leader who will deceive everyone at the end of time. It is, rather, a believer of the late first century who has themselves been deceived and who now misleads others by preaching a wayward gospel. 'So where', asks Henry Asgar Kelly, 'did the infamous Antichrist come from?' Perhaps he can be found in Revelation, the final book of the Bible that Christians regard as revealing what the end times will be like (hence the book's alternate name of 'Apocalypse', from the Greek for 'unveiling'). But there is no mention at all of The Antichrist in Revelation; he does not appear and his name is not used. There is instead a creature called the Beast, which Christians often blithely assume is the same as The Antichrist, but who is actually a symbol of the Roman Empire and a caricature of the Emperor Nero.

While some Christians claim that the European Union is a reconstituted Roman Empire (governed from that centre of Roman power, Brussels) in a comical and futile attempt to make Revelation's macabre predictions apply to unrelated circumstances thousands of years in the future, it remains the case that the true Roman Empire disappeared 1600 years ago, while Nero has now been dead for two millennia. Predictably, there are Christians who believe he will be reincarnated as the end-time Antichrist, but in the real world neither he nor the long-defunct Empire can possibly be The Antichrist of a still future apocalypse.

In answering the question, therefore, about where the end-time Anti-Christ comes from we can only conclude with Henry Asgar Kelly that 'he is an invention of creative readers of Prester John's Epistles and John the Divine's Book of Revelation, who fuse two texts into one'. But when Revelation's Beast is no more than a long-dead Roman Emperor and an antichrist is simply a believer who has gone astray, this fusion produces nothing more than a emphatically non-biblical, fictional baddie. Naturally, this doesn't deter Christians from looking out for The Antichrist's impending appearance on the world stage, and 'waiting in the wings' turns out to be a particularly apposite metaphor for an unconvincing pantomime villain.

Poor Christians; they can't even get their own mythology straight.

PART FIVE: LOSING SIGHT OF TRUTH

Chapter 10

God Is Not The Default Setting

(though Christians would like us to think he is).

Christianity in crisis perpetually sets God as the default, the explanation of everything. If something cannot be explained, then God is working in his renowned mysterious ways; if it can be explained, God is graciously revealing his mysteries; if it can be explained without recourse to God, then plainly the explanation is wrong. However, as Christopher Hitchens points out, 'arguments that explain everything, explain nothing'...

The so-called 'cosmological argument' says in broad outline that the reason there is something rather than nothing is because a supreme being must have created the something. Christians suppose that the supreme being in question can be none other than their own pet deity.

Admittedly the idea is almost biblical, though the creator God in Genesis is one of the Jewish versions of God and not really the God of today's Christians. Nonetheless the presumption is breathtakingly staggering: because, according to Christians, science cannot yet explain why there is 'something rather than nothing', the something that exists must therefore be the work of the Christian God. There is no 'therefore' about it. In *The Grand Design*, renowned physicist Stephen Hawking offers an explanation of the universe's God-free creation:

> *Because there is a law like gravity, the universe can and will create itself from nothing... Spontaneous creation is the reason there is something rather than nothing, why the Universe exists, why we exist. It is not necessary to invoke God to light the blue touch paper and set the universe going.*

Rowan Williams, who is not a renowned physicist but an archbishop, responds to this suggestion by saying:

> *Belief in God is not about plugging a gap in explaining how one thing relates to another within the universe... It is the belief that there is an intelligent, living agent on whose activity everything ultimately depends for its existence. Physics on its own will not settle the question of why there is something rather than nothing.*

Even if Hawking is wrong and physics does not 'settle the question of why there is something rather than nothing', this does not lead us, by some sort of magical default, to the Christian God. It is no more logical to say it does than to claim that because there is an Athens there must be a Zeus, or that the existence of tea-shops proves Bertrand Russell's celestial teapot must really be orbiting the sun. Equally, if the universe has supernatural origins then it is just as likely that Allah lies behind its creation, or Brahma or Amun, or even a deity of which we cannot conceive or comprehend. Hawking's explanation that 'something' was brought into existence from 'nothing' by unimaginably powerful physical forces is far more plausible than insupportable assertions that an 'agent' invented by a pre-scientific culture (take your pick) was hard at work.

The Christian counters with his second argument, that the fact the universe is fine-tuned for life proves that God exists. It is of course self-evident that the universe supports life; we are it and we are here. Life would not have arisen, so the argument goes, if the universe wasn't set 'just right' for producing it; if gravity was either only slightly stronger or weaker, for example, it would have failed to appear. This gives rise to the notion that we live in a 'Goldilocks' universe, where conditions are 'just right', and that, in turn, creates the impression that it must have been *deliberately* finely-tuned to enable life, and human life in particular (the so-called 'anthropic principle'). But how fine-tuned is fine-tuned? If I have a garden of several acres and because of very poor soil, irrigation problems and large expanses of concrete only a single plant grows in one small corner of it, to what extent can it be claimed my garden is fine-tuned for life and growth? The universe may be fine-tuned for small pockets of life (as far as we know, and despite of Stephen Hawking's optimism, we may be the only one) but it is much more 'finely-tuned' for gas clouds, inanimate lumps of rock, dark energy, dark matter, dark magnetism and unimaginably vast tracts of 'nothingness' (which inevitably must be 'dark' too). If whatever the universe is fine-tuned for reflects God's priorities, then he has far greater interest in non-life than he has life.

It does not follow that because one small planet and perhaps a handful of others support life does not mean the *universe* is fine-tuned for it. Most of it is positively hostile to life. While scientists posit the existence of multiple universes, among which our Goldilocks version is the one that is 'just right' for life, perhaps it is not necessary to go to such lengths, given it supports life so exceedingly sparingly. The fine-tuned argument also presupposes that life is a Good Thing. Certainly to us it is, but to the universe as a whole it seems to be both insignificant and inconsequential. From the universe's perspective - if we can impose an entirely human way of looking at it onto an inanimate cosmos - it might even be that life is no more than a form of infestation, suffered by planet Earth alone.

As creatures intelligent enough to appreciate it, we are prone to overstate fine-tuning and over-rate life, which is just one of an incredible number of phenomena in the universe. As remarkable as it is to us, the presence of life on Earth does not demonstrate, much less prove, the existence of a fine-tuner. Even if it did, all it would indicate is what most atheists already know: that human beings are physical, not spiritual entities. As Steve Zara points out, all that the fine-tuning argument leads to is

> *the most absurd position of all – theists claim that we are far more than material beings, that we can exist beyond death of our bodies, that our true selves have a supernatural foundation, and yet they insist that we could not exist unless God had tuned the universe just so, to make the physical, natural world perfect for our existence, an act which would seem absurd if our true*

selves were non-physical.

Not only is it absurd, it's unnecessary when, according to many Christians, our supposedly non-material, supernatural essence is ultimately independent of the natural world.

That world too is compelled to conform to what Christians believe about it, hence their regularly exercised 'Evolution is just a theory' mantra. In excitedly jumping up and down exclaiming that evolutionary theory is a theory and not fact, they demonstrate their ignorance of the scientific use of the term. 'Theory' means 'explanation of observable events', and not, as Christians would have you believe, 'woolly, unproven idea'. While others provide far much more knowledgeable expositions of evolution, I want to note here that evolution happens, in that it can be seen, measured and demonstrated (see Richard Dawkins's *The Greatest Show On Earth*, for example) and that Darwin's theory, and all that follows from it, is an explanation - a description if you like - of a process that goes on in the natural world regardless of whether human beings acknowledge it or not. As Michael Shermer points in *Why People Believe Weird Things*, the description of any natural event is in the mind, while the event itself operates indifferently and independently in nature. Gravity serves as a good example: it existed and operated long before Newton was able to offer a description of how it worked. As with gravity, so with evolution.

Evolution is problematic for Christians because it runs contrary to what the Bible says about how life came about in the two conflicting accounts in Genesis. Neither of these is compatible with what evolution shows us. More than this, however, it undercuts the theology of salvation, which relies on the idea that the 'creation', and human beings in particular, 'fell', from a state of perfection to imperfection, and from being in harmony with God to being lost in sinfulness. The direction of evolution, however, runs in the opposite direction: it demonstrates that life began with simple organisms and developed over vast expanses of time into complex life-forms. There is a significant and irresolvable contradiction between the Bible's teaching that life was originally perfect and subsequently degenerated, and evolution's demonstration that life began simply and became complex. The theories are mutually exclusive and both, as a result, cannot be correct (in case you need a clue: the one that is is corroborated by large amounts of evidence; the one that isn't relies on myths written by pre-scientific tribesmen). It is understandable, therefore, that Christians are so concerned about evolution and its implications, and why some hate 'Darwinism' with a passion. (Generally speaking, Christians avoid the term 'evolution', preferring 'Darwinism', which has much more of a cultist sound to it). They are compelled to insist that of the two explanations, the biblical account(s) must be right, because if it is wrong, and evolution correct, there is no need for Jesus' atoning death, because humans are not fallen, sinful creatures but evolved beings with the complexities and behaviours that come from an animal nature; we would be, as David Attenborough suggests, 'quarrelsome primates'.

This doesn't stop believers as disparate as Australia's most senior Catholic, Cardinal George Pell and biblical literalist Ken Ham of *Answers In Genesis* from bleating about how life, and human life in particular with all its soul, sophistication and moral awareness, cannot have arisen by chance. Setting aside whether the mechanics of natural selection can be thought of as 'chance', this is just the sort of argument we would hear from any creature that had developed sophistication and moral awareness (let's leave 'soul' out of it, given there's no evidence it exists) from a *different* sequence of chance mutation and selection. If one of the other social apes instead of ourselves had reached what we humans are wont to regard as the apex of evolution it too might want to claim its existence was planned and no accident; Pierre Boulle has the hyper-evolved simians in his *Planet of the Apes* do just this. Pell, Ham and their ilk can claim we humans were God's bullseye all along, but that is to draw the target around evolution's chance arrow long after it has landed in the long grass.

The evidence then is not on the side of the Bible's supporters, however much they try to make it fit or denigrate it with alternative explanations; it overwhelmingly demonstrates that evolution is the process by which all life has developed. This means, as Joel Heck of Concordia University Texas and supporter of the anti-science *Answers In Genesis* recognises, that 'if evolution is true... you have death long before you have the first human being, and that makes Paul's statement in Romans 5.12 (that death entered the word only when Adam sinned) false'. Yes, it does and it is. The implications are significant for humans as creatures 'made in God's image' and in need of restoration. Evolution means there is no need for a creator God, nothing to restore us to and no need for a sacrificial death, if indeed that's what Jesus' crucifixion was, to bring about that restoration.

Chapter 11

How Christians Inflict Their Extra-Curricular Beliefs On Us All
(and why we shouldn't let them)

In spite of their claims of allegiance to a Bible they seem not to know, Christians evidently feel free to believe anything they want. This might be acceptable if, firstly, they didn't insist that such beliefs find support in the Bible when they don't, and secondly, there weren't implications for the rest of us in some of their extra-curricular imaginings. Here's how it works: individuals, groups and institutions are inclined to believe that a particular view they hold is actually the case. Developing a resolute conviction between themselves that they are right, they then look for independent corroboration of their conviction. This is not as scientific as it might sound. In fact, it's not scientific at all. The scientific approach would be to look for evidence that refuted the original view, which would itself be based on prior evidence. Christians, however, do just what Francis Bacon described as long ago as the sixteenth century, and look only for verification of their predetermined notions:

> *The human understanding when it has once adopted an opinion... draws all things else to suggest and agree with it. And though there be a greater number and weight of instances to be found on the other side (of the argument) yet these it either neglects and despises, or else by some distinction sets aside and rejects, in order that by this great and pernicious predetermination the authority of its former conclusions may remain inviolate... And such is the way of all superstitions whether in astrology, dreams, omens, divine judgements, or the like...*

And so it is that, even today, Christians turn not to the scientific method of gathering evidence, but to the 'wisdom' of God's Word.

It isn't actually necessary for them to find the corroboration they seek in its pages, and indeed they might not even read it. But that doesn't matter; they find the corroboration of their conviction by interpreting what they assume to be there, through 'the guidance of the Holy Spirit' or whatever flawed cognitive process confirms their original bias. Two convictions without any empirical basis now support one another: the original belief about factor x and the supposition that the Bible must necessarily substantiate that belief.

This leads, through a complete abandonment of logic, to a third conviction: that because the Bible is deemed to support the original view of x, a moral stance needs to be taken on it by everyone, whether or not they share the original conviction or recognise the authority of scripture. Armed with their convictions and extrapolated morality, Christians attempt, often successfully it has to be said, to impose them both on society at large. More often than not, however, the Bible does not support Christians' convictions, which they would know if they took the trouble to read it carefully or, assuming some of them do, were more honest about what it says.

Bishop John Quinn of Minnesota, a celibate, single male and thus an expert in matters matrimonial, writes that 'from the beginning, the church has taught that marriage is a lifetime relationship between one man and one woman... It is a sacrament, instituted by Jesus Christ to provide the special graces that are needed to live according to God's law and to give birth to the next generation". Alas, the bishop doesn't know his Bible, nor his Lord's teaching. He is not alone in superimposing his own views of marriage on the Bible; it is a common practice among Christians today: Stephen Green of *Christian Voice* is fond of making the same assertion. Should you be inclined to do so, you will once again search in vain either for Jesus 'instituting' modern marriage or for the early church promoting it.

Jesus does indeed paraphrase and augment Genesis 2.24 when he says in Matthew 19.5-6,

> *"a man shall leave his father and mother and be joined*

to his wife, and the two shall become one flesh". So they are no longer two, but one flesh. Therefore what God has joined together, let no one separate.

In context, however, this statement is part of a discussion about divorce in which Jesus makes the point that Jewish law permits divorce only because men and women are weak. This prompts the disciples to observe that 'if such is the case of a man with his wife, it is better not to marry', with which Jesus concurs, adding,

not everyone can accept this teaching, but only those to whom it is given. For there are eunuchs who have been so from birth, and there are eunuchs who have been made eunuchs by others, and there are eunuchs who have made themselves eunuchs for the sake of the Kingdom of heaven. Let anyone accept this who can.

In other words, Jesus thinks it is better to be sexless than to marry, the better to pursue the interests of the Kingdom. While his view of marriage reveals him to be a product of his culture, in that he sees it from an entirely male perspective and only in terms of sexual union, he evidently regards it as the inferior option. In case we are mistaking his intent here, here's another of his pronouncements about marriage, this time from Luke 20.34-35:

Jesus said to them, 'Those who belong to this age marry and are given in marriage; but those who are considered worthy of a place in that age [i.e. that of the Kingdom] and in the resurrection from the dead neither marry nor are given in marriage.

This is even less ambiguous in its denigration of marriage; it is for this world only, for those who will not be part of the Kingdom, who will not survive death. Those who live in anticipation of the Kingdom, who would be resurrected from the dead, will have nothing to do with marriage in this life, as in the next. Far from 'instituting' marriage as Bishop Quinn claims, Jesus heralds the end of the institution. Of course, the Kingdom didn't come when Jesus said it would and the newly formed bodies of believers found themselves having to decide what to do about marriage in a world that was lasting longer than they anticipated. Consequently, 'from the beginning', the early church's position was that marriage would do if believers couldn't manage to control their sexual urges. But, Paul declares in 1 Corinthians 7.8-9, it is better to remain celibate and not to marry at all:

> *to the unmarried and the widows I say that it is well for them to remain unmarried as I am. But if they are not practising self-control, they should marry. For it is better to marry than to be aflame with passion.*

While it is true Paul assumes any marriage will be between a man and woman, this is hardly the ringing endorsement of marriage we might expect after reading the bishop's remarks. Perhaps he has in mind the views of the church after Paul's time, though 'from the beginning' implies otherwise. The forger of 1 Timothy, writing many years after Paul's death, has this to say about 'younger widows' in the second century church: 'when their sensual desires alienate them from Christ, they want to marry, and so they incur condemnation for having violated their first pledge [of celibacy?]' (5.11-12). In this writer's eyes, 'condemnation' (by God?) is the result of a desire to marry.

So, Jesus, Paul and the leaders of the early church did not see much point to marrying when they were convinced they lived in the end times. As Paul goes on to say in 1 Corinthians, 7.28-29:

> *But if you marry, you do not sin, and if a virgin marries, she does not sin. Yet those who marry will experience distress in this life, and I would spare you that. I mean, brothers and sisters, the appointed time has grown short; from now on, let even those who have wives be as though they had none...*

'Distress' when the end comes is more likely to be the married person's lot, as opposed to those who are without a spouse to worry about. Paul is not sanctioning marriage because he anticipated that any marriage could only be short-lived and traumatic; as he goes on to explain in 1 Corinthians 7.32-34, marriage is little more than a distraction from 'the affairs of the Lord'. He is not therefore promoting 'life long' commitment in the sense Bishop Quinn means it, because those to whom Paul writes are not, in his view, going to continue in their existing lives for very much longer. Above all, Paul is most definitely not establishing rules for marriage for the rest of time, simply because, for him, there was no 'rest of time'.

This leaves us with the notion of 'becoming one flesh' from Genesis 2.24 that Jesus makes use of in Matthew. The verse, about the creation of Eve, reads 'therefore a man leaves his father and his mother and clings to his wife, and they become one flesh', which is rather a curious moral to draw from the example of the only two people never to have had parents. Be that as it may, how successfully has this recommendation been adhered to by God's people? In spite of its position at the beginning of the Christian Bible, Genesis was completed after several other of the Old Testament's books, round about 500 BCE. Nonetheless, if God ordained that marriage was to be between one man and woman when he created human beings, as Genesis and today's Christians claim, then we can reasonably expect to see the principle being adhered to whenever and wherever we discover his obedient people. Alas, a quick survey of a mere handful of the Bible's heroes is sufficient to disabuse us of any such view:

No sooner has God supposedly endorsed the one-man, one-woman arrangement for marriage, a character called Lamech, in Genesis 4, takes up instead the two wives option (What do you mean there is no two wives option? You think you know better than everyone else in this list?)

Not long afterwards, in Genesis 16.1-3, Abram demonstrates how the one-man, one woman model of marriage really works. He marries his half-sister, Sara. Then, at her behest, he takes a second wife, the handmaid Hagar, when Sara proves to be infertile. We're still in Genesis and already incestuous polygamy is the favoured 'lifestyle'. Later, in Genesis 21, Sara makes Abram cast Agar and her son out when she decides she doesn't like them any more. Abram, evidently committed to marriage for life, meekly obeys.

A change of name and another wife; Abraham marries Keturah, while still married to the other two unfortunate women (Genesis 25.1).

Genesis 32.22 records that Jacob has taken unto himself two wives, with two women-servants on the side in case he gets bored.

Gideon, the guy who leaves his Bibles in modern-day hotel rooms, is recorded in Judges 8.30 as having 'many wives' who were obliged to provide him with seventy sons.

David shows his commitment to marriage for life in 2 Samuel 11.2-5 when he lusts after and sleeps with Bathsheba, even though both are already married to other people. In David's case, several other people (1 Samuel 25.42-44).

Solomon, renowned for his wisdom, shows in 1 Kings 11.2-3 just how wise he is in disregarding the idea of one-man, one-woman marriage. The horny old goat - and there is something very animalistic about an alpha-male and his harem of females - marries seven hundred wives and keeps three hundred concubines on stand-by, just in case he wears the wives out. Surely one of the Bible's more interesting models of marriage: one man and one thousand women.

Rehoboam, though he has eighteen wives and sixty concubines, plays favourites and sleeps with Maacah, daughter of Absalom, far more than he does the rest. Still, the others do get a look in because they produce for him, according to 2 Chronicles 11:21, twenty-eight sons and sixty daughters. Perhaps some of the daughters were fortunate enough to become concubines for some other over-aggrandised troop leader.

While married to Zipporah, a Midianite woman (from present day Arabia), Moses helps himself to an Ethiopian wife (Numbers 12.1).

But enough of this. There are innumerable other examples of polygamy as the favoured marital arrangement in the Old

Testament. You can find a more comprehensive list on the *Skeptic's Annotated Bible* web-site. The point here is that the so-called heroes of the Old Testament knew little of one-man, one-woman marriage. They regarded their wives as property and subscribed with gusto to the polygamous arrangements that the scriptures speak of so approvingly: Exodus 21.10 even has instructions for taking on an extra spouse or two.

But wait, I imagine Christians are saying, this is the old 'covenant', these are ancient people who don't know any better. Quite so: yet Christians would have us believe they do know what they're about when it comes to their equally primitive religious beliefs and brutish 'morality'. Well, yes, says the Christian, but in the case of marriage God had not, in those quaint Old Testament times, made clear his requirements for the one-man, one-woman marriage that we know he really wanted. Clearly not – but then, why not? Did he just forget to add it to his interminable law-making and from both his stabs at those ten, special commandments? Why doesn't he mention it in his confidential chats with one patriarch after another? This is a really serious slip-up over something that today's Christians say is central to God's purposes for mankind.

In fact, the one-man, one-woman concept of marriage evolves: it is becoming the norm by New Testament times, but is still not sufficiently established, even among Christians, that the writers of both 1 Timothy and Titus can't assume would-be bishops will confine themselves to one wife. The leaders of second-century churches have to be *told* that 'a bishop then must be blameless, *the husband of one wife*, vigilant, sober, of good behaviour, given to hospitality, apt to teach' (1 Timothy 3.2, KJV). Meanwhile Jesus himself gives tacit approval to the polygamous model of marriage in one of his parables: 'then shall the Kingdom of heaven be likened unto ten virgins, which took their lamps, and went forth to meet the bridegroom' (Matthew 25.1, KJV). Ten virgins for one bridegroom? A parable, to be sure, of believers welcoming the returning Son of Man (those lamps are going to need to burn for a lot longer than they might think), but one that nonetheless assumes and rests upon an acceptance of polygamy.

The assertion by Southern Baptists in the United States that 'relaxed attitudes toward human sexuality have turned the biblical notion of wholesome and monogamous sexual relations between husbands and wives on its head', is pure self-deception because there is no divine revelation in the Bible about one-man, one-woman marriage. Rather, it is a 'notion' arrived at over time, with later Christians retrospectively resorting to the 'one flesh' pronouncement about Adam and Eve as evidence that the one-man, one-woman arrangement was God's plan all along. But to do this means vaulting over all of the polygamy of the Old Testament and ignoring the awkward fact that Adam and Eve, even taken literally, were not married in any formal sense. The terms 'became as one flesh' and 'took unto himself a wife' appear to have nothing to do with formal marriage as we know it today, but are, rather, euphemisms for sex (see Genesis 16.3 and 30.9 for example). In the ancient world of the Old Testament, individuals were deemed to have become man and wife when they copulated.

More than this, the purpose of 'marriage' in the pre-fall world, as the poet John Milton points out, seems to have been companionship rather than procreation (Genesis 2.18). This companionship would seem to have included, if the euphemistic language of Genesis is anything to go by, recreational as well as reproductive sex.

Genesis 2.24, then, is far more about the symbolism of leaving one's parents, through becoming someone else's sexual partner, than it is about specifying the number of individuals to be involved in a marriage. If it referred to the latter, the rest of Genesis would not be quite so replete with stories of men with multiple wives. Christians who are concerned that legalising gay marriage means abandoning biblical standards and opening the doors for polygamy - an absurd claim they like to make when scare-mongering - need have no worries: polygamy is as biblical as the Ten Commandments.

Christians like Bishop Quinn, Southern Baptists and the divorced Stephen Green are free to advocate the idea that marriage is a wonderful, God-ordained institution between one man and one woman, for all of their lives, but they cannot, in truthfulness, claim that the Bible advocates such a view. Quite the opposite, in fact.

Of course all such assertions are used as a stick with which to beat gay people who want to marry, because even monogamous marriage in Jesus' time bore little resemblance to the idealised form promoted by modern-day marriage-advocates. Marriage in New Testament times was controlled by men. It involved them at the outset negotiating the price of a woman, a prospective husband offering her father what he considered a fair price for her. If the father agreed, this is what he'd sell her for and the deal would be sealed with a toast, not unlike the purchase of a new donkey or camel. Only at this point in the proceedings would the woman be asked if she was willing to become the bride of her purchaser. In reality she had little choice in the matter, the contract between the two men having been finalised.

There would then follow a lengthy period of betrothal (usually a year) during which time the couple were considered committed to each. The groom traditionally spent the time preparing quarters for himself and his bride in his father's house, while she prepared for her wedding. When the time was up, the man picked up his goods from her father's house and took her to his own father's, where the wedding took place. After the ceremony he would take his new wife into the bed chamber and consummate the marriage while his friends waited outside the room, waiting to see how he'd got on. The deed done, he and the wedding party celebrated both his prowess and eye for a bargain, while the bride remained in the bedroom for a week, waiting for an occasional conjugal visit. After seven days she was allowed to leave the room, finally discarding her veil so that everyone could see whether or not she was the bargain they'd all supposed. She then embarked on a short and demanding life of child-bearing and rearing.

This is the model of marriage - that of ancient tribesmen and first century Jews - that the Bible takes as the norm. It is the same model New Testament writers use consistently for their illustration of Jesus as redeemer: all four gospels refer to him as 'the bridegroom', while Paul says he purchased his bride – the church –

with his own blood (1 Corinthians 6.20); the deal is sealed with wine (Matthew 26.28) and Jesus speaks of the betrothal absence (Matthew 9.15), when he goes to prepare rooms in his father's house (John 14.2). In the same spirit, the still-to-come marriage of bride and groom is described by the deranged author of Revelation (19.7-9):

> *...the marriage of the Lamb has come, and his bride has made herself ready; to her it has been granted to be clothed with fine linen, bright and pure - for the fine linen is the righteous deeds of the saints. And the angel said to me, 'Write this: Blessed are those who are invited to the marriage supper of the Lamb'.*

All very clever symbolism, no doubt. But do we really want to return to the kind of marriage Jesus and the New Testament writers accepted as the norm? Do you, ladies, want to be haggled over by your father and would-be husband before being purchased for an agreed sum? Of course you do, because this is what biblical marriage looks like: it is the way the disciple Peter acquired his wife, it is how all of the other disciples acquired theirs. Any married Christians today who didn't come by their partners in this way have failed to follow the biblical pattern. While some, like the members of the Quiverfull Movement in (where else?) the United States follow the procedure stringently, buying and selling women into marriage without their having any say in the matter, most do not because they really don't, as we are seeing with weary regularity, believe what the Bible says. Instead, and as usual, they cherry-pick the parts that are palatable to the modern mind and impose an equally modern concept of marriage on the rest. What they don't do is adhere to its example.

Still, even if those ancient societies had their own quaint ideas about marriage, the family as we know it today has been ordained by God. Christians tell us it has, so it must surely be so. In reality, the idea that our modern social-construct of the family is the one God approves of is about as accurate as the assumption that the Bible unequivocally supports one-man, one-woman marriage. The modern nuclear family, however much we might cherish it, is not the model reflected in the Bible. Let's see just what that is by taking a closer look at some of the wholesome, and most certainly not dysfunctional, families we find there:

First, there's the Noahs. Noah passes out after a drinking bout and inadvertently allows his son, Ham, to see him naked. Ham does something unspeakable to his unconscious, naked father - the account doesn't specify what - which results in his father cursing him for evermore (Genesis 9.20-26). That Noah is an impulsive, drunken slob of a father who strips off before passing out so that his a son can abuse him should not detract from the fact that God regards him as righteous and blameless (Genesis 6.9). He's good with children too.

In the Lot family, Lot offers his daughters to a mob of potential rapists to keep them from assaulting his guests (Genesis 19.4-8). While Lot and his family are the only inhabitants of Sodom whom the Lord regards as righteous, Lot's daughters later get their father drunk, have sex with him over two nights and become pregnant (Genesis 19.31-38). Just the kind of incestuous but indisputably righteous family you'd want living next door.

And there's that paragon of moral rectitude, Abraham, who, when his wife turns out to be temporarily infertile, has children with slave-girls, only to throw them out when his wife produces the goods herself and objects to the competition (Genesis 21.9-12). Clearly the model for infertile couples everywhere (it's in the Bible, isn't it?).

Abraham, again, imagines Yahweh wants him to sacrifice his son, Isaac. He has the knife at the boy's throat when he comes to his senses, helped, according to the story in Genesis 22, by the Lord sending a message with an angel telling him he's changed his mind. This is evidently the example we should all follow in the raising of children; they are expendable in the service of a despotic God. (Advice for selling your daughter as a slave can be found in Exodus 21.7).

Onan reluctantly takes on the task of impregnating his brother's widowed wife, as was the requirement at the time (Genesis 38.9). When he spills his semen on the ground instead of inside the hapless woman, who, incidentally, would have had no say in whether she participated or not, God immediately strikes him down dead. Others were evidently more successful in complying with this peculiar practice, given that we have no other accounts of punishments for floor-messing, so it is difficult to understand why this adorable 'family' arrangement has dropped out of use in Christian circles.

After some successful smiting in the name of the Lord, Jephthah promises in Judges 11 that he will sacrifice whoever comes out of the doors of his house to greet him on his return home. This, perhaps not entirely unpredictably, turns out to be his only daughter, whom Jephthah has the temerity to blame for the resulting awkwardness. Being a psychopath of principle, however, he decides he must honour his vow to Yahweh, the God whom Christians claim has always disapproved of human-sacrifice, and proceeds to burn her alive. We can only hope that, as with all the animals sacrificed to him, Yahweh enjoyed the aroma of the young woman's bubbling, sizzling flesh.

Again, Christians will argue that these were primitive practices by primitive people, all of which have been superseded by Jesus. This, once more, is selective use of this defence; Christians don't, for example, apply it to other aspects of Old Testament 'morality' that they choose not to regard as primitive for no other reason other than it suits them (like the gay-bashing Leviticus 18.22). Nor do they apply it to the ancient Jewish belief in a murderous, tribal God, even though it bears little relationship to their own happy-clappy faith. On the other hand, perhaps little has changed if the findings of recent research by Koch and Ramirez of Texas Tech University are to be believed. They report in *Religiosity, Christian Fundamentalism, and Intimate Partner Violence Among U.S. College Students* their discovery that 'Christian fundamentalism was positively associated with both violence approval and acts of intimate partner violence, but not psychological aggression'. Thank God these Christians don't resort to 'psychological aggression' but like their role-models in the Old Testament, limit their violence to the physical sort. Meanwhile, Scottish bishop Joseph Devine points out that 'more than 75% of all sexual abuse of minors happens in the family, perpetrated by family members, mostly those who are married, and by others known to the victims'. Incredibly, the good bishop offers this bleak portrait of the family as a defence of the abuse of children by Catholic clergy: 'sexual abuse of minors is not', he writes, 'a "Catholic Church" problem'. So that's all right then.

While arguing that we should not look to the Old Testament for a model of family life, but to Jesus, Christians seem to be ignorant of what he actually says about it. To be a follower of Jesus involves abandoning one's family: in Luke 14.26 Jesus declares that 'whoever comes to me and does not hate father and mother, wife and children, brothers and sisters, yes, and even life itself, cannot be my disciple'. As we've come to expect, Jesus fails to provide any endorsement of the ideal promoted by groups like *Focus on the Family* and *Family Life*. 'Hate' is a strong word, and even if Jesus is here using hyperbole, he is using it for a reason - to express how family, and even life itself is of little value compared with following him. He is either very arrogant or is again speaking as one who believes the end of the age is coming, when none of the old arrangements, family and marriage included, are going to matter for very much longer.

On another occasion, recorded in Mark 3.31-35, Jesus illustrates the attitude one should have towards one's family when his turns up uninvited to one of his love-fests - how embarrassing must that have been for a young man on a mission!:

> *Then his mother and his brothers came; and standing outside, they sent to him and called him. A crowd was sitting around him; and they said to him, 'Your mother and your brothers and sisters are outside, asking for you'. And he replied, 'Who are my mother and my brothers?'. And looking at those who sat around him, he said, 'Here are my mother and my brothers! Whoever does the will of God is my brother and sister and mother'.*

These verse and others demonstrate the fallacy of the Roman Catholic doctrine that Mary remained a virgin not just through the conception and birth of Jesus but throughout her life. Unless – and perhaps I'm being too sceptical here - she produced his 'brothers and sisters' as miraculously as she produced him. The tale does not recall what happens to his family after Jesus' dismissal of them. Presumably they had no choice but to leave, while Jesus continued to enthral his adoring fans, or, as he preferred to call them, his real family. How many Christian cults have isolated new converts from their natural families with his irresponsible words, dangerous and hostile towards the family in every conceivable way?

Versions of the family serve as the basic unit of all human social arrangements. The Bible's bizarre and dysfunctional families, however, are far from the model modern Christians want them to be. Nor is the family as they see it the ideal endorsed by their leader, who scoffs at the notion whenever it does not conform to his own peculiar extremism. Shouldn't Christians be following his lead and abandoning the notion of family too?

We can be fairly certain though, can't we, that however much he prevaricates on the family, God is without doubt a protector of the unborn, condemning abortion unreservedly. We have already seen how the commandment prohibiting killing is qualified to such an extent - by Yahweh, the Israelites and later Christians - that it is stripped of any value. God's edict forbidding abortion must be somewhere in the Bible, surely, given contemporary Christians' noisy conviction that he is utterly opposed to it.

Perhaps it is in Exodus 21.22-24 where God makes known his thoughts on the sanctity of the life of the unborn:

> *When people who are fighting injure a pregnant woman so that there is a miscarriage, and yet no further harm follows, the one responsible shall be fined what the woman's husband demands, paying as much as the judges determine.*

What? Paying a fine is the only penalty for causing an abortion?

And that fine payable to the husband too, not even the unfortunate mother? What happened to death as the punishment for murder (and just about everything else)? Could it be that Yahweh doesn't regard the loss of an unborn child as murder? Sounds like it; in fact he seems to regard the unborn as rather trivial if these verses are anything to go by. They're certainly not the possessors of souls on a par with those who've made it to full-term.

God really needs to reconsider his position on this one if he's to meet the expectations of pro-life Christians. By the time the issue arises again, in Hosea 13.16, he'll surely have sorted out his position. Speaking through a favoured 'prophet', he announces there that a tribe he doesn't care for 'shall fall by the sword, their little ones shall be dashed in pieces, and their pregnant women ripped open'. Now, I may be misinterpreting here a God for whom all life is sacred, but demanding the ripping open of expectant mothers with swords, and ordering the smashing of babies' heads doesn't read to me like he's a protector of defenceless children, nor an opponent of abortion. Better luck next time.

In Jeremiah 16.3-4, Yahweh proclaims that:

> *the sons and daughters who are born in this place, and... the mothers who bear them and the fathers who beget them in this land: they shall die of deadly diseases. They shall not be lamented, nor shall they be buried; they shall become like dung on the surface of the ground. They shall perish by the sword and by famine, and their dead bodies shall become food for the birds of the air and for the wild animals of the earth.*

Then again, maybe that's not where he condemns abortion either.

So perhaps it's evident in Psalm 137.9 where, with vengeful relish, the exiled psalmist declares, 'O daughter of Babylon... happy shall they be who take your little ones and dash them against the rock!' There's clarity all right, but of the wrong sort; the kind of God who condones the violent murdering of young children is not one who places a high value on life generally, let alone that of the unborn.

It could be argued that God, being God, is entirely at liberty to carry out such despicable acts, though this hardly equates with the Loving Father Jesus believes in, nor his admonition to 'suffer little children'. That in turn doesn't quite fit with the Christian view that everyone is a sinner from the point of conception. Anti-abotionists who claim that abortion takes the life of innocent children have little conception – no pun intended – of the biblical view that even a foetus is a sinner. (The theology is as complex as it is barmy, but rests on the premise that humanity as whole became tainted with sin through the rebelliousness of Adam). As John MacArthur, 'American Protestant Minister and Educator', expresses it:

> ...*the Bible is absolutely crystal-clear that all children are sinners from conception - all children. The principle of iniquity is embedded in the human race. Children are born morally corrupt. They are born with an irresistible bent towards evil. And any notion that children are born morally neutral and free from a predisposition to sin is absolutely contrary to Scripture.... All humans are born in sin. If infants were not sinful, if they were not morally corrupt, then they wouldn't die. If they were born innocent or pure or morally neutral, there would be no basis for their death! The very fact that they die indicates that the disease of sin is there in them, because sin is the killer. It is in their inherited sin nature that the seeds of death are planted.*

While none of this condones or advocates abortion it is of no support for the Christian pro-lifer's claim that God opposes it. Indeed, as the creator of all, God must ultimately be responsible for the significant number of natural or 'spontaneous' abortions that occur worldwide on a daily basis – 'between 15% and 20% of all clinically recognised pregnancies', according to *The American Pregnancy Association*. How can we conclude anything other than God really is not bothered about the unborn? Unless it's that there is no God to *be* bothered.

PART SIX: CONCLUSIONS

Chapter 12

Facing The Truth

How did I get here?

Flies contributed to my giving up faith. I could never understand how a good God could create carriers of disease who plague every other living thing, from the animals we share our lives with to the malnourished children in the third world who, with pitiful regularity, appear on our TV screens. It's not enough that these emaciated and distended children suffer from starvation and disease, but they have to endure the risk of further infection and the awful indignity of flies crawling into the moisture in their eyes, up their nostrils and round the corners of their mouths. What sort of God creates creatures like this? Where is the loving father Jesus speaks of, who cares for little ones as he cares for sparrows but allows them to suffer not only from malnutrition but from these vile, opportunistic creatures? It might be, as some Christians argue, that flies weren't originally created to be blood-sucking nuisances and disease carriers, but became this way as a result of the Fall. So what were they like before the Fall? What function did they serve?

According to Paul and orthodox theology, death didn't exist prior to Adam's sin, so flies couldn't have been created to dispose of carrion. Excrement maybe - but that would mean there was such stuff in the Garden of Eden, and flies were created then to be like they are now. If not, where did they fit in the web of life? Did they stick to biting and siphoning off blood – horse perhaps and the odd bit of human? An Eden with shit-eating, blood-sucking flies around doesn't sound very much like paradise to me. If, however, they were anything other than they are now, they weren't flies at all and their present, post-Fall form can only have been arrived at through a process remarkably like evolution (or, if you prefer, devolution).

Of course, evolution - mindless, heartless evolution - *is* how flies came to be, like every other living thing on the planet, and while this fact doesn't make them any more pleasant, it does explain their existence and place in the scheme of life without the entirely unnecessary recourse to a god. All of 'creation' can be satisfactorily accounted for in this way, including that which is useful to us and that which we find unpleasant, injurious and detrimental - microbes, viruses, parasites, ticks, mites and flies, as well as the birds of the air and beasts of the field. God was, and is, superfluous to their existence and to their 'relationships' with us.

And so, for me, God began to slip away. I was still attending church, listening to the Reverend Woodhouse tell me and his congregation what dreadful sinners we all were and how we needed Jesus to save us from our sins. With God receding, I had two problems with this. Sin, it was becoming increasingly apparent, was no more than a Christian code-word for human behaviour. 'Sin' didn't just mean the less desirable forms of human behaviour, but all of it. Christian preachers and teachers made it known that any behaviour that they themselves objected to was sinful, sex being a perennial favourite. Inconsistently, they rarely saw sin as synonymous with truly wicked behaviours, like those with which the Bible is replete; murder, genocide, torture, brutality, heartlessness. Instead, the church's version of sin seemed to ignore real immorality (unless it was sexual 'immorality') and the lack of any concern for others - but with finnicky little behaviours; things like failing to respect God, neglecting to give to the church, lacking spiritual stamina in serving the Lord (whatever that meant).

Overall, the sin preached against seemed just to describe human beings as they are, and those in the church who had had their lives 'turned round' by Jesus were just as capable of demonstrating selfish, self-centred behaviour as anyone else: the Rev. Woodhouse wouldn't have needed to rail against it otherwise. Were they, like me, just self-deluded fakes? Possibly, but I soon came to realise that what they were was human, with the all faults, flaws and foibles that we humans have. Their encounters with Jesus hadn't changed that, because having one's 'sins forgiven' doesn't get us anywhere in our attempt to run away from what we are.

There were, to be sure, good people in the church, but I soon began to recognise that they would be good even if they weren't Christians - there were, and are, plenty outside the church who were good without God. Similarly, the self-absorbed and mean-spirited were self-absorbed and mean-spirited with Jesus just as they would have been without him. In short, I realised, Jesus changes nothing. Conversion to Christianity does not produce 'new creatures', just the old ones with new superstitions and new prejudices. Human beings continue to behave like human beings whether Jesus forgives sins or not.

My other problem was with the Jesus preached. He was almost exclusively Paul's 'Christ' and was at odds with the rather more earthy character of the synoptic gospels, who was hardly mentioned in sermons and Bible studies. He in turn was different from the ephemeral mystic portrayed in John's gospel. There were too many Jesuses. The church seemed to know this and so ignored the Jesus that made demands on people. Supernatural Christ was the better option because 'gaining a right standing with God' is an easier game to play than serving others. It was impossible to tell which, from those available, was the 'real' Jesus, even though he supposedly lived in my heart. I could only conclude that none of the Jesuses on offer was real; they were all just interpretations of an idea, possibly of a real person who existed long before any of the New Testament writers put pen to paper, possibly not. But if the Bible hadn't got a grip on what its central figure was all about, what else was it confused or wrong about?

My questioning and my slow awakening to truth and sense were given added impetus when I faced a significant crisis in my life. Throughout it I prayed earnestly and sincerely to my Father in Heaven to help me deal with it. I didn't, however, ask him to resolve the situation. Because I had a degree of 'spiritual maturity' and had been taught not to take Jesus' words literally when he said to pray for anything and it would be given (because everyone really knows that that doesn't work), I sought wisdom to deal with the situation instead. It made no difference. God did not hear and did not respond to any request, and the crisis deepened. After all my praying – and there was a lot of it – God had not shaken off his bed to listen to my petition. I had no more of an idea about how to deal with things than before I started. And so I could only conclude that God was not there, neither in Heaven nor in the hearts of believers, certainly not in mine. I began to ask myself what a world without a god would look like: if God did not exist, human beings would frequently behave like territorial primates; nature would be the result of a mindless and heartless process; sex and death would be the drivers of its development; life would be a cruel struggle for most living creatures, including many humans; the world would be largely indifferent to human aspiration; the brain would find pattern and impose order where none existed. In short, the world without God would be the world exactly as it is. As I much later discovered Julia Sweeney to say, 'the world behaves exactly as you expect it would if there were no Supreme Being, no Supreme Consciousness, and no supernatural'.

Rather than being a disappointment, however, all of this turned out to be an invigorating release. It wasn't that I stopped believing in God, I stopped believing there was a God to believe in. He was gone; he was never there; he isn't there. Much followed from this as my faith - that house of cards (built on sand) - began to tumble: Jesus, whoever he was, was not the son of God because a non-existent being doesn't produce offspring (unless they are similarly non-existent); the promises of the Bible are false and I was a dupe to have believed otherwise; people are good or bad irrespective of 'salvation'; the universe can be more than adequately accounted for by cosmology, and life, including human behaviour, by evolution. I had discovered Occam's razor, without knowing the term, and was finally free from religion as an explanation of life and as a necessity in my own. I knew without a shadow of a doubt that Christianity was not - and is not – true. I have been free of it ever since.

So what am I saying in this book? That all Christians are hypocrites? That is really for you, the reader, to judge. If a hypocrite is defined as a person who preaches one thing but does another then there really is a significant body of evidence that points to the hypocrisy of Christian believers. I've attempted throughout this book to present some of that evidence. If you are not convinced by what I've had to say, maybe the conclusion drawn by evangelical writer Ronald J. Sider will persuade you. In *The Scandal of the Evangelical Conscience,* he writes: 'whether the issue is divorce, materialism, sexual promiscuity, racism, physical abuse in marriage or neglect of a biblical world-view, the polling data point to widespread, blatant disobedience on the part of people who allegedly are evangelical, born-again Christians'.

My intention in writing has not been, however, to draw attention to the hypocrisy of Christians, pronounced as that may be. My point is that while they find themselves unable to practise much of what they preach, of equal significance is that which they neither preach nor practise, even though the one they claim as saviour demands that they should: they don't sell all they have to give to the poor, don't love their enemies, don't pray for those who persecute them, don't lend without expectation of any return, don't cut off body parts that offend them, don't attend to the log in their own eye before the speck in their neighbours'.

I've suggested that most of Jesus' requirements are unrealistic and impractical, and that is why his followers today are inclined to disregard them, as did most of their predecessors throughout history. But Christians must exercise a rigorous cognitive dissonance (call it 'faith') that prevents them from admitting this: how else can they continue to believe that Jesus is, at least, the Son of the living God, and, at most, that same God in human form, while blithely ignoring his expectations of them? This is the same cognitive dissonance that prevents them from recognising the complete failure of Jesus' prophecies, in particular those of his early return and the establishment within his own generation of God's Kingdom on earth; the same blind spot that prevents them from acknowledging, in the face of overwhelming evidence, that his promises too – of miracles, of receiving whatever is asked for, of healing powers – have never delivered.

So I am not calling Christians hypocrites; the 'fruits' of their faith do that without any accusation on my part. Their belief in Jesus does not extend to their doing what he tells them to do, in terms of the morality he demands and the beliefs he requires. It's as if he's speaking directly to them when he says in Luke 6.46, 'Why do you call me 'Lord, Lord' and do not do what I tell you?'.

And why does this matter? Matthew spells out the implications:

> *Not everyone who says to me, 'Lord, Lord', will enter the Kingdom of heaven, but only one who does the will of my Father in heaven. On (judgement) day many will say to me, 'Lord, Lord, did we not prophesy in your name, and cast out demons in your name, and do many deeds of power in your name? Then I will declare to them, "I never knew you; go away from me, you evildoers".* (Matthew 7.21-23)

Believers needn't worry too much though. Jesus is long dead; he will not judge them or cast them out, because, being dead, he can't. There is no heaven to worry about getting into, nor will God's Kingdom be imposed on the earth. Christians who have so easily abandoned the extreme morality Jesus demands could just as easily dispense with these supernatural elements of faith. Indeed, there is no point to their hanging on to them, because, according to Jesus, it is not belief or being extraordinarily spiritual that will save them but doing what he commands. Having thrown out this particular baby, there is no point in them insisting on keeping the bath water.

Even if cognitively dissonant Christians think they can, we cannot escape the conclusion that Jesus was a disaster: his prophecies were wrong, his promises untrue, his morality, as his followers demonstrate to this day, impossible. His mission, to herald the arrival of the Kingdom of God for the Jewish people, was a failure that led, ultimately, to untold evil being committed in his name. He was responsible for the stultification of mankind's cultural and intellectual development, and, still today, the suppression of reason, autonomy and equality. The world would have been a better place if he had never lived, or at least if those who followed him hadn't made a religion out of his failure. He believed that the root cause of illness was sin and demonic possession: he was uneducated and unsophisticated. He was inconsistent, unpleasant to those who opposed him, dismissive of those outside his own circle. He was, in all of this, thoroughly human. He was not God, nor the Son of God, and he was not delivering any divine salvation plan. He was a charismatic, Jewish fanatic from a superstitious backwater of the first century. He has, or should have, no more relevance to the lives of people today than any of the other itinerant preachers of the time. I say this not because I'm choosing to 'reject' him - he can no more be 'rejected' than other divine men like Mithras, Krishna and Superman - or because I want to revel in my own 'sin', as Christians assert of those of us who really don't see what all the fuss is about, but because this is what the evidence tells us. Read the synoptic gospels without preconceptions, without the interpretive gloss invented by Paul and later Christians, and this is the Jesus you'll see.

For all that, an end to Christianity, the cult that caught on and just wouldn't go away, seems unlikely. Religion survives because of the human capacity to believe any old mumbo-jumbo in the name of self-preservation. So long as that capacity survives, religion, Christianity included, will persist.

GLOSSARY

Or, how words mean what Christians say they mean and not what everyone else thinks they mean.

Bible-based values: Judgemental intolerance, arrived at by cherry-picking the bits of the Bible that confirm one's existing prejudices.

Biblical Exegesis: the neat trick of reinterpreting bits of the Bible - under the guidance of the Holy Spirit, naturally - so they say whatever you want them to say. Perhaps the closest believers come to changing water into wine.

Blessing: a) Feeling good, euphoria. Attributed to God.

b) Aspects of a comfortable life. Attributed to God

Born Again: Converting to Christianity, switching off your critical faculties, and imagining you're having a meaningful relationship with a person who's been dead for two-thousand years. Unfortunately for Christians, Jesus never says anyone should be born 'again': the entire point of his fabricated exchange with Nicodemus in John 3.3 is that one needs to be born 'from above' because 'above', beyond the canopy of the sky, is where Jesus and his contemporaries believed God and heaven to be (see, for example, Hebrews 7.26).

A Day: a period of time similar in length to a thousand years (see 2 Peter 3.8)

Family: Opposition to sex outside traditional marriage. Christian organisations with 'Family' in their titles, for example the *Family Research Council*, the *American Family Association,* and *Focus on the Family*, also get very agitated about 'homosexual advocacy'.

The Flesh: the dictates of the body and the unregenerate or 'carnal' mind. It also stands for the life lived by an unsaved person whose existence is determined by 'baser needs'. Christians, on the other hand, never succumb to the flesh and as a result are known never to eat, experience lust or have sex of any sort. The idea is Paul's - see Romans 5.24 - and doesn't sit easily with Jesus' own enjoyment of eating, drinking and making merry (Matthew 11.19). As disparaged as the flesh is, Christians are promised a new *physical* body come the resurrection (1 Corinthians 15.53-54).

The Gay Agenda: An invention of right-wing Christians designed to frighten more impressionable brothers and sisters into thinking gay people want to take over the world so that they can convert and recruit others into being homosexual too. Overlooking the fact that converting and recruiting are what Christians do, this hateful nonsense galvanises opposition to any sort of rights for gay people, whose 'agenda' is usually just the same as everyone else's; to be treated fairly and get peaceably through the day.

Holy Ghost: Not that non-believers have much use for this one, but in case you're not as up-to-date as you'd like to be, the artist formerly known as the Holy Ghost is now, after a recent make-over and re-branding, the Holy *Spirit*. The shedding of its former association with non-existent entities like apparitions and phantoms – which, of course, it most emphatically is not - produces a concept that's much more hip for today's with-it believer.

Lifestyle: Homosexuality. Occasionally applied more broadly to refer to any sex outside traditional marriage.

Marriage: The union of one man and one woman for life (even though this is not actually advocated in the Bible) with the right to divorce when the participants want to. *Not* the formalisation of loving same-sex relationships. What would become of marriage if that were allowed?

New Age: the disparaging term used to describe any wacky spiritual beliefs that are not of Christian origin (see also 'pan' and 'kettle').

Outpouring (of the Holy Spirit): Euphoria/hysteria.

Pro-life: Anti-abortion

Pro-marriage: Anti-gay

Pro-family: Anti-abortion *and* anti-gay

The Rapture: The ultimate high. When Jesus first appears in the sky at his second coming he will use his power of mass-levitation to draw his followers up into the air to be with him. Not all Christians are convinced this will happen, however, even though it's based on an idea of Paul's in 1 Thessalonians 4:17.

Righteous:
    a) Irritable, prone to jealousy, murderous. As God is all of these, it must be what Christians mean when they say he is righteous.
    b) Self-induced feelings of superiority, enjoyed by many Christians. Closely related to 'hypocritical'.

Slain in the Spirit: the compulsion to fall over while in a state of euphoria and attribute this to the Holy Spirit. A favourite trick of faith healers, it has nothing to do with faith or healing

A Thousand years: Pretty much the same as a day (see 2 Peter 3.8 again).

The World: Not the Earth or its populations as we might normally refer to them, but unredeemed mankind living in godless societies that do not follow Christ nor the Christian way. Also known as 'normality'. Christian use of the term based on verses such as 1 John 2:15-16.

Notes:

Introduction

Page 6. **Sam Harris on the soul/self and the brain**: *The Moral Landscape*, pp158-159.

Page 9. **Dating the four canonical gospels**: a subject of perpetual debate. I have worked with a chronology for the creation of the gospels and the rest of the New Testament collated from a range of scholarly sources (see the appendix).

Page 9. **The developed theology of the late, fourth gospel**: Wright, *The Evolution of God*, p254.

Page 9. **The King James Bible:** Despite the belief that it is the 1611 original that is still in use today, it is only the 1769 revision that is available.

Page 9. **KJV - good enough for God**: originally intended flippantly, I have subsequently been made aware, by Gordon Campbell's *Bible: The Story Of The King James Version 1611-2011,* that there are indeed groups of Christians who believe that the KJV 'preserves the very words of God in the form in which he wished them to be represented in the universal language of these last days: English' (p265).

Chapter 1

Page 14. **Bart Ehrman on Jesus' end-times pronouncements**: *Jesus Interrupted*, pp156-162.

Page 16. **David Wenham**: *Paul: Follower of Jesus or Founder of Christianity?,* p296.

Page 18. **Tom Wright on second coming**: *Surprised by Hope*, pp137-138.

Page 18. **Tom Wright on heaven's appearance**: *Surprised by Hope*, pp115-116.

Page 18. **Tom Wright on the Ascension**: *Surprised by Hope*, pp120-128.

Page 19. **Tom Wright on first century concerns**: *Surprised by Hope*, p133.

Page 22: ***RaptureAlert.com* on the restoration of Israel**: http://raptureforums.com/index.cfm

Page 22. ***Renew America* sees the Second Coming as imminent**: http://www.renewamerica.com

Page 23. **Ken Daniels on reinterpreting Jesus' first century return**:
http://www.infidels.org/library/modern/ken_daniels/why.html#Jesus

Page 24. **Stephen Green plays the man**:
http://www.christianvoice.org.uk/

Page 24. **Dominionism**: see, for example,
 http://www.scholarscorner.com/Critical/dominion.html
http://www.publiceye.org/magazine/v08n1/chrisre1.html and http://www.discernment-ministries.org/Newsletters/NL2010NovDec.pdf

Page 27. **Forcing the gospel narrative to fulfil prophecy**: the most well-known example is Jesus being born of a 'virgin', based on a mistranslation of 'young woman' in the Latin version of Micah that Matthew consulted. Another is his doubling up of the animals on which Jesus rides into Jerusalem. The original 'prophecy' simply uses synonyms - donkey and colt – for the same animal, but Matthew mistakenly thinks it means Jesus must somehow ride on both a donkey *and* a colt at the same time. So that's what he has him do (Matthew 21.2-7).

Page 30. **Barrie Wilson on Roman attitude to novelty**: *How Jesus Became Christian*, p238.

Page 31. **Divine rape in ancient mythologies**: Paul Tobin in *The Christian Delusion*, p158.

Chapter 2

Page 34. **Figurative language and literal truth**: http://www.james-dave.com/literal.html

Page 34. **Tom Wright on moving mountains**: *Jesus and the Victory of God*, p274.

Page 35. ***Justification by Grace* source:**
http://justificationbygrace.com/2010/07/30/oh-desire/

Page 37. **Authors of John's gospel, plural**: Several hands are at work in John's gospel (not to mention the others). Note the use of the pronoun 'we' in John 1.14 and the third person reference to 'he who saw this' in John 19.35. If the author of the gospel is himself the eye-witness to events, why does he refer to himself in the third person? There are actually very good reasons for supposing John's gospel is not an eye-witness account (it differs widely from the synoptic gospels, for example) and that, at best, it is the product of a later Christian community.

Page 37. **Dissent in the early church**: John W. Loftus in *The Christian Delusion*, pp191-202.

Page 37 & 127. **34,000 Christian groups:**
http://www.religioustolerance.org/worldrel.htm#wce

Page 37. **Apostasy and disunity**: according to the *Apprising Ministries* website (http://apprising.org/), too many churches have strayed from the 'truth' of the gospel.

Page 38. Details of this **appalling litany of failed prayer** can be found here:
Neil: http://www.katu.com/news/20461264.html
Madeline: http://www.foxnews.com/story/0,2933,341574,00.html

Zachery:
http://www.heraldnet.com/article/20090827/NEWS03/708279491
Ava:
http://www.oregonlive.com/clackamascounty/index.ssf/2009/07/jury_hears_father_recount_fait.html

Page 39. **Francis Collins on prayer for healing**:
http://onfaith.washingtonpost.com/onfaith/guestvoices/2010/09/praying_for_my_friend_christopher_hitchens.html

Page 40. **Snake handler fatalities**:
http://news.nationalgeographic.com/news/2003/04/0407_030407_snakehandlers_2.html

Page 41. **Later additions to Mark's gospel**: see, for example, Ehrman (2005) *Misquoting Jesus: The Story Behind Who Changed the Bible and Why*, p66.

Page 44. **Online Bible study**:
http://www.biblestudymanuals.net/first_last_last_first.htm

Page 45. **Dominionist ambitions**: North, G. (1989) *Political Polytheism: the Myth of Pluralism*, p87, cited on http://en.wikipedia.org/wiki/Gary_North_%28Christian_Reconstructionist%29

Page 45. **Christians -**
a) reacting aggressively to criticism:
http://www.suite101.com/content/persecution-of-christians-in-britain-a218905
b) whingeing at mild, unintended slights:
http://www.express.co.uk/posts/view/218290/Furt-over-BBC-s-Nativity-insult
c) claiming persecution:
http://www.telegraph.co.uk/news/newstopics/religion/8226444/The-Christians-who-felt-discriminated-against.html
d) suing:
http://www.dailymail.co.uk/news/article-1270364/Christian-preacher-hooligan-charge-saying-believes-homosexuality-sin.html

Page 45. **Nick Baines refutes persecution claims**:
http://www.ekklesia.co.uk/node/13680

Page 47. **Augustine on resurrected hair**: *Wherefore, if the hair that has been cropped and the nails that have been cut would cause a deformity were they to be restored to their places, they shall not be restored; and yet no one will lose these parts at the resurrection, for they shall be changed into the same flesh, their substance being so altered as to preserve the proportion of the various parts of the body. However, what our Lord said, "Not a hair of your head shall perish," might more suitably be interpreted of the number, and not of the length of the hairs, as He elsewhere says, "The hairs of your head are all numbered."* (*City of God*, chapter 22).

Chapter 3

Page 49. *Exploring Christianity* **on morality**:
http://www.christianity.co.nz/morality.htm

Page 49. **Ray Cotton on morality**:
http://www.leaderu.com/orgs/probe/docs/god-ethi.html

Page 54. **Bradlee Dean on homosexuality**: *The Minnesota Independent*, 25/05/10 -
http://minnesotaindependent.com/58393/gop-linked-punk-rock-ministry-says-executing-gays-is-moral

Page 54. **Ugandan Anti-homosexuality Bill**:
http://www.martinssempa.com/warren-response.html

Page 54. **Pope Benedict XVI on same-sex marriage**: UK *Daily Telegraph*, 13/05/10

Page 55. **Association of Orthodox Experts in Moscow**:
http://www.interfax-religion.com/?act=news&div=7178

Page 56. **Alfred Mohler on the ten commandments**:

http://www.albertmohler.com/2009/09/11/words-from-the-fire-the-10-commandments-for-christians-today/

Page 57. **Ronald J. Sider's** *The Scandal of the Evangelical* cited on: http://www.mrgoodman.com/articles/christianliving.html

Page 58. **Ohio Sceptics**: 28/05/10. Unfortunately, this information has now been removed from the site.

Page 58. **Creflo Dollar's dollars**: *New York Times*, 15/01/06

Page 58. **Creflo Dollar's arrest on family violence charges**: http://www.myfoxatlanta.com/story/18738248/rev-creflo-dollar-arrested-on-family-violence-charges

Page 59. **Benny Hinn's hotel guest**: http://www.thestar.com/news/gta/article/839668--married-toronto-preacher-benny-hinn-romantically-linked-to-healer?bn=1

Page 61. **The nurse Chaplin saga**: http://www.timesonline.co.uk/tol/comment/faith/article6841549.ece
http://www.timesonline.co.uk/tol/comment/faith/article7089691.ece

Page 62. *The IVP Bible Background Commentary*: http://www.keyway.ca/htm2003/20030320.htm.

Page 62. *Church of God Online Daily Bible Study*: http://www.keyway.ca/htm2006/20060203.htm

Page 64. **Sunday becomes the Sabbath**: http://www.religioustolerance.org/sabbath.htm

Page 65. **Public stonings**: http://www.nytimes.com/2010/08/17/world/asia/17stoning.html?ref=world

Page 66. **Tom Wright and Jewish peasant culture**: *Jesus and the*

Victory of God, p278

Page 71. **George Tiller's murder**:
http://en.wikipedia.org/wiki/George_Tiller

Page 72. **Albert Mohler on the death penalty**:
http://www.abpnews.com/content/view/6760/53/

Page 72. *Good News* **magazine on the sixth commandment**:
http://www.gnmagazine.org/booklets/TC/sixthcommandment.asp

Page 74. **Christian divorce statistics**:
http://www.religioustolerance.org/chr_dira.htm

Page 74. *Barna Research Group's* **divorce statistics**:
http://www.barna.org/family-kids-articles/42-new-marriage-and-divorce-statistics-released

Page 74. **Newt Gingrich's hypocrisy:** http://www.newt.org/

Page 75. **Robert Stein fudges eye-gouging commandment**: cited on
http://georgepwood.com/2008/09/25/if-your-right-eye-causes-you-to-sin-matthew-529%E2%80%9330/

Page 77. **Tim McHyde's revolutionary thoughts**:
http://timmchyde.com/gods-name-in-vain/

Page 78. **Clerical abuse in Belgium**:
http://www.telegraph.co.uk/news/worldnews/europe/belgium/7994705/No-Belgian-church-escaped-sex-abuse-finds-investigation.html

Page 79. *Louisville Institute* **reports collection plate theft**:
http://www.villanova.edu/business/assets/documents/excellence/church/catholicchurchfinances.pdf

Page 79. *International Bulletin of Missionary Research* **reports fraud**: http://www.internationalbulletin.org/

Page 79. *Center for the Study of Global Christianity* reports financial crimes:
http://ockenga.gordonconwell.edu/ockenga/globalchristianity/staff.php

Page 79. **Christian fraud increasing**:
http://christianheadlines.com/blog/2011/01/08/an-overview-of-religious-financial-fraud

Page 79. *Word Of Truth Radio Network* reports stealing from God: http://www.eternallifeministries.org/lrs_stealing.htm

Page 80. **University of Michigan report on church attendance**:
http://ns.umich.edu/htdocs/releases/story.php?id=8155

Page 81. **Pope excuses church paedophilia**:
http://www.belfasttelegraph.co.uk/news/world-news/popersquos-child-porn-normal-claim-sparks-outrage-among-victims-15035449.html

Page 81. **The deplorable Martin Ssempa on YouTube**:
http://www.youtube.com/watch?v=q1wwe9-be2Y

Page 82. **Martin Ssempa faces blackmail charges**:
http://www.monitor.co.ug/News/National/-/688334/1077294/-/cjw8roz/-/index.html

Page 82. **Stephen Green says gay people not marginalised**:
http://christianvoiceuk.blogspot.com/

Page 82. *Focus on the Family*'s **alarmist agenda**:
http://truetolerance.org/p9_June_Jul_Citizen_10_antibullying.pdf

Page 83. **William Lane Craig on 'the absurdity of life without God'**:
http://www.bethinking.org/suffering/intermediate/the-absurdity-of-life-without-god.htm

Page 83. *Kansas Express Way Church of Christ* on a world

without God: http://www.kecoc.org/

Page 83. **Comparative studies of morality**:
http://www.latimes.com/news/opinion/commentary/la-oe-lobdell-religion-20100808,0,3621871.story
and
http://www.pitzer.edu/academics/faculty/zuckerman/Zuckerman_on_Atheism.pdf

Page 83. **The rather good *Friendly Atheist* blog**:
http://friendlyatheist.com/

Page 84. **Non-believers help Japan**:
http://givingaid.richarddawkins.net/,
http://foundationbeyondbelief.org/

Page 85. **Trade and compassion**: Ridley, *The Rational Optimist,* p116

Page 86. **Benny Hinn covets a jet**:
https://www.bennyhinn.org/donate/default.cfm?referrer=na_dove1&CFID=28601541&CFTOKEN=87786284
and http://www.bennyhinn.org/finances/articledesc.cfm?id=1000

Page 87. **Stephen Green and *Christian Voice* seek a return to iron age customs**:
http://www.christianvoice.org.uk/Articles/A%20Model%20Nation.html

Page 87. **Erecting the ten commandments in -**
a) **Illinois**:
http://www.wsiltv.com/p/news_details.php?newsID=10859&type=top
b) **Virginia**:
http://www.washingtontimes.com/news/2011/jan/23/ten-commandments-restored-at-virginia-schools/
c) **classrooms**:
http://www.daflynn.com/Press/20101109~Filing82nd.pdf

Chapter 4

Page 90. **Revelife says Christians 'shouldn't respond in kind'**:
http://www.revelife.com/677549933/can-christians-fight-back/

Page 90. **Not so *Provocative Christian Living***:
http://provocativechristian.wordpress.com/2009/01/23/provocative-bible-verses-turn-the-other-cheek/

Page 90. **Turning the other cheek means guns**:
http://www.gac.20m.com/self-def.htm

Page 92. **The less than merciful *House of Mercy***:
http://news.change.org/stories/georgia-shelter-confirms-gay-people-deserve-to-be-homeless

Page 92. **Paster Himes anti-gay campaigning**:
http://www.advocate.com/News/Daily_News/2011/02/19/Montana_Lawmakers_Consider_LGBT_Antidiscrimination_Bill/

Page 95. **The Dave Mcalpine incident**:
http://www.bbc.co.uk/news/10174393

Page 96. **The litigious *Christian Institute***:
http://www.christian.org.uk/who-we-are/

Page 96. **C. S. Lewis on Jesus as 'great human teacher'**: *Mere Christianity*, p52

Page 100. **The early church and morality**: Paul spends most of his first letter to the Corinthian Christians telling them off for their lack of morality and inability to follow Jesus' (or perhaps it's his own) teaching. Why is this, when they are being guided by the indwelling Holy Spirit?

Page 100. **Stoning as penalty for adultery in the modern world**:
http://www.iium.edu.my/intdiscourse/index.php/islam/article/view/139/140

Page 101. **The death penalty in Jewish law**: under the Roman rule the Jews did not have the right to execute anyone: that the Pharisees seek to do so in the encounter with the woman caught in adultery points to the story's inauthenticity.

Page 102. **Ricky Gervais and 'he who is without sin'**: http://www.wired.co.uk/news/archive/2011-04/14/ricky-gervais-why-im-a-good-christian

Page 103. **Use of the word 'church' in Matthew 18**: The word translated 'church' is *ecclesia,* which has no other meaning other than 'church'. There is no getting around the fact that this can only be a later addition to whatever Jesus' original teaching on this subject was.

Page 105. **Desmond Tutu quotation**: *God Is Not A Christian*, p38.

Page 111: **Jim Jones's People's Temple Christian Church mass suicide**: http://news.bbc.co.uk/onthisday/hi/dates/stories/november/18/newsid_2540000/2540209.stm

Page 112: **David Koresh's Branch Davidians death by fire**: http://news.bbc.co.uk/1/hi/world/americas/431311.stm

Chapter 5

Page 115. **Q90fm knows better than Jesus**: http://www.q90fm.com/lifest2010.asp

Page 118. **Dave Wenham on judgement**: *Paul: Follower of Jesus or Founder of Christianity,* p297

Page 120. **Tom Wright seen to get it all wrong**: http://www.svchapel.org/resources/book-reviews/4-christian-living/688-radical-taking-back-your-faith-from-the-american-dream-by-david-platt

Page 120. **Tom Wright on gospel practicalities**: *Surprised by Hope, p216*

Page 120. **Gary Gilley asserts Christians not commissioned to rectify injustices**: http://www.svchapel.org/resources/book-reviews/4-christian-living/688-radical-taking-back-your-faith-from-the-american-dream-by-david-platt

Chapter 6

Page 121. **Beliefs not founded on Jesus' teaching**: Davidson, *Gospel of Jesus: In Search of His Original Teachings*, p7. Not that we can ever know what Jesus' 'original teachings' were.

Page 124. **Nothing beyond what is written**: see also Deuteronomy 12.32 and Revelation 22.18-19.

Page 121. ***Way of Life* Christian website on inspiration**: http://www.wayoflife.org/wayoflife/statement.html

Page 123. **The Bible's late compilation**: Freeman, *Heretics, Pagans and the Christian State*, p42

Page 123. **Inspiration of non-canonical texts?**: Ehrman, *Jesus Interrupted: Revealing the Hidden Contradictions of the Bible*, chapter 4

Page 124. **The trouble with 2 Timothy**: http://www.earlychristianwritings.com/2timothy.html

Page 124. **Peter's illiteracy**: Ehrman, *Forged* (pp75-76).

Page 124. **Ehrman forgeries and lies quotation**: http://www.huffingtonpost.com/bart-d-ehrman/the-bible-telling-lies-to_b_840301.html

Page 124. **Forgeries in the New Testament**: Ehrman, *Forged: Writing in the Name of God - Why the Bible's Authors Are Not Who We Think They Are*: The Pastoral letters – pp96-103; 2 Thessalonians - pp105-108; Ephesians - pp108-112; Colossians – pp112-114; Jude – pp186-188; James – pp192-198.

Page 125. **Alterations to scripture**: Ehrman, *Misquoting Jesus: The Story Behind Who Changed the Bible and Why* in its entirety!

Page 128. **Tim Keller proposes a decent commentary**: *The Reason for God*, p110

Page 128. **John MacArthur says Genesis is literally true**: http://apprising.org/2010/07/22/john-macarthur-everything-evolution-cant-explain-in-genesis-11/

Page 128. **The *Christian Research Network***: http://christianresearchnetwork.com/

Page 129. **Albert Mohler on the 'inerrancy war'**: http://www.albertmohler.com/2010/08/16/the-inerrancy-of-scripture-the-fifty-years-war-and-counting/

Page 129. **Rob J. Hyndman on biblical consistency**: http://robjhyndman.com/bible/BRB/chap6.pdf

Page 130. **Explaining (away) biblical contradictions**: innumerable web-sites attempt this, concentrating almost exclusively on conflicting incidental detail. Very few seem aware of the much more serious doctrinal contradictions. The 'Contender Ministries' site is representative:
http://contenderministries.org/discrepancies/contradictions.php

Page 131. **Bart Ehrman on the meaning Luke ascribes to Jesus' death**: *Jesus Interrupted: Revealing the Hidden Contradictions of the Bible,* pp93-94

Page 134. **Ken Pulliam asks if the Bible couldn't be a little clearer**:

http://formerfundy.blogspot.com/2010/09/is-bible-clear-on-how-someone-can-be.html

Page 135. **Jonathan Knight on interpretation**: *Jesus: An Historical and Theological Investigation*, p194

Page 135. **Deliberate copyist changes**: Ehrman, *Forged: Writing in the Name of God - Why the Bible's Authors Are Not Who We Think They Are*, pp240-245

Chapter 7

Page 139. **Nick Page on Jesus' baptism**: *The Wrong Messiah: The Real Story of Jesus of Nazareth*, p79. Page correctly points out that the inclusion of the baptism in the gospels indicates its authenticity on the basis of the 'criterion of embarrassment': a 'divine' being in need of repentance and forgiveness is extremely problematic for the Christology of later believers.

Page 140. **Ehrman on Jesus as 'legend'**: *Jesus Interrupted: Revealing the Hidden Contradictions of the Bible*, p142

Page 141. **Paul's contribution to the Jesus myth**: Wilson, *How Jesus Became a Christian: The Early Christians and the Transformation of a Jewish Teacher into the Son of God*, p111

Page 141. **Paul's inner vision (Galatians 1.15-16)**: Knight, *Jesus: An Historical Theological Investigation*, pp204-5

Page 143. **Mark's tampered-with ending**: *ibid*, p207

Page 143. **Mark 14. 25, 'I will never again drink of the fruit of the vine until that day when I drink it new in the Kingdom of God'**: Before any Christians claim otherwise, we know that Jesus could not possibly have been referring to any delayed second-coming; you think he's got time for a drink when he's got the rapture to see to?

Page 147. **The conformist bias in human nature**: Robert Wright, *The Evolution of God*, p478.

Page 149. **'The Trinity' appears 350 years after Jesus' lifetime**: Freeman, *AD 381: Heretics, Pagans and the Christian State*, p100

Page 150. **The Holy Spirit only just makes it**: ibid, p68

Page 146. **The Catechism and the 'mystery' of the Trinity:** http://www.vatican.va/archive/ccc_css/archive/catechism/p1s2c1p2.htm#II

Page 154. **Reformed Baptists' interpretation of the gospel**: https://reformedontheweb.wordpress.com/2011/01/17/what-is-the-gospel/

Page 155. **Keith Ward on Jesus' version of 'the gospel'**: *The Word of God: The Bible After Modern Scholarship, p105*

Page 156. **Paul not universally held in high regarded in the early church?**: Freeman, *AD 381: Heretics, Pagans and the Christian State,* p158-159

Chapter 8

Page 157. **Oremus Bible Browser**: http://bible.oremus.org/ . I am indebted to the browser for many of the biblical references that occur in this book.

Page 157. **Old Christian rock song**: this is 'Reader's Digest' by the late, great Larry Norman on the album *Only Visiting This Planet* (1973): Solid Rock Records.

Page 157. **Sam Harris on the illusion of free will**: *The Moral Landscape,* pp102-106. Quotation from p103.

Page 159. **Footprints in the sand**: http://www.footprints-inthe-sand.com/index.php?page=Poem/Poem.php

Page 160. ***Bible-Knowledge.com***'s suspect guidance:
http://www.bible-knowledge.com/god-s-guidance/

Page 161. **Tom Wright on heaven**:
http://www.time.com/time/world/article/0,8599,1710844,00.html#ixzz0uEK1bit7

Page 162. ***Way of Life Literature* on heaven**:
http://www.wayoflife.org/wayoflife/statement.html
Note the relish with which the site relates the fate of the wicked unbeliever!

Page 162. **Bart Ehrman on the 'immortality of the soul'**: *Jesus Interrupted: Revealing the Hidden Contradictions of the Bible*, p266

Page 166. **William Lane Craig and the inner witness of the Holy Spirit**: http://formerfundy.blogspot.com/2009/11/witness-of-spirit-and-burning-in-bosom.html

Page 166. **William Lane Craig quotations**: *Reasonable Faith*, 3rd ed., pp. 48-50

Page 168. **Attributing agency to random acts of nature**: Robert Wright tracks the evolution of this tendency in *The Evolution of God*, pp473-476

Page 168. The ludicrous claims about natural disasters can be found on the following sites:
http://mediamatters.org/research/200509130004

http://www.cbsnews.com/8301-504083_162-12017-504083.html

http://www.interfax-religion.com/?act=news&div=7178

http://www.youtube.com/watch?v=V17WGTvPHGg&feature=player_embedded

http://catchthefire.com.au/blog/2011/01/08/are-the-qld-floods-the-result-of-kevin-rudd-speaking-against-israel/

http://www.religiouswatch.com/rw_latest.htm#Faulty_Religion_7638 (original site now shut down)

http://www.generals.org/news/single-view/article/a-perspective-on-the-earthquake-in-japan/

Page 168. *Mountain Retreat* on faith:
http://www.mountainretreatorg.net/faq/eviden.html

Page 170. **Supplementary beliefs 1 and 2**:
http://www.creationists.org/dinosaurs-humans-coexisted.html

Page 171. **God controls the weather**:
http://www.christiananswers.net/q-eden/edn-c023.html

Page 171. **Sam Harris on faith**:
http://www.samharris.org/site/full_text/afterword-to-the-vintage-books-edition/

Page 171. **Reason as a clue to God's existence**: Tim Keller in *The Reason For God*, p141

Page 174. **Tony Blair says Terry Jones is not a proper Christian:**
http://www.channel4.com/news/articles/politics/international_politics/obama+condemns+plans+to+burn+koran/3763377.html

Page 174. **Sam Harris on the dangers of moderate religious belief**: *The End of Faith*, p45

Page 175. *Guardian* **comment**:
http://www.guardian.co.uk/commentisfree/2010/may/02/muslim-veil-religion

Page 176. **Christians claim persecution**:
http://www.telegraph.co.uk/news/religion/7531293/Senior-bishops-call-for-end-to-persecution-of-Christians-in-Britain.html
and
http://www.telegraph.co.uk/comment/letters/7528487/The-religious-rights-of-Christians-are-treated-with-disrespect.html

Page 176. **Christians indulge in some persecution of their own**:
http://www.guardian.co.uk/society/2010/aug/19/catholic-adoption-agency-gay-parents

Page 177. **77% of Americans are Christians**:
http://www.gallup.com/poll/117409/easter-smaller-percentage-americans-christian.aspx

Page 177. **American Christians lament the stripping way of 'religious liberties'**:
http://blog.christianitytoday.com/ctpolitics/2010/05/christians_defy.html

Page 180. *Answers In Genesis* **side-splitting cartoon**:
http://www.answersingenesis.org/media/image/cartoons/after-eden/thanks-for-nothing

Page 182. **Richard Dawkins on Christian ingratitude**:
http://www.salon.com/2005/04/30/dawkins/
Dawkins is here talking about being thankful *for* life, not about being grateful *to* a fictitious divine creator. Not all Christians understand the difference:
http://open.salon.com/blog/jeffrey_dach_md/2009/02/09/newsflash_dawkins_disavows_atheism)

Page 184. **Gossiping**: see Romans 1.29 and 2 Corinthians 12.20 if you think the Bible treats gossiping lightly.

Page 184. **Matt Ridley on the causes of homosexuality**: *Nature via nurture: Genes, experience, and what makes us human,"* HarperCollins, (2003), p159, cited on:
http://www.religioustolerance.org/hom_caus4.htm

Page 184. *Got Questions?Org* **equating homosexuality with violence and rage**: http://www.gotquestions.org/homosexuality-Bible.html

Page 184. **Exodus International statement**:

http://www.exodusinternational.org/content/view/33/57/

Page 185. **Lee Grady's claims**:
http://www.charismamag.com/index.php/fire-in-my-bones/29039-say-goodbye-to-the-untouchable-preachers#ixzz0voIsciff

Page 186. **Tom Wright on Jesus' welcome to sinners**: *Jesus and the Victory of God*, p274

Page 188. **Ken Silva and *Apprising Ministries'* 'speaking the truth in love'**: http://apprising.org/. There should also be reference to the Westboro Baptist church here, but I can't bring myself to include it. Google it if you really must see for yourself what it says.

Page 189. **Richard Dawkins and Christopher Hitchens experience the 'spirit of love'**:
http://richarddawkins.net/letters/ugly,
http://www.vanityfair.com/culture/features/2010/10/hitchens-201010

Page 191. **Alan Dershowitz on the 'unchanging' nature of God's truths**: http://www.c-spanvideo.org/program/159474-1

Chapter 9

Page 192. **In this world but not of it**: the expression does not appear in this form in the Bible but the sentiment behind it is used both by Paul and the creators of the fourth gospel. The sense of dislocation evidently came early in the faith's development.

Page 192. **The decline in Sabbath observance**: Miller, *The Peculiar Life of Sundays*, p264

Page 193. ***Religious Tolerance* and dates for the end of the world**: http://www.religioustolerance.org/end_wrld.htm

Page 193. ***Family Radio Worldwide* guarantee that judgement**

day is or was 21st May 2011:
http://www.familyradio.com/index2.html

Page 194. **God's Final Witness guarantee that the end will be in 2012**:
http://theend.com/2008GodsFinalWitness/gclid=CK2XpaeorqcCFQoY4QodRjLGCA

Page 194. **Rod Parsley sees the Antichrist waiting in the wings**:
http://www.youtube.com/watchfeature=player_embedded&v=SP57i-ohDRI

Page 194. **The non-biblical nature of the Antichrist**: this section owes a great deal to Henry Ansgar Kelly's *Satan: A Biography* (2006), particularly pages 161-164, from where quotations are taken. Kelly also demonstrates how Christians subscribe to a wider mythology that finds little support in the Bible: *'We should also note what we do **not** find in the Old and New Testament. There is no pre-mundane fall of the angels. There is no connection of Satan with the Serpent of Eden or the sin of Adam... There is no Antichrist, only antichrists, who are human and not directly associated with Satan. There is no rebellious Lucifer, only Jesus, the good Lucifer'* (p172).

Page 196. **Nero as the Beast of Revelation**: Robert Wright, *The Evolution of God*, p186

Chapter 10

Page 197. **Stephen Hawking on the self-creating universe**: *The Grand Design*, p180

Page 198. **Rowan Williams invokes God**:
http://www.telegraph.co.uk/news/religion/7979093/Stephen-Hawking-religious-leaders-dismiss-God-not-needed-comments.html

Page 198. **Fine-tuning**: for a discussion of the various forms of the anthropic argument, see Shermer, *Why People Believe Weird*

Things, pp262-265

Page 199. **Steve Zara on the absurdity of the theist position**:
http://zarbi.posterous.com/god-and-evidence-a-strident-proposal

Page 200. **Description all in the mind**: Shermer in *Why People Believe Weird Things*, p33

Page 201. **David Attenborough and quarrelsome primates**: 'Primates are just like us - intelligent, quarrelsome, family-centred'. Episode 10 of *Life*. BBC, 2009

Page 201. **Joel Heck remarks about death from lecture *The Genesis Account of Creation* on**:
http://issuesetc.org/tag/evolution/

Page 201. *Answers in Genesis'* **beliefs**:
http://www.answersingenesis.org/articles/affirmations-denials-christian-worldview

Chapter 11

Page 203: **Francis Bacon**: cited in Shermer, p296

Page 204. **Bishop John Quinn, expert on marriage**:
http://www.catholicnewsagency.com/news/minnesota-bishop-encourages-catholics-to-act-against-same-sex-marriage-dangers/?utm_source=feedburner&utm_medium=feed&utm_campaign=Feed%3A+catholicnewsagency%2Fdailynews+%28CNA+Daily+News%29

Page 204. *Christian Voice*'s **Stephen Green, expert on marriage**:
http://www.express.co.uk/posts/view/194537/Gay-vicar-s-marriage-is-an-abomination-say-Christians

Page 207. **Probable date of Genesis' completion**:
http://atheism.about.com/library/chronologies/blchron_ot2.htm

Page 209. *Skeptic's Annotated Bible* **list of polygamous**

marriages:
http://skepticsannotatedbible.com/says_about/polygamy.html

Page 210. **Southern Baptists' self-deception**:
http://au.christiantoday.com/article/christians-urging-obama-government-to-crack-down-pornography/10240.htm

Page 210. **Same-sex marriage and polygamy**: David Kupelian of the right-wing Christian web-site, *World Net Daily* claims, for example, that *once gay marriage is legalized in America... polygamy will inevitably be legalized also, since there simply will no longer be any legal basis for keeping polygamy illegal... Beyond man-man, woman-woman and polygamous "marriages," every other type of degenerate combination imaginable – and unimaginable – will be civilly sanctified in America as marriage. If two men can be married, then three men can be married. It's difficult to grasp just how perverse life will be in that kind of nightmare America.*
http://www.wnd.com/index.phpfa=PAGE.view&pageId=192221

Page 214. **Jerome R. Koch and Ignacio Luis Ramirez**: *Religiosity, Christian Fundamentalism, and Intimate Partner Violence Among U.S. College Students* (2009):
http://courses.ttu.edu/jkoch/Research/Koch%20Ramirez%20Religion%20and%20Partner%20Violence%20Final%20Feb%2009.pdf

Page 215. **Bishop Joseph Devine excuses Catholic violence**: *The Sunday Herald*, 30/05/10 on:
http://www.heraldscotland.com/news/home-news/devine-slams-anti-catholic-agenda-in-child-sex-abuse-row-1.1031394

Page 218. **John MacArthur says all children are sinners**:
http://www.ondoctrine.com/2mac0142.htm

Page 218. ***The American Pregnancy Association* on spontaneous abortion**: http://www.suite101.com/content/miscarriage-facts-and-statistics-a120921#ixzz14shHZswz

Chapter 12

Page 222. **Julia Sweeney on the world without a Supreme Being**: http://www.juliasweeney.com/letting_go_mini/

Page 223. **The Scandal of the Evangelical Conscience**: a summary of Ronald J. Sider's (2005) book can be found at http://www.onthewing.org/user/Ev_Scandal%20of%20the%20Evangelical%20Conscience.pdf, cited in Pinsky, p96.

Glossary

Page 225. **The impossibility of Jesus' 'born again' discussion with Nicodemus**: As Bart Ehrman explains in *Jesus, Interrupted* (p 155), the misunderstanding central to this exchange, between 'born again' and 'born from above' occurs only in Greek. As Aramaic speakers, Jesus and Nicodemus would not, if they knew any, have resorted to Greek for this one conversation, just so this very confusion could be created.

The word in question is 'anothen', which can mean both 'again' and 'from above', and it is this double meaning that prompts Nicodemus to ask if he is expected to crawl back into his mother's womb so he can be born 'again'. The contrivance allows Jesus to make a show of correcting him and to make his real point; 'No, Nic, you dumbkoff. Not 'born again', but 'born from above'. What do they teach you at synagogue school these days?'.

So in a conversation he never had, depending as it does on a misunderstanding of the Greek he didn't speak, 'born again' is not what Jesus means: his point, as the writers of John make clear (in the Greek Jesus didn't speak, but they did), is that one has to be 'born from above'.

New Testament chronology

While Bible scholars routinely allude to books of the New Testament written before or after others, it is difficult to pin down dates of composition, either actual or estimated, for all of them. Nevertheless I found in the early stages of writing this book that I needed both a chronology and a record of likely authorship to which I could readily refer. I compiled that which follows from a wide range of sources, synthesising their stated or implied dates for each book of the New Testament and other significant events in the evolution of Christian theology, as well as author attribution. I include it here so you can see the chronology with which I worked.

Event/Book	Approximate date	Author	Comment
Jesus' birth	6 - 4 BCE	-	
Jesus' death	27 - 31 CE	-	
First letter to Thessalonians	51	Paul	
Letter to Galatians	54	Paul	
First letter to Corinthians	54 - 55	Paul	
Second letter to Corinthians	56	Paul	
Letter to Romans	57	Paul	
Philemon, Philippians	60 - 62	Paul	
Death of Paul	64	-	Date contested
Gospel attributed to Mark	70	Unknown	
1 Peter	70 - 90	Unknown	Pseudonymous: not written by Peter

Letter of James	70 - 100	James	Pseudonymous: not written by James, brother of Jesus
Colossians	75 - 85	Unknown	Pseudonymous: not written by Paul
Gospel attributed to Matthew	80 - 85	Unknown	
Hebrews	80 - 90	Unknown	Not written by Paul and does not claim to be
Gospel attributed to Luke and Acts of the Apostles	80 - 95	Unknown	
Ephesians	80 - 100	Unknown	Pseudonymous: not written by Paul
1, 2 and 3 John	80 - 100	'The Prester'	Not the same author as John's gospel.
2 Thessalonians	80 -100	Unknown	Pseudonymous: not written by Paul
'The Writings'	90	Various	Books of Old Testament accepted as part of Christian heritage
Jude	90 - 100	Jude	Pseudonymous: not written by Jude, brother of Jesus
Revelation	95	John of Patmos	
Gospel attributed to John	100 - 125	Unknown	
1 and 2 Timothy, Titus	100-150	Unknown	The 'Pastoral' Epistles. Pseudonymous: not written by Paul
2 Peter	140	Unknown	Pseudonymous: some scholars think 2 Peter as late as 160
Collation of four canonical gospels	150	-	

Formal declaration of Jesus' divinity	325	Council of Nicaea	
Twenty-seven books of 'New Testament' fixed	367	-	Canon first referred to by Athanasius
Doctrine of Trinity formulated	381	First Council of Constantinople	

Bibliography

Ali, Ayaan Hirsi (2007) *Infidel.* New York Free Press. New York.

Ariely, Dan (2008) *Predictably Irrational: The Hidden Forces That Shape Our Decisions.* London:HarperCollins.

Barker, Dan (2008) *Godless: How An Evangelical Preacher Became One of America's Leading Atheists.* Ulysses Press: Berkeley, CA.

Barker, Dan (2011) *The Good Atheist: Living A Purpose-Filled Life Without God.* Ulysses Press: Berkeley, CA.

Campbell, Gordon (2010) *Bible: The Story Of The King James Version 1611-2011.* Oxford University Press: Oxford.

Davidson, John (2004) *Gospel of Jesus: In Search of His Original Teachings.* Clear Books,
revised edition: New Delhi.

Dawkins, Richard (2006) *The God Delusion.* Bantam Press: London.

Dawkins, Richard (2010) *The Greatest Show on Earth: The Evidence for Evolution.* Black Swan: London.

Ehrman, Bart, D. (2005) *Misquoting Jesus: The Story Behind Who Changed the Bible and Why.* Harper Collins: New York.

Ehrman, Bart, D. (2009) *Jesus Interrupted: Revealing the Hidden Contradictions of the Bible.* Harper Collins: New York.

Ehrman, Bart, D. (2011) *Forged: Writing in the Name of God - Why the Bible's Authors Are Not Who We Think They Are.* Harper Collins: New York.

Freeman, Charles (2008) *AD 381: Heretics, Pagans and the Christian State.* Pimlico: London.

Freke, Timothy & Gandy, Peter (1999) *The Jesus Mysteries: Was The Original Jesus a Pagan God?* Thorsons: London.

Harris, Sam (2004) *The End of Faith: Religion, Terror, and the Future of Reason.* Free Press: London.

Harris, Sam (2007) *Letter to a Christian Nation: A Challenge to Faith. Bantam Press*: London.

Harris, Sam (2010) *The Moral Landscape: How Science Can Determine Human Values.* Transworld: London.

Harris, Sam (2012) *Free Will.* Free Press: London.

Hawking, Stephen & Mlodinow, Leonard (2010) *The Grand Design.* Bantam Press: London.

Humphreys, John (2007) *In God We Doubt: Confessions of a Failed Atheist.* London: Hodder & Stoughton.

Keller, Tim (2009) *The Reason For God: Belief in an Age of Scepticism.* London: Hodder & Stoughton

Kelly, Henry Ansgar (2006) *Satan: A Biography.* Cambridge University Press: Cambridge.

Knight, Jonathan (2004) *Jesus: An Historical and Theological Investigation.* T&T Clark International, Continuum imprint: London.
Son of Man discussion in above from p112 to 123.

Kurtz, Paul (2008) *Forbidden Fruit: The Ethics of Secularism.* Prometheus Books: Amhurst.

Lewis, C. S. (1952) *Mere Christianity.* Fount, William Collins Sons: Glasgow.

Loftus, John [Ed] (2009) *The Christian Delusion: Why Faith Fails.* Prometheus Books: New York.

Miller, Stephen (2008) *The Peculiar Life of Sundays.* Harvard: London.

Mills, David (2006) *Atheist Universe: The Thinking Person's Answer to Christian Fundamentalism.* Ulysses Press: Berkeley, CA.

Page, Nick (2011) *The Wrong Messiah: The Real Story of Jesus of Nazareth.* Hodder & Stoughton. London.

Pinsky, Mark, I. (2006) *A Jew Among the Evangelicals: A Guide for the Perplexed.* WJK: Kentucky.

Ridley, Matt (2010) *The Rational Optimist: How Prosperity Evolves.* HarperCollins: London.

Shermer, Michael (2002) *Why People Believe Weird Things: Pseudoscience, Superstition and Other Confusions Of Our Time.* Souvenir Press: London.

Tutu, Desmond (2011) *God Is Not A Christian: Speaking Truth In Times Of Crisis.* Rider. London

Ward, Keith (2010) *The Word of God: The Bible After Modern Scholarship.* SPCK: London.

Wenham, David (1995) *Paul: Follower of Jesus or Founder of Christianity?* Eerdmans: Cambridge, UK.

White, Mel (2006) *Religion Gone Bad: The Hidden Dangers of The Christian Right.* Tarcher/Penguin: New York.

Wilson, Barrie (2008) *How Jesus Became a Christian: The Early Christians and the Transformation of a Jewish Teacher into the Son of God.* Weidenfeld & Nicholson. London.

Wright, N. T. (1996) *Jesus and the Victory of God.* SPCK: London.

Wright, Robert (2009) *The Evolution of God: The Origins of Our Beliefs.* Little Brown (Abacus): London.

Wright, Tom (2007) *Surprised by Hope.* SPCK: London.

Printed in Great Britain
by Amazon.co.uk, Ltd.,
Marston Gate.